Hypermedia As a Student Tool

Hypermedia As a Student Tool
A Guide for Teachers

Marianne G. Handler, Ed.D.
National-Louis University
Technology in Education Department
Wheeling, Illinois

Ann S. Dana, Ed.D.
Adjunct Faculty, National-Louis University
Educational Computing Consultant
Hinsdale, Illinois

Jane Peters Moore, M.Ed.
Adjunct Faculty, National-Louis University
The North Shore Country Day School
Winnetka, Illinois

Teacher Ideas Press
A Division of
Libraries Unlimited, Inc.
Englewood, Colorado
1995

Dedication

This book is dedicated to teachers who struggle in their efforts to integrate technology into their instructional practice. They are risk-takers who model for their students what it is to be a life-long learner. We hope we have made that struggle a little easier.

TEACHER IDEAS PRESS
A Division of
Libraries Unlimited, Inc.
P.O. Box 6633
Englewood, CO 80155-6633
1-800-237-6124

Production Editor: Kevin W. Perizzolo
Copy Editor: Tama J. Serfoss
Typesetting and Interior Design: Kay Minnis

Library of Congress Cataloging-in-Publication Data

Handler, Marianne G.
    Hypermedia as a student tool : a guide for teachers / Marianne G.
Handler, Ann S. Dana, Jane Peters Moore.
    xviii, 272 p. 22x28 cm.
    Includes bibliographical references and index.
    ISBN 1-56308-138-5
    1. Computer-assisted instruction. 2. Hypertext systems.
3. Interactive multimedia. 4. Curriculum planning. I. Dana, Ann
S. II. Moore, Jane Peters. III. Title.
LB1028.5.H3166   1995
371.3'34--dc20   94-35586
                                                          CIP

Contents

Acknowledgments

The authors want to thank all the teachers and students who have worked with us. We particularly want to thank Marta Evans, Mickey Tandent, Karen Jump, Joan Hoexter, and Diane Cederlund for letting us into their classrooms and computer labs. Although the majority of the lessons have been developed by the authors, we are grateful to Bonnie Thurber, Linda Earnest, Vito Dipinto, Sally Ryan, Elisa Denja, and Ricky Crown for sharing the multimedia lessons they have been using with students. Roger Wagner has been more than generous in supplying us with many versions of HyperStudio during the development of this book. Our thanks to Larry Burkness for providing Multimedia ScrapBook and SuperLink for our use, to Pierian Spring Software for sharing Digital Chisel, and to EduQuest for providing LinkWay Live! Linda Manlove and Sheila Cory were helpful in critiquing portions of the book. Special thanks to our editor, Kevin W. Perizzolo, who kept us going through the development and completion of this book. We want to thank Ron Handler, Clint Moore, and Jennifer Nelson for their patience and tolerance through all the days we spent away from home during the writing of this book.

The authors wish to thank the following people or publishers for the use of graphics and material in this book.

Lara Crock, Emma Huspelhorn, and Claire Weingarden.

Roger Wagner Publishing, Inc. for the HyperStudio® menus and clip art examples.

Dover Publications, Inc., New York, NY, for *Classroom Clip Art* in the *Educator HomeCard*.

©Apple Computer Inc. 1990. Used with permission. Apple and the Apple logo are registered trademarks of Apple Computer, Inc. All Rights Reserved.

What Is This Book All About?

It is the intent of this book to provide support for the classroom teacher who wants to use hypermedia as a tool for student involvement as authors and designers. Teachers working with a new medium need such ongoing help and support. This book is intended to help the teacher, in operating a hypermedia program, and in using instructional strategies and learning environments that could provide opportunities for student collaboration. This book will provide a framework for offering students ways to share information with a real audience.

The curriculum ideas presented here have been used by real teachers with real students. They may not have worked the first time, but they have been shaped and reshaped by the teachers who created them. You are welcome to reshape them to fit your needs and to use them as models in your own classrooms. There is no right or wrong way to use these lesson models, which can be adapted to any idea that a teacher feels fits their curriculum and teaching style. For the teacher who developed these lessons, hypermedia was seen as a way to expand and extend opportunities for involved student learning. Technology is meant to serve the goals and objectives of the instructional program. It is not in the best interest of learners to build the curriculum around the technology.

This book provides support for a variety of hypermedia programs. They do not all use the same terminology. As you read through the curriculum ideas, you will find that we have used the terms *stack, screen,* or *card.* Those of you who are using DOS-based or Windows-based programs will be using the terms *folder* and *pages. Stack* and *folder* are the same concept just as *card* and *page* refer to the screen.

Student directions will be provided for at least one hypermedia program for each of the computers used in schools: HyperScreen (Scholastic) for the Apple IIe/GS computer; HyperStudio for AppleGS and the Macintosh; HyperCard for the Macintosh; Digital Chisel for the Macintosh; and LinkWay Live!, SuperLink, and Multimedia ScrapBook for the IBM and compatibles. The student instruction sheets presented here are provided only as models. Your students may need support materials for other parts of the hypermedia programs.

Appendix A contains three assessment instruments to evaluate hypermedia projects. They can easily be used for peer evaluation or assessment by the teacher. All have been successfully used in classrooms. Each one looks at a project a little differently; the more in-depth assessments are for older students. We leave it to your discretion which ones to use with your students; perhaps the provided assessments will give you ideas on how to develop one of your own.

We encourage you, the teacher, to work through each of the steps before you use them with students. As computer-using teachers, our goal in creating this book was to support other teachers who might not have a real person to walk alongside them as they take the risk of trying new and exciting instructional strategies. We would like to hear from you about what works well, and about new ideas you come up with that could be added to this book.

Marianne Handler
National-Louis University
Wheeling, IL 60090
e-mail: mhan@wheeling1.nl.edu

Ann Dana
P.O. Box 209
Hinsdale, IL 60522
e-mail: adana@icebox.ncook.k12.il.us

Jane Moore
The North Shore Country Day School
Winnetka, IL 60093
e-mail: jmoore@icebox.ncook.k12.il.us

Introduction

Hypermedia tools have been developed to help teachers create new kinds of learning environments. Most of the commercial materials have been designed to help teachers use hypermedia tools to build classroom applications. This book is designed to help teachers integrate hypermedia into their classrooms as a student tool.

Actively involving students in their own learning has proven to be an educationally sound and highly motivating way of teaching. Hypermedia provides a learning environment that encourages active participation on the part of the student. When students use hypermedia programs designed by others to give them problem-solving situations, they become more actively engaged in learning. Students can also become more involved by designing their own hypermedia projects. In either situation, an important element for successful use of hypermedia in the classroom is the teacher. The teacher should be comfortable with the technology and have the skills needed to integrate technology into the curriculum. When using hypermedia in a classroom setting, educators confront a variety of educational issues, problems with the hypermedia itself, and problems that accompany education in an unstructured environment (Heller 1990).

Advantages and Constraints

As students collaborate to create stacks in a hypermedia environment, they are engaged in the kinds of activities that teachers have been wanting to promote. Four particular components of a positive learning environment can be contained in these activities. Children are involved in learning by doing; they are problem solving as they learn to communicate in this new medium; they are transforming and using prior knowledge, both in terms of what they have learned about the software, and in selecting the content area-material that best meets the criteria of the project; and they are learning in a highly supportive environment, supported by the teacher and by their peers.

To make all of this come to pass requires effort and time on the part of teachers. It means learning how to use hypermedia software, deciding how it can best be used within the curriculum, and providing opportunities for students to learn how to work with others and to develop the skills necessary for successful peer collaboration.

Hypermedia in the Literacy Curriculum: Communication Skills

Students use hypermedia to communicate information to their peers in a creative way. Students get to make many of their own choices in determining how they can relate an idea or specific piece of information to a chosen audience. When teachers prepare children to speak to or write for others, they provide students with tools to do the task. Students are taught eye contact, how to stand, and how to use notecards and key words to help them in their presentation. In their writing, students are taught to consider the audience, to think about the message they want to share, and the importance of clarity and good sentence structure. As students begin to develop their own hypermedia stacks teachers should help students develop the skills needed to use this new form of communication effectively.

Planning a hypermedia stack involves choosing the topic, identifying the audience, making a storyboard of possible screens, and selecting or creating visuals appropriate for the project. With this freedom of expression, and knowing that someone besides the teacher is going to share the results of their efforts, students have more interest in researching their topic. It is important for students to consider the audience who will "read" their stacks as they create their screens and consider the various paths through the stack. These elements are particularly emphasized in Quilts (page 18) and Poetry and Images (page 23), although communication through good writing is a part of all lessons in this book.

Visual Literacy

Teachers and students need to understand the importance of incorporating the design elements of visual literacy into the planning and implementation of hypermedia projects. "Visual literacy is the learned ability to interpret visual messages accurately and to create such messages" (Heinich, Molenda, and Russell 1989, 70-71). Children are bombarded with visual messages everywhere. During their work with hypermedia, students develop a sense of how to communicate using visuals and how to recognize the meaning of visuals in the work of others. Being visually literate includes the ability to think, learn, and communicate through visuals (Baca 1990, 99–106).

Emphasis on critical elements of screen design is one component of helping students to share ideas through this new medium. It is important for the teacher to demonstrate how to create original graphics and visuals as well as to display visual samples created by others. The activities in this book are designed to support the teacher as he or she models the planning process and interacts with students during their own planning. Students should be made aware of the elements that are important in a well-designed display of information. These elements include simplicity, clarity, balance, space, emphasis, shape and form, and the use of color. During the development of their stacks, students learn to incorporate text and graphics to improve the clarity of the screens and of the stack for the user.

Standards have been developed for print media and are in the process of being adjusted for software. Instructional media for schools should follow these standards more closely than is probable in the entertainment media. It is important to create hypermedia following good design as it is to plan good instruction.

The first consideration for both is the user. Who are the learners, what are their characteristics, and what is their background knowledge? The second consideration is the subject area. From then on, the differences will be in the presentation. On the screen, text should be limited to important points; white (empty) space is an asset. Graphics should support the purpose; on the screen, one picture balanced with the text is more effective than several pictures. Messages as to the location of a screen and the method of navigation within the program are always clearer when consistency of placement is observed. It is the *information* that is valuable, not the experience of discovering how to move through the program.

Designing a template for students that allows specific space for titles, graphics, text, navigation icons, and questions and responses may be the solution that ends confusion for the user. One important idea to get across to students is that simplicity in text and graphics is better than too much of anything. Sounds that have no relationship to the screen's content are confusing to the user; good design allows the message to be clearly and quickly understood. The Visual Literacy project (page 95 in chapter 6) emphasizes these elements.

Student Designers

In hypermedia environments, students frequently work in groups, making decisions cooperatively and constructively, a skill that is useful in real work environments (Bellan and Best 1992). They are able to share their efforts with many others rather than reporting only to the teacher, in the traditional manner, limiting them to an audience of one. "Collaborative activities by their very nature lend themselves to authentic activity, situated cognition, and socially based learning strategies" (Bellan and Best 1992, 313).

Involvement in the design process gives students new opportunities to consider the information they want to communicate to others. Students must recognize and select the relevant knowledge that should be included in the project (Harel 1991). The collaborative nature of learning is encouraged by social activity where the information in the project is developed through the interactions between peers and between the teacher and the students (Turner and Dipinto 1992).

The Role of the Teacher

The teacher has a multifaceted role during this design time. He or she serves as coach, design consultant, organizer, keeper of the tools, editor of accuracy, evaluator, and audience. No one who observes this process can claim that using the computer within the instructional setting is an easy task for the teacher. There are many, however, who do believe that the time and effort are worthwhile because of the positive impact on student learning and engagement. The teacher must be familiar with the selected program, and comfortable enough with the software to help students explore and experiment. Later, the teacher will need to act as troubleshooter. Beyond an understanding of the software itself, basic knowledge of screen design is necessary.

All of the research skills needed to produce a well-prepared oral presentation or a well-written report must be used when working with hypermedia. The students need to select the information that best conveys the idea they are trying to communicate. The traditional role of helping children to organize, analyze, and synthesize information is not usually a problem for the classroom teacher. It is in the area of incorporating technology into the instructional process that teachers need support. Brooks (1990) describes the difficulty teachers may have in striking the balance between teaching for skill acquisition and teaching for independent thinking. Although difficult to incorporate at the beginning, hypermedia quickly becomes a tool to help the teacher strike that balance.

Hypermedia in the Mathematics Curriculum

In March 1989, there was a revolution in mathematics. After three years of study and work, the National Council of Teachers of Mathematics (NCTM) set forth its *Curriculum and Evaluation Standards for School Mathematics*. The most significant change for students and teachers alike is the recommendation that mathematical power be developed in all students.

> Mathematical power includes the ability to explore, conjecture, and reason logically; to solve nonroutine problems; to communicate about and through mathematics; and to connect ideas within mathematics and between mathematics and other intellectual activity. Mathematical power also involves the development of personal self-confidence and a disposition to seek, evaluate, and use quantitative and spatial information in solving problems, and in making decisions. Students' flexibility, perseverance, interest, curiosity, and inventiveness also affect the realization of mathematical power (NCTM 1992, 1).

Routine lessons where homework is checked, problems are worked on the blackboard, and students are given explanations before they complete seatwork do not fit into this new schema. Students need to become engaged in mathematical tasks, investigating concepts and ideas and making connections to previous and developing knowledge. Another significant change in mathematics is the emphasis on communicating mathematical knowledge. Writing the answers on a separate sheet of paper does not qualify! Students of mathematics need to assess their own thinking processes, talk through their conjectures with others, and develop an easily understood explanation. Hypermedia can be a way to communicate this mathematical knowledge.

NCTM points out the need for teachers to model the use of technology and to help students become users of technology and related tools as they pursue mathematical innovations. It has long been known that before one can teach a subject, one must know the subject well. Hypermedia can be used to promote peer teaching about mathematical topics between students. This is a splendid way for encouraging students to wrestle with ideas and promoting mathematical discourse.

In addition, the thought and planning required by students who are creating hypermedia stacks is, in itself, the type of logical thinking that the *Standards* call for. The problems that students must explore as they prepare their information for presentation requires communication, connection, and spatial information.

Technology is attractive to children. They can achieve a great deal of self-confidence through the manipulation of this tool. Hypermedia is a great way to engage students and allow them to communicate their understandings.

The math lessons on Multiplication Word Problems (page 27), Fractions (page 30), and Perimeter and Area (page 32) are good examples of how mathematics and hypermedia can interrelate.

Hypermedia in the Science Curriculum

Not since *Sputnik* has the need to teach science and mathematics been so clearly stated. President Bush declared that the goals of the America 2000 program are to overhaul math and science teaching, to improve literacy, and to make American students the best-educated in the world. Only high-quality, universal education can produce great minds, promote innovations, and develop a workforce capable of handling the technological tools of the future (Sosinsky 1992).

Teaching science to better prepare students for their future involves them in as many ways of thinking and doing as possible. Investigating questions and phenomena that are interesting and familiar to students is the best way to begin. Students need to get acquainted with the things around them—to observe, collect, handle, describe, question, and argue about them and then try to answer their questions (Rutherford and Ahlgren 1990, 188).

Students need to have many and varied opportunities for collecting, sorting, and cataloging; observing, note taking, and sketching; interviewing, polling, and surveying; and using hand lenses, microscopes, thermometers, cameras, and other common instruments. They should dissect; measure, count, graph, and compute; explore the chemical properties of common substances; plant and cultivate; and systematically observe the social behavior of humans and other animals.

Science teaching should include in any discussion the history or the influence society has had on the development of science and technology and the influence of science on society. It is important to include oral and written communication at all levels, with teachers insisting that students' reports include clear, unambiguous replication of their supporting evidence. Scientists work mainly in groups, so it is natural to have students work collaboratively to question and discuss their own procedures and findings.

Understanding science as a process, rather than just a set of terms, gives students knowledge that will accumulate while they continue to extend their understanding by questioning and pursuing answers.

In learning science, students need time for exploring, making observations, taking wrong turns, testing ideas, and doing things over again; time for building things, calibrating instruments, collecting things, and constructing physical and mathematical models for testing ideas; time for learning whatever mathematics, technology, and science they may need to deal with the questions at hand; time for asking around, reading, and arguing; time for wrestling with unfamiliar and counterintuitive ideas, for coming to see the advantage in thinking in a different way. For new concepts to take hold of students and mature within them, individually, the new concepts must not just be presented to students from time to time but must be offered to them periodically in different contexts and at increasing levels of sophistication (Rutherford and Ahlgren 1990, 193). Ocean Creatures (page 46) is a collaborative project in which students must investigate questions, decide how to complete the project, and to explain their choices.

Warn, Whiting, and Coutts (1991) discuss what happens when children are given the opportunity to enter a real-world dialogue about issues that concern them. First-graders were involved in a science lesson on gears. One student commented, "The teeth have to fit." Given more opportunity to explore, another student related, "The gears only turn when another one turns around." Just as the movement of one gear affects others, collaboration and a shared vision are essential ingredients in integrated planning. Real-world problems and real-life issues are clearly important in the Tropical Rainforests (page 36) and Mammals (page 41) projects.

Anderson-Inman (1989) reported that hypertext offers students at least three ways to link information. Although the author was referring to an already written stack, students creating hypermedia documents also benefit from an understanding of these types of links. Referential links are used to connect a specific chunk of information in a document; these links can be retraced. An organizational link is designed to connect one section of a hypertext document with other sections. The third type is the key word link, designed to search a hypertext document and pull together all chunks of information containing a specified keyword. As students plan their webs, the cards can be specified as to the type of link needed to connect the cards.

Hypermedia in the Social Studies Curriculum

Hypermedia is an appropriate tool for use within the social studies curriculum. One goal of social studies teachers everywhere is to help students learn to work and live in the information-rich society that we have become. It is clear that students need skills in information retrieval, interpretation of information, management of information, and storage of that same data. As students work on their projects, they need to seek a variety of information sources, find the meaning of this information in terms of their project or question, determine the best way to share it and the key issues for the audience, and how to present it. To achieve these goals, students will have to apply the critical-thinking skills that have been modeled and taught in their classrooms. In addition, during the data-collection and planning stages, students will find it necessary to work with others and to clearly communicate their ideas to others. Research is a necessity as students work on such lessons as Pioneers (page 61), The States Projects (page 65), and The '60s (page 77.)

In her book *Constructing Buildings, Bridges and Minds: Building an Integrated Curriculum Through Social Studies*, Katherine Young (1994) describes the importance of community spirit. She describes the variety of learning styles in a classroom, and how students learn from one another while struggling to solve a variety of problems. The collaborative nature of children learning from each other and planning together is a part of the hypermedia environment as well, an environment that encourages and supports active and involved learning for the participants.

According to Welton and Mallan (1992), the variety of thinking skills important within social studies can be placed into four categories:

- Data-gathering skills
- Intellectual skills
- Decision-making skills
- Interpersonal skills

Hypermedia is a communication tool through which students can develop the skills that fall within each of these categories. By building assessment strategies into the projects, the teacher can help students recognize their own strengths and weaknesses in each of these areas and help them develop the skills in which they need practice. The participation skills each student needs to become a working part of the larger community are inherent in the process of becoming a hypermedia collaborative author. Peer evaluation and collaboration are an important criteria in all the lessons. The City (page 68) and the Chinese Lunar Calendar (page 84) are good examples of both.

As students become more aware of other cultures and begin to use languages of other countries, hypermedia is an excellent environment for practicing foreign-language skills. Sounds can be added easily to most of the programs. Travel Mates (page 52) and An Animal Habitat Alphabet Book (page 14) can be easily adapted to other languages.

References

Anderson-Inman, L. 1989. Electronic studying: Information organizers to help students to study "better" not "harder"—part II. *The Computing Teacher* 16 (9): 21–29, 53.

Baca, J. C. 1990. The Delphi study: A proposed method for resolving visual literacy uncertainties. In *Perceptions of visual literacy*, edited by R. A. Braden, D. G. Beauchamp, and J. C. Baca. Blacksburg, VA: International Visual Literacy Association.

Bellan, J., and T. Best. 1992. Pixels instead of pens and paste. In *Visual communication: Bridging across culture*. Blacksburg, VA: International Visual Literacy Association.

Brooks, J. G. 1990. Teachers and students: Constructivists forging new connections. *Educational Leadership* 47 (5): 68–71.

Curriculum and Evaluation Standards for School Mathematics. 1992. Reston, VA: National Council of Teachers of Mathematics.

Harel, I. 1991. *Children designers: Learning through design and production*. Paper presented at the annual conference of the American Educational Research Association, Chicago, April 1991.

Heinich, R., M. Molenda, and J. E. Russell. 1989. *Instructional media and the new technologies of instruction*. 3d ed. New York: Macmillan.

Heller, R. S. 1990. The role of hypermedia in education: A look at research issues. *Journal of Research on Computing in Education* 22 (4): 432–441.

Nicol, A. 1989/90. Children's hypermedia compositions. *Journal of Computing in Childhood Education 1 (2): 3–17.*

Rutherford, F. J., and A. Ahlgren. 1990. *Science for all Americans.* New York: Oxford University Press.

Sosinsky, B. 1992. Kids' stuff: Buying computers for children. *Boston Computer Society Update*: 6–14.

Turner, S. V., and V. M. Dipinto. 1992. Students as hypermedia authors: Themes emerging from a hypermedia study. *Journal of Research on Computing in Education* 25 (2): 187–99.

Warn, G., L. Whiting, and M. Coutts. 1991. Integrating technology. *Schoolhouse Monitor on Cue* 6 (3): 13, 17.

Welton, D. A., and J. T. Mallan. 1992. *Strategies for teaching social studies.* 4th ed. Boston: Houghton Mifflin.

Young, K. 1994. *Constructing buildings, bridges, and minds: Building an integrated curriculum through social studies.* Portsmouth, NH: Heinemann.

Curriculum Ideas

1
About Me

About Me for Elementary Students

Curriculum Connections:
Language arts, communication skills, art, problem solving, planning

Purpose:
Students are introduced to hypermedia as a communication tool. They will work in pairs to practice several specific skills within the hypermedia program they are using and to create a single hypermedia stack that will introduce each of them to the user.

Content Goals:
- Developing communication skills.
- Developing a knowledge of self and a sense of self-esteem.

Planning Forms:
About Me for Elementary Students Planning Form

Student Experiences:
- Choosing a graphic to define oneself.
- Writing descriptive text to accompany a graphic.
- Planning for an audience.
- Sharing with an audience.

Hypermedia Skills Needed for This Project:
The "Software Support Materials" section of this book contains handouts appropriate to the hypermedia program being used by the class, covering the following areas:
- Starting up
- Creating a stack or folder
- Adding a border (optional)
- Using the Text tool
- Importing or creating graphics
- Using Paint tools
- Adding transitions (optional)
- Creating buttons:
  1. To display text
  2. To add sounds
  3. To link to screen or card
  4. To link to stack or folder
- Saving the work

Social Skills Emphasized in This Project:
1. Sharing information about self and family.
2. Working with partners.
3. Planning and executing a plan within a time framework.
4. Sharing equipment and time.
5. Peer coaching.

6. Peer editing and evaluation.
7. Group assessment.

Note: Even if students work independently at computers, numbers 5, 6, and 7 will still apply.

Suggested Time-Frame:

Five sessions of 40 minutes each, including one classroom session for selecting graphics and borders and creating texts for buttons.

Description of Sessions:

Session 1—An introduction to Hypermedia (computer session): Two students share a computer. Using the Starting Up handout, students enter the program and each creates a stack named either *AM.YourInitials.# of disk* (if there is a number) or *About.Me.YourInitials.# of the program/stack disk*. Each student takes a turn using the computer to experiment with the Text tool, writing his or her name on the screen. One student reads the step-by-step instructions for importing a graphic while the partner performs the necessary actions. Then the paint program "fill" or "flood fill" is introduced individually as children complete the graphic import. These screens are for practice only and should either not be saved or be deleted, depending on the particular program.

Session 2—Planning the About Me screen (classroom session): Students should discuss what they have learned about hypermedia from their time at the computer. Students should view hard copies of the resident graphics, fonts, and borders in the program, if available. Using the planning sheet for this activity, they can design the layout of the screen, plan the graphic they will use, and write the two or three lines of text needed to describe themselves. Each screen will feature a graphic and a button icon. The button will reveal text that will identify and introduce the student. Later, students try to guess the identities of the creators of other stacks. The planning sheets are edited by peers or teachers.

Session 3—Creating the About Me screen (computer session): Students use their planning sheets and work in pairs at the computer. They start up the program, insert the disk containing their files, and open the stacks created in Session 1. A reasonable goal for the session is to have each child place and color a border and add clip art for his or her screen.

Session 4—Completing the screens (computer session): Students use the Creating a Button handout and work in pairs to prepare the button that will trigger their text. Instructions should be read aloud by one student while the partner creates the button. After the text is entered, partners switch roles.

Session 5—Linking the stacks (computer session): The goal of this session is for student pairs to create buttons to link their two screens together. The first student links his or her stack to the partner's stack. The second student creates a button to link their stack to the stacks created by other students. By this point, students should be working with minimal support from the teacher.

Assessment:

Student assessment for this project can involve several elements:

- Peer assessment: Have the class (or another class) view the merged stack as though they had never seen it before. In a general discussion, ask the students what they liked about the presentation and what could be improved. What did they learn about the students who were featured in the stack? Was the information presented clearly? What would the students change about their individual screens if given the chance to do them again? Which screens did they really like? Why? This is a good time to discuss the importance of a clear link between the selected graphics and the information in the text field.

- Teacher assessment: This evaluation should be based upon criteria emphasizing the specific skills explored in the activity and the other goals decided upon by the teacher and class.

- Self-evaluation: Have each student write a critique of his or her own stack.

Additional Notes:

It should be noted that, in this exercise, the stacks were linked linearly. Further class discussions and viewing of the merged stack brought new questions and ideas to the surface. Students wanted to be able to view their own screens without having to view all the preceding screens. Within the parameters of the program, it was possible to introduce another stack that listed the students' names in pairs. These names served as Link to Stack buttons so that the users could immediately go to the screen of their choice.

This project was successful in many ways. The students were able to produce a pleasing and gratifying presentation in a few short lab periods, and they developed many basic programming skills that were essential to further use of hypermedia. Their parents were impressed with their use of the technology. And through the About Me stack, the teacher was able to get parental and administrative support for hypermedia use.

Through several years of experimentation, we found that the initial project was most effective when followed by two to three weeks of exploration. The students were eager to explore the options afforded them by the program. In the weeks that followed, they were introduced to the drawing and sound features of the program. Very little direction was necessary. Once a student "discovered" a tool, others immediately began to use it. After this exploration period, the students were ready to move into another organized project.

The creating a Menu Stack handout (see appendix C), explains how to combine the work of all students into one presentation, with instructions for each of the various hypermedia programs. If you are comfortable using computers, the directions should see you through. If not, seek out a school colleague or computer coordinator who can give you a hand the first time. If using HyperScreen, call Scholastic for directions.

Extensions:

The About Me stack is an example of the instructional philosophy represented by this book in that it provides the students with real experiences and the opportunity to apply newly learned skills. The About Me stack happened to fit the aims and time-frame of this classroom. Other ways to achieve the same end might include: riddles with pop-up answers, a dictionary of school or academic terms, or an I'm Special stack.

About Me for Elementary Students Planning Form

Name: _____

Border Line-color: _____

Border Fill-color or pattern: _____

Graphic to be used:_____

The text that will go into the field where you describe yourself:

_____

_____

_____

_____

_____

_____

_____

_____

_____

_____

_____

_____

_____

_____

_____

About Me for Middle-School Students

Curriculum Connections:
Social studies, language arts, communication skills, planning, art, problem solving

Purpose:
Students are introduced to hypermedia as a communication tool. They practice several specific skills within the hypermedia program they are using.

Content Goals:
- Developing communication skills.
- Developing knowledge of self and a sense of self-esteem.

Planning Forms:
About Me Planning Sheet

Facts About Me form

Screen Planning Form (see appendix B)

Student Experiences:
- Choosing graphics to define oneself.
- Writing text that is descriptive and related to the graphics.
- Peer evaluation.
- Sharing.

Hypermedia Skills Needed for This Project:
The "Software Support Materials" section of this book contains handouts appropriate to the hypertext program being used by the class, covering the following areas:
- Starting up
- Creating a stack or folder
- Adding a border (optional)
- Using the Text tool
- Adding transitions
- Importing or creating graphics
- Using Paint tools
- Creating buttons:
    1. To display text
    2. To add sounds
    3. To link to a new screen
    4. To link to another stack
- Saving the work

Social Skills Emphasized in This Project:
1. Sharing information about self and family.
2. Developing and executing a plan within a time framework.
3. Peer editing and evaluation.

Suggested Time-Frame:

Eight computer lab sessions of 40 minutes each plus one period for sharing.

Description of Sessions:

Session 1: Students are given the About Me Planning Sheet to use as a reference and a guide during the project. Then, after a classroom discussion about the project, students fill out the Facts About Me form, including information about themselves, their families, and their personal interests.

Session 2: Discuss the software and procedures for booting, using the samples as guides. Students create a data disk, referring to the Creating a Stack handout.

Session 3: Using the Screen Planning Form, students plan the title screen. They should investigate available backgrounds or graphics that can be imported.

Session 4: Students can plan and start a new stack or folder, name the first screen, and add a background. Then students learn how to save the stack.

Session 5: Students add buttons to the title screen—a Display Text button, and a Link to Next Screen button. The next screen they create contains facts about themselves.

Session 6: The students continue to follow the steps on how to add backgrounds, graphics, text, and buttons. Then students add a third screen, about their families.

Session 7: In this session, students learn how to add a sound button. They create the final screen, adding a transition. The final screen is about their interests, with appropriate text and graphics. A button is added to link back to the title screen.

Session 8—Peer evaluation and editing: Students pair up and evaluate each other's stack or folder. Where changes are needed, time should be made available for editing.

Session 9—Class presentations: Whole-class presentation and sharing of finished project.

Assessment:

- Peer assessment: Have the each member of the class view and comment on at least three other projects using the Peer Evaluation Form (see appendix A).

- Teacher assessment: This evaluation should be based upon criteria emphasizing the specific skills explored in the activity and the other goals decided upon by the teacher and class.

- Class assessment: The class should engage in discussion during whole-group presentations.

Additional Notes:

This was a linear project. Each screen was linked to the next. Students were comfortable sharing information about themselves. Most students were willing to express their personal feelings, especially about their families. Most students were able to finish the four screens within the allotted time. A few students added additional screens. When students are learning a new media, it is important to use subject matter that is familiar—there is nothing they know more about than themselves.

As this was a tutorial in how to use the software, it was followed by a more in-depth project to put these newly learned skills to immediate use.

These projects can be used as a display during an open house; see appendix C for information on how to combine all the student projects onto one disk.

About Me Planning Sheet

1. Obtain the following:
   - Facts About Me form
   - Software program disk
   - Student data disk
   - Screen Planning forms
   - Starting Up handout

2. Fill in the Facts About Me form.

3. Plan your first screen:
   a. The opening screen is the title screen. It should include your name and text to let users know that they will find information about you and your family in this stack or folder.
   b. The title screen should have two buttons—a Display Text button, to give additional information, and a link to the Next Screen button. Plan where to place these buttons. Obtain a hard copy of resident graphics, fonts, and borders for your program. This will help you to make the appropriate choices for text size and style and for graphics to represent the buttons.
   c. Use the Starting Up handout for your software to help you create the first screen you planned. This first screen may include a graphic, and it should be in color, if available. Use the Creating a Button handout to help you make a button to display text that tells a fact about you or that describes you.

4. Plan the second screen.
   a. The second screen will display facts about you. This can be done with text or with a combination of text and graphics. Use the hard copy of graphics, fonts, and borders to find the appropriate graphics, or you may want to draw your own with the Paint tools.
   b. The two buttons for the second screen should be interesting; one should reveal additional text or graphics, and one should connect to a third screen.

5. The third screen should be about your family. One of the buttons should reveal additional text or graphics, and one should connect to the fourth screen.

6. The fourth screen should be about your personal interests (dance, reading, sports, camping, horseback riding, etc.). One of the buttons should reveal additional information, and the other button should connect back to the title screen.

7. Assessment.
   a. Obtain the Peer Evaluation Form (see appendix A)
   b. With a partner, look at each other's stacks or folders and do a helpful critique.
   c. Make any corrections or additions to your own stack as suggested by your partner.

8. Whole-class presentation.
   a. Check your stack or folder again to make certain all buttons work as planned.
   b. Check your stack or folder for any spelling or grammatical errors.
   c. Decide the order in which you would like to present your stack or folder and sign up.

Facts About Me

Fill in the blanks with information about you and your family.

Name:_____ Nickname:_____

Birthdate:_____ Place of birth:_____

Address:_____ House/Apartment:_____

Parents names: _____

Brothers' names and ages:_____

_____

_____

Sisters' names and ages:_____

_____

_____

Pets, kind and names:_____

Describe Yourself

    Hair:_____ Eyes:_____ Height:_____ Weight:_____

Any special characteristics: _____

_____

Favorite vacation spot: _____

Favorite school activity: _____

Favorite family activity: _____

Other favorites: _____

Best friend: _____

Special talents:_____

What you would like to learn to do? _____

_____

If you had a wish, it would be? _____

_____

2
Language Arts

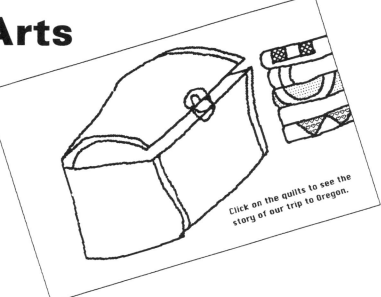

Click on the quilts to see the story of our trip to Oregon.

Endangered Animals.... from A - Z

An Animal Habitat Alphabet Book

Level: Elementary

Curriculum Connections:
Language arts, science, research skills

Purpose:
Students study the habitats of a variety of endangered animals, which are selected or assigned according to letters of the alphabet. To foster sharing of research results, each students creates a stack that tells about one animal and its habitat. As in traditional written reports, the individual stacks will each include a list of bibliographic references used by the student. The individual stacks are joined together to create a single class presentation that contains all of the letters the alphabet and the animals they represent.

Content Goals:
- Understanding influence of habitat on animal life.
- Developing higher-order thinking skills.
- Thinking in a nonlinear fashion.
- Developing an awareness of audience in planning a project presentation.

Content Forms:
Screen Planning Forms (see appendix B)

Note-taking sheets*

Bibliography form*

Student Experiences:
- Using multiple sources for gathering data.
- Creating a bibliography.
- Students are familiar with creating a list of references for a traditional report. During this project, they learn that a reference list is necessary in all media environments when the work of others is included. Each teacher must determine what will be included in the bibliographic format. In the third grade, for example, students might only list the author and name of the source.

Hypermedia Skills Needed for This Project:
The "Software Support Materials" section of this book contains handouts appropriate to the hypertext program being used by the class, covering the following areas:
- Starting up
- Creating a stack or folder
- Adding screens or cards
- Using the Text tool
- Using the Paint tools
- Importing or creating graphics (optional)

---

* Depending on the age of the students, teachers should provide appropriate note-taking sheets and bibliographic forms.

- Adding a border (optional)
- Adding transitions (optional)
- Using icons
- Creating buttons:
    1. To display text
    2. To add sounds (optional)
    3. To link to screen
    4. To link to stack

Social Skills Emphasized in This Project:
1. Peer coaching.
2. Peer editing.
3. Cooperative planning.
4. Developing an awareness of your audience.

Suggested Time-Frame:
The amount of time necessary for this project will depend on the grade level of the students and the depth of the research required. All research should be completed prior to planning the hypermedia project.

Description of Sessions:
Early sessions of this project are spent in the classroom or library media center gathering information about the habitat of the animal to be researched.

Session 1 (computer session): Students follow their planning sheets, making it easier for them to follow through the activities in order. During this session, students will:

- Create the stack.
- Design the opening screen, which contains the letter followed by ellipsis points. It is also decorated in whatever way the student chooses. Students should be encouraged to create their letter using both traditional and unique forms.

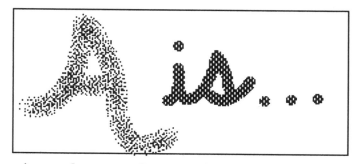

A sample screen from an alphabet stack.

The second screen continues from here and contains the name of the animal and a student drawing of it. Students frequently enjoy creating their own graphics; however, if clip art is available, the teacher may allow the students to import the clip art onto the screen or card.

Session 2 (computer session): Students begin from where they left off at the first session. The last card (or screen) to be created will contain the text about the habitat of the animal. Depending on the hypermedia program that is being used, this card may have text only, text and a border, a scrolling text field with color text, or, possibly, a small graphic depicting the particular type of habitat.

Session 3 (computer session): If this is the first time all the student stacks will be combined into a single, larger classroom stack, a discussion should be held with students about what information the menu should contain and the process for mapping and creating the menu. Ask the students in what ways they think users of the stack will want to navigate through the stack. This could include going from stack to stack linearly, looking for the stack of a particular student, a particular animal, or a particular letter of the alphabet. As a class, determine who will create the menu stack to aid users (probably you, if this is an elementary class and if this is their first experience). In addition, students will need to consider how the consistent use of the same button icons in each of their individual stacks will help users to know where they are going in the larger, combined stack. Information on how to create this kind of stack is included in the "Software Support Materials" section under the specific hypermedia program.

As a class, before the students place buttons on the cards (or screens), choose the arrow and home icons that will be used and determine where they are to be placed on the students cards.

During the third session, buttons are created to link all the cards in the stack. Students will need to create different buttons on each of the cards.

The opening screen with letter will need:
- an invisible button to cover 3/4 of the screen that will link to the next screen. Clicking anywhere on that 3/4 of the card will move the user to the next screen.
- an arrow button that will move to the next stack, which should be placed in the bottom 1/4 of the screen.
- a home icon button to move to the menu for all the stacks should also be placed in the bottom fourth of the screen.

The alphabet letter screen will need:
- an arrow button that will move the user to the next card.

The animal screen will need:
- a curved arrow button that will return the user to the opening screen. This curved arrow is the standard return icon. Helping students learn which functions have standard icons helps them as they design stacks.

Do not be surprised if it takes more than one session to create buttons on all three screens. The age of the students and how much prior experience they have had will determine how long this step will take. Each teacher will have to make this determination.

Assessment:

When the project is introduced, students and teachers agree upon the content goals and the criteria for a well-designed stack. Criteria for the content can be provided by the teacher before the actual research begins. Students, using the knowledge of design gained during other projects, could be responsible for developing the design criteria.

- Peer assessment: Have students assess each other's stacks, using the agreed-upon criteria, and fill out Peer Evaluation Forms (see appendix A).

- Teacher assessment: The teacher also uses the agreed-upon criteria to evaluate the individual stacks. The Peer Evaluation Forms completed by the students can also be considered in the final assessment of each stack.

- Class assessment: At various times during the designing and mapping of the stacks, students should share what they consider to be successes and problems in their stacks and ask for peer feedback. At the end of the project, evaluate the final, combined stack as a class, based on the same criteria that were used to evaluate the individual stacks.

Additional Notes:

This project can be completed by students individually or in pairs.

Extensions:

This project can be used with any content area and it provides an opportunity to pull together information on any theme or topic previously introduced. Reading of alphabet books can provide the stimulus for this project. Another possibility is to have older students create alphabet books for younger students.

Have students create alphabet books by themselves or collaboratively. Another possibility is for pairs of students to create one stack each, with the teacher then putting them all together into a single stack.

Suggested Alphabet Books:

Edwards, Michelle. *Alef-bet: A Hebrew Alphabet Book*. New York: Lothrop, Lee & Shepard, 1992.
This Hebrew alphabet book features three siblings and their parents in their everyday life at home.

Ehlert, Lois. *Eating the Alphabet: Fruits and Vegetables from A to Z*. San Diego, CA: Harcourt Brace Jovanovich, 1989.
An alphabetical tour of the world of fruits and vegetables.

Pallotta, Jerry. *The Ocean Alphabet Book*. Chicago: Children's Press, 1991.
Introduces the letters A to Z by describing fish and other creatures living in the North Atlantic Ocean.

Quilts

Level: Elementary

Curriculum Connections:
Language arts, social studies

Purpose:
Students create a story based on a quilt created in hypermedia by the teacher. Students then write a story and embellish the quilt picture.

Content Goals:
Students should see the quilt as a story. They will use the quilt provided by the teacher as a story starter.

Planning Forms:
Screen Planning Form (see appendix B)

Plans for Making a Fabric Quilt from Hypermedia Designs (for the teacher, see appendix C)

Student Experiences:
- Classroom study of quilts and quilters' stories.
- Reading of children's literature related to quilts.
- Directed writing.
- Peer editing.

Hypermedia Skills Needed for This Project:
The "Software Support Materials" section of this book contains handouts appropriate to the hypertext program being used by the class, covering the following areas:
- Starting up
- Creating a stack or folder
- Adding a border (optional)
- Using the Text tool
- Importing or creating graphics
- Using Paint tools
- Adding transitions (optional)
- Creating buttons:
  1. To display text
  2. To add sounds
  3. To link to screen or card
  4. To link to stack or folder
- Saving the work

Social Skills Emphasized in This Project:

1. Working with partners.
2. Planning and executing a plan within a set time.
3. Sharing equipment and time.
4. Peer editing and evaluation.

Suggested Time-Frame:

Two or three computer lab sessions, 40 minutes each; one or two classroom periods for planning, story writing, and editing.

Description of Sessions:

(These directions are for use with Scholastic's "HyperScreen." They can be adapted for other platforms.)

Session 1 (classroom session): Students are paired to practice collaborative skills. The teacher gives each pair a paper printout of a simple, six-patch quilt. This is the graphic that each pair will have as background in their hypermedia stack. Students are asked to talk about the quilt and then write its story.

Session 2 (classroom session): Student pairs continue their writing, if necessary, then edit and revise their stories. They submit the final stories to the teacher for comments.

Session 3 (computer session): Each student pair is assigned a number. Prior to this session, the teacher creates a new stack for each pair of students labeled *Quilt#* (the number corresponds with the pair's number) and imports a simple quilt graphic as a background using the Import Graphics feature (see the Quilt Graphic sheet at the end of this section). The students open Graphic Background and select Quilt. The quilt graphic will appear with a horizontal arrow (link to screen) in the lower right corner. Students create a Link to Screen button located at the arrow and connect to a new text screen, which they should name "Page 2." They should then select a border and an opening transition and begin typing in their text. The students should be reminded to create a button labeled "More" or "Next" in the lower right-hand section of the screen that will connect this screen to the next screen or stack, depending on the length of the text. At the end of the session, screens are saved.

Session 4 (computer session): Students continue typing in their text. Partners can take turns typing, or they may want to schedule the time in the lab so that both partners are working together, with one typing and the other checking the work. Before the stacks are completed, the partners should embellish the simple quilt graphic using the Paint tools.

Session 5 (computer session): Optional, depending on the needs of the group. If only a few students need to complete work, it might be more practical to have them work on the classroom computer or in private sessions in the lab.

Assessment:

- Peer assessment: Have students evaluate each other's stacks, based on both the content and the presentation of the story. Have them write down what they like best about the stack and what could be improved.

- Teacher assessment: Teacher assessment should be made based on design, the relevance of the story to the graphic, elements in the story, and the overall appearance. Conventional methods of assessing student's writing seem most appropriate, although a project of this kind might be the impetus to using a less traditional method.

Additional Notes:

This project requires that the teacher use the Plans for Making a Fabric Quilt from Hypermedia Designs (found in appendix C) to provide a common first screen for all the stacks. Perhaps suggest designs that can represent several things (e.g., a spiral can be a snail, a rose, or a gem). Following the completion of the stacks, the teacher can opt to link the stacks in a linear fashion. Discussions from previous projects might have brought up the suggestion that students would like to view their own project without having to go through the entire stack. One easy way to do this is to create an opening stack with an introduction and a second page featuring the names of the partners. Buttons can be created around those names to connect the user to that particular opening screen.

A follow-up quilt activity would be to have students design a quilt square in hypermedia. They can then write a story based on the quilt square. Students have to show a wide range of ideas with this assignment. Some of them are: a quilt found by an antique dealer many years after it was created, a story of the fabric pieces in the quilt, how a quilt brought luck to generations in a family, and the story that was shown on the quilt cover.

Extensions:

This stack provides an opportunity for the reluctant writer to be teamed with one who is more enthusiastic. Viewing one's story on the computer screen is a powerful incentive for writing.

There are many children's books that center around the topic of quilts and quilting. Two books of special interest are:

Jonas, Ann. *The Quilt.* New York: Greenwillow Books, 1984.

Coerr, Eleanor. *The Josefina Story Quilt.* New York: Harper & Row, 1986.

This project is a good model for hypermedia extensions of other thematic units. Simple teacher- or student-created graphics can be used by pairs of students as a stimulus for writing. Suggestions for thematic units with ties to literature can be found in the publication *Booklinks,* ALA Subscription Services, 50 E. Huron St., Chicago, IL 60611.

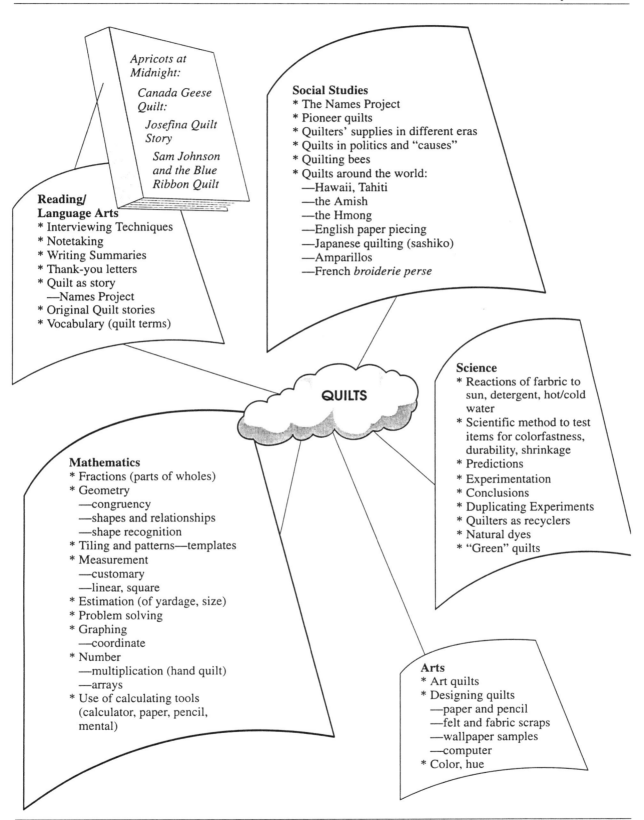

**Reading/
Language Arts**
* Interviewing Techniques
* Notetaking
* Writing Summaries
* Thank-you letters
* Quilt as story
  —Names Project
* Original Quilt stories
* Vocabulary (quilt terms)

Apricots at Midnight:

Canada Geese Quilt:

Josefina Quilt Story

Sam Johnson and the Blue Ribbon Quilt

Social Studies
* The Names Project
* Pioneer quilts
* Quilters' supplies in different eras
* Quilts in politics and "causes"
* Quilting bees
* Quilts around the world:
  —Hawaii, Tahiti
  —the Amish
  —the Hmong
  —English paper piecing
  —Japanese quilting (sashiko)
  —Amparillos
  —French *broiderie perse*

QUILTS

Science
* Reactions of farbric to sun, detergent, hot/cold water
* Scientific method to test items for colorfastness, durability, shrinkage
* Predictions
* Experimentation
* Conclusions
* Duplicating Experiments
* Quilters as recyclers
* Natural dyes
* "Green" quilts

Mathematics
* Fractions (parts of wholes)
* Geometry
  —congruency
  —shapes and relationships
  —shape recognition
* Tiling and patterns—templates
* Measurement
  —customary
  —linear, square
* Estimation (of yardage, size)
* Problem solving
* Graphing
  —coordinate
* Number
  —multiplication (hand quilt)
  —arrays
* Use of calculating tools (calculator, paper, pencil, mental)

Arts
* Art quilts
* Designing quilts
  —paper and pencil
  —felt and fabric scraps
  —wallpaper samples
  —computer
* Color, hue

Quilt Graphic

Use the Paint tools in your hypermedia program to create a quilt top. This quilt will be the stimulus for student writing, and the students will also use the hypermedia Paint tools to embellish the graphic. Make the designs vague enough to allow for as many student interpretations as possible. Use this graphic as a first card in the stack or folder, or import it as a background, depending on your program. This will allow you to place it in every student's stack or folder. See the illustration below, created in HyperCard, for an example of a quilt graphic.

Twelve-square quilt example.

Poetry and Images:
A Thanksgiving Experience

<u>Level: Elementary</u>

Curriculum Connections:
Language arts, social studies, visual literacy

Purpose:
Students listen to a Thanksgiving poem and use their own imagination to create images in hypermedia to accompany the text. The poem should be appropriate for the grade level and allow students to visualize a variety of images. The poem used in this example, "Song of the Osage Woman," attributed to an Osage Indian, is included in the book *Thanksgiving Poems* from Holiday House (1985).

Content Goals:
- Developing listening skills.
- Developing imagery skills.
- Creating visual images inspired by poetry.
- Increasing understanding of another culture.
- Increasing vocabulary.
- Considering Thanksgiving from the perspective of the author.

Planning Forms:
Screen Planning Forms (see appendix B)

Student Experiences:
- Listening to a variety of poetry.
- Interpreting poetry.
- Linking verbal images with visual images.

Hypermedia Skills Needed for This Project:
The "Software Support Materials" section of this book contains handouts appropriate to the hypertext program being used by the class, covering the following areas:
- Starting up
- Creating a stack or folder
- Adding a border (optional)
- Using the Text tool
- Importing and creating graphics
- Using Paint tools
- Adding transitions (optional)
- Creating buttons:
  1. To display text
  2. To add sounds
  3. To link to screen or card
  4. To link to stack or folder
- Saving the work

Social Skills Emphasized in This Project:

1. Working with partners.
2. Planning and executing a project within a time framework.
3. Sharing equipment and time.
4. Peer coaching.
5. Peer editing.
6. Group assessment.

(If students work independently at computers, numbers 2, 4, 5, and 6 should still apply.)

Suggested Time-Frame:

Two class sessions of 40 minutes each.

Description of Sessions:

Session 1 (classroom session): In a manner determined by the teacher (see "Additional Notes"), the poem "Song of the Osage Woman" is read to the class. After jotting down key words to help them remember the images, students use the generic planning sheets to plan their screens (or cards) with sketches, word notes for placement, or other inclusions. They also plan the text that will explain the element or phrase from the poem they have chosen to illustrate.

Session 2 (computer session): After hearing the poem for a second time, students use their completed Screen Planning Forms to transfer their ideas to the screen. As they save their work, it is important to have students name the stacks in a manner that makes them easy to identify. For example, the word *Poem* followed by the student's initial or verse numbers may be sufficient, but if there is a possibility of confusion later, the naming might be more specific, such as *OsagePoem.MH.vs2–4*. If students have not had a great deal of experience creating new stacks, remember to discuss the difference between *stacks* and *screens*. Until you are certain that each student understands the difference, it is important to include such a discussion in each lesson.

Assessment:

- Peer assessment: During the session in the computer lab, stop and ask the students if they have a screen they would like to share. This sometimes stimulates questions and provides an opportunity for both assessment and shared learning. At other times, ask students if they are having difficulty creating an image or idea and if they would like to ask the group for suggestions. Again, this provides an opportunity for brainstorming and collaborative experiences.

Combine the screens so that they can be shown on a large-screen monitor in class. Ask the students if they would like to guess which parts of the poem are being illustrated. Another possibility is to show the stack to students who have not heard the poem and let them tell or write what they, as the audience of the stack, think the poem may be about.

Additional Notes:

This activity could be used to teach poetry appreciation, or it could be used during the celebration of a particular holiday, or it could be used with any other content area. The assignment described here was used in two third-grade classrooms and one fifth-grade classroom. As a result, a variety of approaches were used to introduce the poem to the students. In one class, the poem was read to the students, but they were not shown the illustrations in the book. In a second classroom, the poem was read to students the illustrations were shown. In the third classroom, the poem was first read to the students without the existing images so that they could begin to envision their own. Then the students were given copies of the poem with illustrations to refer to as they designed their screens. Some teachers used this as an individual project. Color printouts of the students' screens were displayed as part of the holiday decorations in several classrooms.

Poetry Collections:

Cooper, Floyd. *Pass It On: African-American Poetry for Children*. New York: Scholastic, 1993.
   An illustrated collection of poetry by such African American poets as Langston Hughes, Nikki Giovanni, Eloise Greenfield, and others.

Gensler, Kinereth D. *The Poetry Connection: An Anthology of Contemporary Poems with Ideas to Stimulate Children's Writing*. New York: Teachers and Writers, 1978.

Hopkins, Lee Bennett. *The Sky Is Full of Song*. New York: Harper & Row, 1983.
   An anthology of poems celebrating the seasons.

———. *A Song in Stone: City Poems*. New York: Crowell, 1983.
   Twenty poems about city life by Eve Merriam, Myra Cohn Livingston, Lillian Moore, and others.

Janeczko, Paul B. *Preposterous: Poems of Youth*. New York: Orchard Books, 1991.
   An anthology of poetry about being a teenager, and adolescent problems and concerns.

Extensions:

This assignment could be modified to have students select images from other sources that support the text. The text could be entered on the screens and linked to images from laser discs. Students could select art that illustrates stanzas or particular words or phrases from the selected poetry.

Pairs of students could select a short poem related to any content area. They could enter it into a stack, and use invisible buttons placed over selected phrases or words, which would link to a variety of images that readers of the stack could view.

3
Mathematics

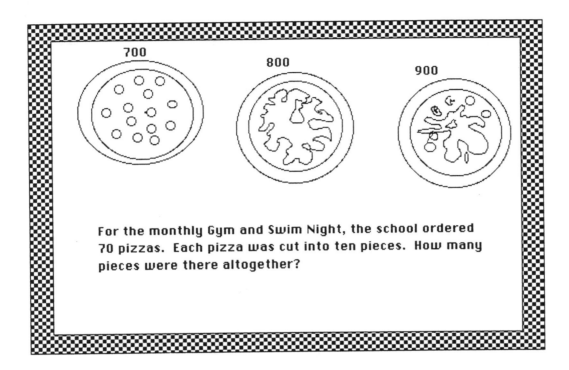

700   800   900

For the monthly Gym and Swim Night, the school ordered
70 pizzas. Each pizza was cut into ten pieces. How many
pieces were there altogether?

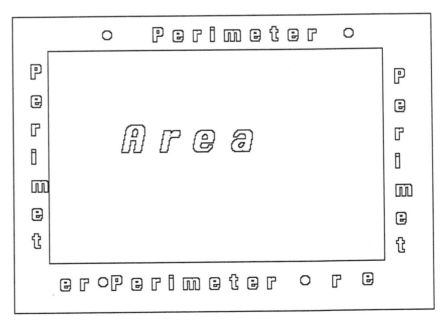

Multiplication Word Problems

Level: Elementary

Curriculum Connections:
Mathematics, writing

Purpose:
Students create multiplication word problems with multiple-choice answers. The hypermedia stack will display a screen for each of the possible answers. The screens linked to wrong answers will provide clues for solving the problem. The mathematics involved will be appropriate to grade level.

Content Goals:
- Identifying situations in which multiplication can be used to solve a problem
- Relating real-world issues to mathematics
- Creating a story or situation that is engaging to peers
- Developing plausible alternative solutions
- Creating clues or hints that assist students in solving the problem

Planning Forms:
Math Story Problem Planning Sheet

Screen Planning Form (see appendix B)

Content-Area Experiences:
- Students will have spent a month or more using math manipulatives to develop an understanding of the concept of multiplication.
- Students will have created original story problems for other mathematical operations, such as addition and subtraction.
- Students will have developed story problems for multiplication in cooperative groups.

Hypermedia Skills Needed for This Project:
The "Software Support Materials" section of this book contains handouts appropriate to the hypertext program being used by the class, covering the following areas:
- Starting up
- Creating a stack or folder
- Adding a border (optional)
- Adding a transition (optional)
- Using Paint tools
- Using the Text tool
- Importing or creating graphics (optional)
- Creating buttons:
    1. To display text (optional)
    2. To link to screen or card
    3. To add sound (optional)
    4. To link to stack or folder
- Saving the work

Social Skills Emphasized in This Project:
1. Working in small groups.
2. Planning and executing a plan within a time framework.
3. Peer editing and evaluation.

Suggested Time-Frame:
Two or three 40-minute classroom sessions for planning, story writing, and editing. Two or three computer lab sessions.

Description of Sessions:
Sessions 1–3 (classroom sessions): Students work in pairs to develop a possible story that meets the criteria on the Math Story Problem Planning Form. After they complete the form, they exchange forms with another pair, who comment on the appropriateness of the task (Is it too hard? Too easy? Does it require multiplication to solve? Is this an interesting task?). The pair must also determine which wrong answers to include in the multiple-choice format and develop screens with clues to help the users arrive at the correct answer.

Sessions 4–6 (computer sessions): Students create cards or screens for their stack and link them according to the planning form.

Assessment:
- Peer assessment: Midway through the project, student pairs each display to the class the screens they have created and tell what still needs to be created. They should ask for feedback and questions from the group. A teacher may help direct this assessment.

- Final assessment: A checklist of the project objectives and the criteria for a successful hypermedia program is given to students in another classroom, as well as other students and teachers who participated in this project.

- Self-evaluation: It would be appropriate for group members to evaluate their own work.

Additional Notes:
It is important for students to remember that the task they create will involve a multiple-choice format. Connected to each of the "wrong" answers should be helpful hints regarding an appropriate way to solve the problem. Students should be encouraged to illustrate their notes for all answers, showing a graphic representation of the problem's solution. For example, one possible graphic representation of a multiplication problem is an array:

• • • • •

• • • • •

• • • • •   3 groups of 5 (3 x 5) = 15

Math Story Problem Planning Form

Names: _____

_____

What is the real-world situation of your problem?

Where does it take place? _____

Who are the characters involved? _____

What is the problem that has to be solved? _____

_____

How will you solve the problem?

_____

_____

_____

What are some other strategies for solving this problem?

_____

_____

_____

What are some ways in which students could solve the problem incorrectly?

_____

_____

_____

How could you help a student get closer to an accurate solution?

_____

_____

_____

Fractions

Level: Elementary

Curriculum Connections:
Mathematics (fractions)

Purpose:
Students create fractions problems for others to solve. Initially, they will create these problems using math manipulatives, then they will "record" the problems and possible solutions using hypermedia. Students will have already explored possible strategies for solving the problems, to help them create the incorrect solutions.

Content Goals:
- Using hypermedia to visually "record" a fraction problem developed using math manipulatives.
- Developing plausible alternative solutions.
- Creating clues or hints to assist users in solving the problem.
- Demonstrating knowledge of fractions through accurate problems and solutions.

Planning Forms:
Screen Planning Form (see appendix B)

Content-Area Experiences:
- Students will have spent several weeks exploring the concept of fractions using math manipulatives such as fraction bars, fraction strips, and pattern blocks.
- Students will have worked in groups to create problems for other groups to solve.
- Students will have developed written strategies for solving similar problems in their math journals.

Hypermedia Skills Needed for This Project:
The "Software Support Materials" section of this book contains handouts appropriate to the hypertext program being used by the class, covering the following areas:
- Starting up
- Creating a stack or folder
- Adding a border (optional)
- Using the Text tool
- Importing or creating graphics
- Using Paint tools
- Adding transitions (optional)
- Creating buttons:
    1. To display text.
    2. To link to screens or cards.
    3. To link to stacks or folders.
- Saving the work

Social Skills Emphasized in This Project:

1. Working in small groups
2. Developing a plan within a time framework
3. Testing solutions and evaluating them as a group

Suggested Time-Frame:

Two or three 40 minute classroom sessions to develop the problem and possible solutions. Two or three computer sessions to create the necessary screens or cards and connect them.

Description of Sessions:

Sessions 1–3 (classroom sessions): Students work in pairs or small groups to develop a fraction problem as a hypermedia stack or folder. The pairs use math manipulatives to visualize the solutions and record the explanations as part of their stack planning, using the generic Screen Planning Forms. After they complete the forms, they will exchange them with another pair of students who assess the appropriateness of the problem (Is it too hard? Too easy? Is this task interesting and clearly presented?).

Sessions 4–6 (computer sessions): Students will follow their planning forms to create the stacks or folders. They should display the problem and a visual recording of it on one card, including a list of possible solutions (a multiple-choice task). They should connect these answers to screens or cards which explain the answer or give helpful hints if the chosen answer is incorrect.

Assessment:

- Peer assessment: Midway through the assignment, student pairs should display the screens or cards they have created and explain what will follow them. Students should ask for feedback, both positive and constructive. A teacher may help direct this assessment.

- Final assessment: A checklist of the project objectives and the criteria for a successful hypermedia program is given to students in another classroom, and to other students and teachers who participated in this project.

- Self-evaluation: It would be appropriate for group members to evaluate their own work.

Additional Notes:

This project asks the students to justify or explain their answer through graphics. This is a way of supporting those students whose mathematical language-communication skills might be lacking.

Extensions:

This format could be appropriate to many strands of mathematics: geometry, measurement, graphing, and so on.

Perimeter and Area

Level: Middle School

Curriculum Connections:
Mathematics, language arts

Purpose:
Students create a geometry stack teaching perimeter and area to be used by an elementary class. They include conceptual information as well as contextual problems. The stack will include at least one sample problem demonstrating the concepts described. The answers will be presented in a multiple-choice format. Each answer will either lead to an explanation of the solution or hints for arriving at the correct answer.

Content Goals:
- Identifying situations in which perimeter and area can be used to solve a problem.
- Developing an understanding of the mathematics involved and an ability to communicate those understandings to a younger student.
- Relating real-world issues to mathematics.
- Creating an engaging story or situation.
- Develop plausible alternative solutions.
- Creating clues or hints that assist students in solving the problem.

Planning Forms:
Perimeter and Area Planning Sheet

Screen Planning Form (see appendix B)

Content-Area Experiences:
- Students will have spent several weeks using math manipulatives to develop an understanding of the concepts of perimeter and area and the relationship between the two.
- Students will have created story problems for other mathematics operations: addition, subtraction, multiplication, fractions, and division.
- Students will have developed story problems for perimeter and area in cooperative groups.

Hypermedia Skills Needed for This Project:
The "Software Support Materials" section of this book contains handouts appropriate to the hypertext program being used by the class, covering the following areas:
- Starting up
- Creating a stack or folder
- Adding a border (optional)
- Adding a transition (optional)
- Using Paint tools
- Using the Text tool
- Importing or creating graphics (optional)

- Creating buttons:
    1. To display text (optional)
    2. To link to screen or card
    3. To add sound (optional)
    4. To link to stack or folder
- Saving the work

Social Skills Emphasized in This Project:
1. Working in pairs.
2. Planning and executing a plan within a time framework.
3. Peer editing and evaluation.

Suggested Time-Frame:
Two or three classroom sessions, 40 minutes each, for planning, story writing, and editing. Two or three computer lab sessions.

Description of Sessions:
Sessions 1–3 (classroom session): Students work in pairs to discuss possible ways to teach the concepts of perimeter and area that meet all the criteria for the assignment, as enumerated on the Perimeter and Area Planning Sheet. When students have a workable strategy, they develop it by completing Screen Planning Forms. Then the pairs exchange forms and assess each other's stacks (Is it too hard? Too easy? Does it clearly explain the concepts of area and perimeter? Are the sample problems appropriate? Are the hints helpful? Is this task interesting?)

Sessions 4–6 (computer session): Students create the cards or screens for their stacks and link them according to their planning forms.

Assessment:
- Peer assessment: Midway through the project, student pairs each display the screens they have created to the class and tell what is still to be created. They should ask the group for feedback and questions. A teacher may help direct this assessment.

- Final assessment: A checklist of the project objectives and the criteria for a successful hypermedia program is given to students in another classroom, as well as to other students and teachers who participated in this project.

- Self-evaluation: It would be appropriate for group members to evaluate their own work.

Additional Notes:
It is important for students to remember that the task they create will involve a multiple-choice format. Helpful hints regarding possible ways to solve the problem should be connected to each of the wrong answers. Students should be encouraged to illustrate their wrong-answer screens, showing a graphic representation of the problem's correct solution.

Perimeter and Area Planning Sheet

Names: _____

_____

With your partner, create a stack to help elementary students understand the concepts of perimeter and area. You should:

1. Define the terms.

2. Illustrate the terms.

3. Compare figures with like perimeters or areas.

4. Present at least two multiple-choice problems to solve.

5. Provide screens behind each of the possible answers, either explaining the solution if the correct answer is selected or providing hints if an incorrect answer is selected.

When you have completed the Screen Planning Forms, find another group and have them check over your work for accuracy and appropriateness.

4
Science

Locomotion(slow speed)

When the river otters move, they move usually at one of two speeds. The first and slower speed is approximately 8 kph and the faster speed is about 13 kph. They also swim in water.

The way the river otters move is very specific. The river otter were observed to have an order of which foot was set down first, second, third, and so on. This order was right front paw, then left rear paw, then left front paw, then right rear paw. There was a 10 cm interval between paws. When the river otters were at the slower speed, its limbs were observed to be at a 90 degree angle at the bend and a 45 degree angle off the ground. The river otter would extend its limbs to a 135 degree angle at the bend and almost a 90 degree angle from the ground. It would repeat this process until it got to its desired location. At this speed, the river otter's tail would be dragging on the ground. This is how it would move on solid ground at the slower speed.

MENU BAR

Table of Contents

Where do I live?

LOCAL MENU BAR

In Water

Fast Speed

1st Card

CREATIONS

movie

Poem

A Day In the Life Of An Armadillo

Just So Story

photo

Haiku

Poem

photo

Cartoon

Tropical Rainforests

Level: Elementary

Curriculum Connections:
Science, social studies, problem solving

Purpose:
Students research the rainforests and identify the various layers of the rainforest life and the animals that inhabit each layer. They discover the importance of rainforests, what problems exist there, and some possible solutions. The students work in groups, each responsible for using a hypermedia stack to illustrate the animal life of each layer of the rainforest.

Content Goals:
- Learning about and describing animals of the rainforest and their habitats.
- Learning other important facts about the rainforests.
- Researching and discussing the dangers to the rainforests.

Planning Forms:
Problems Research-Planning Sheet

Animal and Forest-Layer Research Form

Screen Planning Form (see appendix B)

Student Experiences:
- Creating a graphic of a rainforest animal.
- Writing a description of the habitat of the animal.
- Collaborating with a partner.
- Sharing with an audience.

Hypermedia Skills Needed for This Project:
The "Software Support Materials" section of this book contains handouts appropriate to the hypertext program being used by the class, covering the following areas:
- Starting up
- Creating a screen
- Creating a border (optional)
- Using the Text tool
- Importing a graphic
- Using Paint tools
- Adding transitions (optional)
- Creating buttons:
  1. To display text
  2. To add sounds
  3. To link to screen
  4. To link to stack or folder
- Saving the work

Social Skills Emphasized in This Project:
1. Collaborative learning.
2. Planning and executing a plan within a time framework.
3. Sharing equipment and time.
4. Peer coaching, editing, and evaluation.
5. Group assessment.

Suggested Time-Frame:
Seven sessions of 40 minutes each, including at least two for research, one for an introduction to the software, one for planning the screens, and two for creating the screens on the computer, all to be followed by evaluation, editing time, and class presentation.

Description of Sessions

Session 1 (classroom session): As a class, discuss how to use hypermedia to portray the animals learned about in the research. Have student pairs join other pairs until there are four groups, one for each layer of the rainforest. Each group identifies the layer they will research. Each pair of students chooses an animal living in their layer that they will research. They research their animal, looking for interesting facts to include in their stack.

Session 2 (research): When each pair of students concludes their fact-finding, they decide how to present this information in text, understanding that only the facts are needed, not lengthy descriptions. Using hard copies of available graphics, they look for pictures of their animal. If none are available, or if the students prefer, they plan how they will create their own image of this animal.

Session 3 (computer session): Students bring their worksheets to the computer. During this session, each pair of students should follow their design plans to create or import a graphic of their animal. At the conclusion of the session, the screen should be ready for the next stage. The screen should be saved on their data disk.

Session 4 (computer session): After bringing up their screen with the animal graphic, the students use the Creating a Button handout to create a button that will go to another screen. Later, a second button is created to link this screen to a main menu. The new page is used to display text and information about the animal and where it lives in the rainforest. To complete the project, two buttons are added to this second page. One of the buttons returns the user to the previous screen, and the second is a Display Text button that can be used to give bibliographic information and the students' names.

Assessment:
- Peer assessment: Pairs of students should view another pair's project and use the Peer Evaluation Form (see appendix A) to see if the project guidelines have been followed, and then offer constructive criticism. After reviewing the evaluation, the students do any editing necessary to improve their projects. When the final corrections have been completed, each pair shares their project with the class and listens to the class's comments.

- Teacher assessment: Takes place continuously as each pair of students is guided through the developmental stages of the project.

Additional Notes:

For a more extensive project, students should import or create the proper rainforest background for their animal. An opening screen for the project might be a map of the world's rainforests that links to the rest of the stack. Another opening screen might include a drawing of a rainforest, with buttons that link to the animals living in a particular layer.

Extensions:

Students could add a third screen to their project that offers explanations as to what should be done to save the rainforests of the world and why such measures should be taken.

Problems Research-Planning Sheet

Name: _____

1. On a map of the world, color the areas covered by tropical rainforests.

2. Describe these areas (temperature, climate, locations, similarities, differences).

3. Why are tropical rainforests important to the world?

4. What are the problems facing the tropical rainforests?

5. What do you think can be done to solve these problems?

6. Research sources (names of books, magazine articles, film, or software used):

Animal and Forest-Layer Research Sheet

Name: _____

Forest Layer: _____

Animal: _____

Find the answers to the following questions:

I. Description

- What does it look like?

- Describe its size, color, and special features:

- How does it move around?

- How does it live (alone, with family)?

II. Habitat

- Where does it live?

- Why is it in this forest layer?

- Does it have a special place to sleep (or does it go to a special place to sleep)?

- Is it found anywhere else?

III. Food

- What does it eat?

- How does it get food?

- Do other animals eat the same food?

IV. Research Sources (names of books, magazine articles, film, or software used):

Mammals

Level: Middle School

Curriculum Connections:
Science, language arts, art, research skills

Purpose:
Students learn about a mammal through research and careful observation. They search available literature, obtaining information to write a complete profile of the animal they have studied and observed at the zoo.

Images that the students import into the stack could come from photographs taken at the zoo, pictures purchased at the zoo, or from a magazine article or book.

Content Goals:
- Learning about mammal behaviors.
- Learning about mammal locomotion.
- Writing a physical description of a mammal.
- Developing research skills.

Planning Forms:
Animal Research Paper Sheet

The Hypermedia Zoo: Reflective Essay Sheet

Screen Planning Form (see appendix B)

Navigation Planning Form (see appendix B)

Student Experiences:
- Each student researches and observes a mammal.
- The students learn specific observation techniques, concentrating on a different aspect of their animal for each of four 1/2-day visits to the zoo.
- Students learn how to observe and take notes, and how to write a classical expository essay based on those observations.

Hypermedia Skills Needed for This Project:
The "Software Support Materials" section of this book contains handouts appropriate to the hypertext program being used by the class, covering the following areas:
- Starting up
- Creating a new stack or folder
- Creating a card or screen
- Creating a field
- Creating a background
- Creating buttons:
    1. To link cards or screens
    2. To add sounds
- Scanning images
- Placing scanned images into a stack

- Using a laser disc (suggested: *BioScience Encyclopedia of Mammals)*
    1. Setting it up
    2. Creating buttons
- Using Paint tools to create a title card

Social Skills Emphasized in This Project:
1. Planning and executing a plan within a time framework.
2. Sharing equipment and time.
3. Peer editing and evaluation.
4. Sharing and synthesizing information.
5. Making decisions and compromises.

Suggested Time-Frame:
Three sessions per week, 40 minutes each, for 10 weeks (a total of 30 sessions). The hypermedia portion of the project begins at the conclusion of all four visits to the zoo.

Description of Sessions:
Prior to the zoo visits and after each zoo visit, there should be a classroom discussion about how to make written observations, and about how to write a classical expository essay in zoology based on observations. Both content and style should be discussed during these sessions. Also, have students practice observation techniques in the classroom prior to each visit. The 1/2-day zoo visits once a week, last for four weeks. During each zoo visit week, one classroom session deals with a specific observation technique to be used.

Each week throughout the project, conduct a classroom session (perhaps using a video lesson) to develop note-taking skills and improve expository essay-writing skills.

The hypermedia portion of the project begins the week after the last zoo observation. Students work on these projects 3–20 times in the computer lab.

Zoo Visits and Research
Prior to visit 1 (classroom session): Students observe animal behaviors in the classroom and describe what they see. This practice should be aimed at helping students describe the animals in ways that are not anthropomorphic: they should not attribute human feelings and characteristics to animals (such as "the dog is smiling," or "the animal is sad"). This practice helps move the students toward making more careful descriptions.

Zoo visit 1: Students observe their animals and takes notes on their behaviors, being careful not to anthropomorphize those behaviors.

Prior to visit 2 (classroom session): Students use text materials to study the variety of ways in which animals move.

Zoo visit 2: Students observe their animals, concentrating specifically on how the animals move. Students take notes and make sketches as necessary.

Prior to visit 3 (classroom session): Students practice observing animals. They describe the classroom examples in detail, including physical measurements. After they have written their descriptions, each student gives their description to another student, who read sit and tries to draw the animal from the description.

A second practice experience includes observing, writing, and exchanging with partners to critique each other's descriptions.

Zoo visit 3: Students observe their animals, taking notes about the animal's physical appearance, possibly including sketches.

Prior to visit 4 (classroom session): In an art class, students work with the art teacher to learn how scientific illustrators work: first the shape is drawn, then the details are filled in, and lastly, the color is added.

Zoo visit 4: During this visit, students focus on the aspects of the animal that they will include in their research project.

Hypermedia Sessions

Sessions 1–2: Using only their essays, students construct a hypermedia document that reflects their experience in observing and learning about their chosen mammal.

Sessions 3–20*: Students work at their own pace and share with one another things that they have discovered about HyperCard. During this time, pairs of volunteers will learn how to use a scanner, laser disc, QuickTime movies, and how to add sound to a hypermedia document. These pairs become the experts that other members of the class go to for instruction.

Assessment:

Most of the assessment is verbal and informal.

- Peer assessment: During the last session, the teacher models how to evaluate a stack because each student is required to evaluate a peer's stack, and not their own. Each student evaluator creates the style of assessment comments to be applied to the stack. The written form contains several features that the assessor likes or areas of improvement that might be needed.

- Teacher assessment: The teacher uses the assessment style developed by the student evaluator of each stack. The teacher reviews each stack with a small group of students, to incorporate the benefits of public assessment and support.

- Self-assessment: Students reflect in writing on what they have learned using the hypermedia program.

Extensions:

Following the completion of the hypermedia projects, students write a formal, traditional research paper on their chosen mammal in a class that is taught cooperatively by the English and the science teacher, and students may choose to present that paper as a multimedia document.

---

* Each teacher should reshape the plan and the number of sessions based on their own goals and objectives.

Animal Research Paper

Purpose

The purpose of this paper is to write a profile of a mammal based on research and observation. Your observations and drawings, and the comments of parent observers during the trips, should serve as primary resource material. Library sources should serve as secondary resource material. You may do all or part of your paper as a hypermedia document.

Content

Your research paper should include, but not be limited to, the following sections:

1. A physical description of the animal.

2. A detailed description of the animal's natural habitat and zoo habitat: to compare and contrast these habitats, include a critique of the zoo habitat, and suggest possible improvements. Drawings and illustrations are necessary.

3. A description of the animal's geographic range, including a map showing the extent of the range and any migration patterns.

4. An analysis of the impact of humans on the animal's survival in the wild.

5. A detailed description of the animal's behavior in the wild and in captivity.

6. A section called "The Amazing Animal Game," which should include 15–20 questions and answers. Remember to write questions first, organizing them from general to specific, based on the information necessary to answer them.

7. Several pieces (at least three) of creative writing, which may include poems, a fictional short story, or a script for a play. These pieces may be intended to alert the reader to the endangered status of your animal, or to elicit public support for your animal in its zoo captivity.

8. A section called "The Facts," which should list 10 essential facts that everyone should know about your chosen animal.

Resources:

Use your own observations and drawings, parent observations, and any books or magazine articles you find. You may *not* use an encyclopedia for reference, although you can use one to get ideas for topics to study.

The HyperMedia Zoo: Reflective Essay

Write an essay reflecting on what you learned while using hypermedia. It is important to describe more than the specific skills you acquired while doing this project. Try to explain what you learned about the way you think, how to write, your understanding of technology and how to use it, and how using hypermedia affects your learning. The questions included below should be addressed in this reflective summary, which is to be in the form of an essay.

How would you describe hypermedia to someone else? What is it like? How would it be useful for doing other school activities?

What was the hardest part of using hypermedia? What was the easiest part? Do you feel you have learned enough hypermedia skills to begin a project of your own choosing and design? What might the topic be? What are some elements of stack design that you would include? Why?

How is using hypermedia different than using a word processor? How is it the same?

Was there any piece of technology (e.g., buttons, sound, scanned graphics, laser disc images, QuickTime movie clips) that effectively enhanced your report? If so, how?

What do you like best about your stack? Why? What did you like least? Why? Did you see any elements of other people's stacks that you wish you had included in your stack?

How did using hypermedia help you understand your animal? Or if it didn't, why not?

Would you use hypermedia again to do another project like this? Would you use hypermedia for a different kind of project? Why or why not?

How much time did you spend outside of class on this project? Did you use a computer at home, the lab at school, or both? What did you know about hypermedia, and computers in general before you started this project?

How did it feel to help someone in the class? How did it feel to teach someone a new skill, such as how to scan or use the laser disc? How did it feel to be helped by another student instead of the teacher?

Your essay must be word processed and is due _____. In addition to this reflective summary, please write an evaluation of my teaching of hypermedia. Tell me what worked and why. Tell me what needs improvement and include suggestions on how I could teach hypermedia better next year. Thanks for all your hard work!

Ocean Creatures

Level: Elementary

Curriculum Connections:
Science, research skills, language arts, art

Purpose:
Students research an ocean creature. They then work with a partner to create a new, fantastic creature by combining the characteristics of both animals that the partners have researched. The student pair creates a hypermedia report that shows and explains the creature, its name and habitat, its growth, its food, and other interesting facts.

The project provides opportunities for creative, divergent thinking; the use of information acquired through traditional research and observation; artistic expression; and nonlinear thinking. Students create their projects to be shared with a real audience other than the teacher.

Content Goals:
- Developing research skills.
- Learning about the appearance, habitat, predators, prey, food, reproduction, and unique characteristics of a specific sea animal.
- Creating a make-believe creature incorporating the characteristics of two real animals.

Planning Forms:
Ocean Animal Facts form

Ocean Creature Project Schedule

Screen Planning Form (see appendix B)

Navigation Planning Form (see appendix A)

Student Experiences:
The whole class should spend several weeks studying the ocean, its various habitats, currents, topography, plant and animal life, and environmental hazards, incorporating the following:
- Researching an ocean-dwelling animal.
- Imagining a new creature, considering all the aspects of that creature's life and environment that need to be described.
- Following a prescribed plan for researching and presenting information through a hypermedia report.
- Observing animals at a local aquarium, if at all possible.
- Presenting a research report to the class.

Hypermedia Skills Needed for This Project:
The "Software Support Materials" section of this book contains handouts appropriate to the hypertext program being used by the class, covering the following areas:
- Starting up
- Creating a stack or folder

- Adding a border (optional)
- Adding a transition (optional)
- Using Paint tools
- Using the Text tool
- Importing or creating graphics (optional)
- Creating buttons:
    1. To display text (optional)
    2. To link to screen or card
    3. To add sound (optional)
    4. To link to stack or folder
- Saving the work

Social Skills Emphasized in This Project:
1. Planning and executing a plan within a time framework.
2. Sharing equipment and time.
3. Peer editing and evaluation.
4. Sharing and synthesizing information.
5. Making collaborative decisions and compromises.

Suggested Time-Frame:
About two months for the entire project, including the initial research, a visit to the aquarium for observation, and creation of an independent project. The hypermedia extension should include five 40-minute sessions, two in the classroom and three in the computer lab.

Description of Sessions:
Session 1 (classroom session): Each student has researched and observed (if possible) his or her animal and then created an individual report on it. While researching the individual project, or after it has been completed, the student should fill out an Ocean Animal Facts form to use in the hypermedia stage of the project. Following this individual work, all student names are placed in a hat and pairs of names are chosen at random.

Each pair must combine their individual research to create a new creature that incorporates some characteristics of each of the two animals. They must:
- name the creature
- describe its appearance
- describe its habitat
- describe its eating habits and predators
- describe its reproduction
- note its unique characteristics

Session 2 (classroom session): The student pairs plan five screens:

1. The opening screen, which names and shows the creature; it also features the authors' names.
2. The habitat screen, which describes and depicts the creature's habitat.
3. The food screen, which describes and shows the creature's eating habits and its predators or prey.

4. The growth screen, which tells about the creature's reproduction and growth.

5. The unique facts screen, which gives interesting and unique information about this creature.

It may be necessary to include more screens because of lengthy text or other information that students wish to include. Students should carefully plan how these screens will be connected. Nonlinear as well as linear sequencing should be discussed and mapped out on the planning sheet.

Session 3 (computer session): Pairs of students, using their planning sheets prepared outside the lab, create a new stack labeled *Ocean (#)*. They then create the five required screens and any additional screens they wish to include, making sure to create the necessary linking buttons as noted in their plan.

Session 4 (computer session): Begin with a brief group assessment. Each pair should display their opening screen for the class, describing any features that remain incomplete. Positive feedback should be given as well as constructive comments about clarity. Pairs should have the opportunity to reassess their stack and make any changes deemed necessary.

Session 5 (computer session): This and any more sessions should focus on completion of the stack.

Assessment:

- Peer assessment: Because a project of this complexity would ordinarily take place after the students have had some experience working with hypermedia, they can provide each other with constructive feedback that will allow them to rethink and redesign projects. Midway through the project, student pairs each display to the class, the screens they have created telling the class what remains to be created. They should ask the group feedback and questions. Similar "stop and look" assessments can take place at other intervals and can be focused on a particular screen or aspect of the project (e.g., "How are your screens linked?").

- Teacher assessment: This evaluation should be based upon traditional criteria emphasizing the specific skills explored in the activity, or upon the criteria determined by the students and teacher in the peer assessments.

Extensions:

This project, which combines independent research and reporting with collaboration, can be followed by a similar combination hypermedia project in other curricular areas. For example, students researching countries or American colonies could then combine their research to create an imaginary country or colony. Those studying folk or fairy tales could combine the key elements to create a new story.

Ocean Animal Facts

Name: _____

My topic is: _____

You should investigate the following:

Description

- What does it look like as an adult? When young?
- What is its size and coloring? Does this vary according to sex?
- Does its appearance provide it any protection? How?

Development

- Where does it reproduce and have its babies?
- Which parent takes care of the young?
- Do babies look different from adults? Are they able to do different things?
- Do babies grow up in a different place than the adults live?

Habitat

- Where does it live?
- Does it move between land and water?
- Does it move between parts of the ocean?
- Does it live throughout the world, or in one specific area or type of area?

Food

- What does it eat?
- How does it get food?
- Is this animal food for any other ocean animal? What are its predators?

Other Unique Characteristics

Research Sources (names of books or magazine articles):

From *Hypermedia As a Student Tool.* © 1995. Teacher Ideas Press. (800) 237-6124.

Ocean Creature Project Schedule

1. Date: _____ You need to decide on a name for your creature and begin to work on the description.

2. Date:_____ You need to work on planning sheets—one for each screen you will be creating.

3. Date:_____ Continue working on your stack. Be sure to decide the best way to link your screens.

4. Date:_____ Complete your individual stack so that we can link all the stacks together.

5. Date: _____ Hopefully we'll have a stack to show!

5
Social Studies

Alaska: The Last Frontier

Chicago
Places to Go!

STOP

N
W E
S

The China Press

CH'IN DYNASTY

The CH'IN Dynasty
started in 221 BC
and lasted until
286 BC.

Travel Mates

Level: All Ages

Curriculum Connections:
Geography, language arts, mathematics, social studies, foreign language

Purpose:
Students send out "Travel Mates," stuffed animals that travel, through the kindness of strangers, for six months. The Mates are equipped with:

- a backpack containing a set of instructions for the people who find them
- a diary in which people can record the Mates' travel adventures
- an address where postcards can be sent and where the mate can be returned.

When the Mate comes home, the students will use the diary and postcards to map their itineraries. Students will gain a perspective on the interests of adults by their participation in the project. Missing Mates also provide teachable moments, by allowing the students to experience loss.

Content Goals:
- Developing map skills.
- Developing interpersonal skills.
- Developing letter writing skills.
- Dealing with loss.

Planning Forms:
Travel Mates Directions (for the teacher)

Travel Mates: Letter to Parents

Travel Mates: Message

Travel Mates: Instructions

Final Mapping Project

Screen Planning Form (see appendix B)

Student Experiences:
- Writing instructions for the Travel Mates.
- Corresponding with people who have aided the Travel Mates' journeys.
- Keeping track of postcards over a period of time.
- Locating points on a map.
- Developing a picture of a journey by piecing together facts from an itinerary.
- Completing a hypermedia project based on the Travel Mates' journeys.

Hypermedia Skills Needed for This Project:
The "Software Support Materials" section of this book contains handouts appropriate to the hypertext program being used by the class, covering the following areas:
- Starting up
- Creating a stack

- Adding a border (optional)
- Using the Text tool
- Importing or creating graphics
- Using Paint tools
- Adding transitions (optional)
- Creating buttons:
    1. To display texts
    2. To add sounds
    3. To link to screen or card
    4. To link to stack
- Saving the work

Social Skills Emphasized in This Project:
1. Working in partnerships.
2. Planning and executing a hypermedia project within a time framework.
3. Sharing information and ownership with those whose Travel Mates have not returned.

Suggested Time-Frame:
Two 40-minute sessions.

Description of Sessions:
Six months before the actual hypermedia project is scheduled to begin, students bring stuffed animals, backpacks, and diaries to be sent on journeys. The students send their Travel Mates on a trip, with instructions for people who find them, who could note in the diary where the Mate was found, send a postcard back to the class, and send the Travel Mate on the next leg of its journey. Included in the diary is a deadline telling the "kind stranger" when the stuffed animal and diary should be returned to the class.

As postcards come in from the Travel Mates, they are read and kept on a bulletin board. Students locate on a map the places where the Mates have been. When the Travel Mates return, students complete their itineraries and map the journeys.

Session 1 (classroom session): About three or four weeks after the Travel Mate return deadline, students should design a screen to honor their Travel Mate. They should include any destinations that are known, an illustration of the Travel Mate, and their own name. They should also include information as to whether the Travel Mate has returned. Toward the end of the first session, students will share their first screens with the group and ask for comments on design and content.

One screen should be about the Travel Mate (name, illustration, etc.) and other screens are dedicated to its travels (itinerary, map, etc.). Individual stacks are linked in a classroom stack dedicated to all the Travel Mates and those who shared their trips.

Sessions 2–5 (classroom sessions): Students are paired at the computer to help each other execute their planned screens. Screens can be completed in additional computer sessions as needed.

Assessment:

- Peer assessment: Students should share their screens and get peer feedback on their screen designs and content. Then the project author should edit his or her screen based on those comments.

Additional Notes:

Further information about the Travel Mates project can be found in:

McCarty, Diane. "Geography for Kids and Stuffed Pets." *Teaching PreK–8* 23 (April 1993): 32–35.

Extensions:

If a teacher does not wish to have all students sending out Travel Mates, one Travel Mate could be sent by the entire class and the resulting hypermedia project could involve having the class as a whole record all the adventures from the one diary.

This activity is particularly appropriate in schools developing thematic curricula. In mathematics, some of the concepts that are addressed include: measuring and computing distances on a map, time, time zones, keeping a chronological list of places visited, and coordinate graphing with longitude and latitude.

In social studies, concepts that would be appropriate are: locating cities on maps, choosing correct maps (state, U.S., foreign, world) for the locations required, climate differences, time differences, language and customs of various locations, using longitude and latitude, and using map keys.

Language arts activities that could support this thematic approach include: the letter format for a diary, writing a letter to those who send postcards from Travel Mates, fictional accounts of Travel Mates' adventures while the animals are "on the road," actual accounts of the journeys when the Travel Mates return, letters to Travel Mates while they are "on the road," and multicultural literature, which would vary depending on where the Travel Mates have gone. This would be a good opportunity to learn about the language of other countries as well as their customs.

Social skills are important in all curricula; these include: patience; perseverance; expression of feelings such as loss and grief, joy for another's happiness, and excitement and surprise; thank you letters; being taken seriously; and faith in humanity (experiencing goodness from a total stranger.

Travel Mates Directions (for the teacher)

Although Travel Mates was conceived and published by Diane McCarty, Jane Moore has developed many classroom aides to strengthen the project. They are contained in the handouts for this activity. When you are preparing materials for students, the following suggestions are helpful to keep in mind:

1. Talk to the students about the idea of traveling. Because none of them can leave school to travel extensively, the Travel Mates can take their places. Ask the students to go through their stuffed animal collections and pick one that they can part with for an extended period of time (or perhaps permanently) to send on the journey. For those who might have a difficult time parting with any of their animals, suggest a trip to a flea market or garage sale to purchase a stuffed animal.

2. Send a letter to parents explaining the process. See the Travel Mates: Letter to Parents Form. Have students fill in the blanks, or you might rewrite the letter, inserting any information needed.

3. Take pictures of the class. Get enough prints so that one copy can travel with each Travel Mate and one can remain at school. Students need to indicate which picture is of them and write their name on a card. The card will have instructions printed on it (see the Travel Mates: Instructions Form).

4. Laminate the pictures to the name cards. After laminating, use a permanent marker to draw an arrow to the owner's face in the class picture. Punch two holes in the top of the card and use ribbon or yarn to tie the card securely to the animal. (It should not be loose enough to be easily removed, or it may get lost.)

5. Have students write a message in the journal (see the Travel Mates: Message Form for a suggestion).

6. Students could write good-bye letters to their Travel Mates. Perhaps hang them on a bulletin board with the pictures of the students together with their Mates.

7. Have a send-off "Bon Voyage" party. Each student can introduce his or her Travel Mate and tell who's taking it where first. Be sure that you get colleagues or friends to offer to take any Mates who are without transportation. Some can even take two, but ask them to give each Mate to a different person. You could make a video of the party and the speeches. Take pictures of each Travel Mate with the owner. These can be used later for bulletin board displays and, perhaps "Missing in Action" posters.

Handout continues on page 56.

8. During the travel mates absence, the following activities could be part of the project:
   - Students write about what they imagine the Travel Mates are doing.
   - Students write letters to their Travel Mates.
   - Create a display of cards and letters as they come in. Put the picture of the student with their Travel Mate at the top of the postcards on the display. If you photocopy the message side they can be displayed as well.
   - Place a "Back Home" sign, with the date of return, next to each Travel Mate's picture.

9. Travel Mate Return Activities:
   - Prepare a manila envelope for each student and Travel Mate to hold all the postcards or letters received.
   - When the Travel Mate returns, the student lists all the places the Mate traveled, in chronological order, using the diary and postcards.
   - Set a date two to three weeks after the return deadline to divide the students into small groups for mapping, so that the tasks can be shared among students who have not received their Mates back.
   - Prepare "Missing in Action" posters for lost Mates.

10. Group Responsibilities:
    - Decide which maps are needed (state, U.S., foreign, world).
    - Make a list of the continents visited for a class graph.
    - Figure the mileage traveled by using map keys.
    - Create a table for each Travel Mate in the group, stating the destinations and mileage traveled.
    - Write an account of each Travel Mate's adventure (true to its travels, but students should indulge their imagination).

11. Student Responsibilities:
    - Write an evaluation of the experience.
    - Take home the Travel Mate and all souvenirs after a celebration party.

You may want to get all the "parents" of missing animals together and talk about loss and grief and maybe have students write letters to their animals as well.

From *Hypermedia As a Student Tool.* © 1995. Teacher Ideas Press. (800) 237-6124.

Travel Mates: Letter to Parents

Date:

Dear Parents:

A special project is being planned. It is called Travel Mates and is designed to correlate with our map skills study. The students will be bringing in a stuffed animal or doll that will become a Travel Mate.

Travel Mates are stuffed animals or dolls (small) that the students send to various parts of the country. Each animal wears a "dog tag" that includes a class picture and a note explaining the project. The Travel Mates also wear a backpack, or else they are placed in a bag for traveling. Students send the Travel Mates around the country (or world) with people who are traveling. For example, if your family were traveling to New York for Thanksgiving, the Travel Mate could come along and you could give it to someone there who was going to another part of the country (or world).

The animals are sent with instructions and with a journal. The instructions and journal are kept in the Travel Mate's backpack or travel bag. The journal itself should be small—about the size of a small assignment pad. Each person who travels with the animal is asked to write in the journal their name and address and a brief message about the area they are visiting. They are also asked to send a small souvenir or postcard to the school to let us know where the Travel Mate has been.

The instructions ask that on or about _____ the Travel Mates be sent back to the school either with a traveler or by mail. Students will be using map skills to plot the voyage of their individual animals.

You and your student should decide together what animal or doll will make the trip. There is always the possibility that the Travel Mate will not return, so this should be considered.

All Travel Mates with their packs and notebooks should be in the classroom and ready to start their travels by _____.

Thank you for your help in this exciting project.

Sincerely,

Travel Mates: Message

In the Travel Mate's journal, you should write a message to your stuffed animal's traveling companion to introduce yourself, your school, and your town. The following is an example that may be used.

My name is _____. I am the person sending out this Travel Mate. I am a _____ grader at _____ School in _____, _____. Let me tell you about _____. It is a _____ suburb of _____, located about _____ miles from _____. I live in _____. I usually _____ to school. Thanks for taking care of _____. Please send me a postcard so I can tell where he has been or e-mail my teacher at teacher@address.

Travel Mates: Instructions

The Travel Mate has a "dog tag" tied around its neck. This dog tag is the owner's picture and a set of instructions that introduces the Travel Mate to its travel companion. The following may be used for the instructions. Fill in the blanks with the proper information.

Hello!

You are probably wondering who I am, what I am, and why you're holding me. Let me take time to introduce myself. My name is

_____. I belong to

_____. I'm part of a geography project

in _____ classroom at _____

School, in _____.

I have been sent on a journey across the country. When I return

to _____ School, the students in

_____ class will plot my travels on

U.S. and world maps.

Please pass me from person to person. This is my method of

traveling. Record your name, city, and state (and your address if you'd

like us to write back) in the journal that's inside my backpack or case.

If you wish, you may add a souvenir from your travels with me. Please

send a postcard to the class at school so that my owner will hear from

me. Then please pass me on to another person who may be traveling

to a different place.

On _____, please mail me to our

school: _____.

Thank you for letting me travel with you and the class thanks

you for your help. Please don't keep me too long.

Final Mapping Project

Name: _____

Travel Mate's Name: _____

Itinerary:

1. List all the places your Travel Mate has traveled. Be sure that you use the diary (if your Travel Mate is back) or postcards (if it has not returned). If you have heard nothing from your Travel Mate, help the members of your group fill in their sheets.

2. Locate all these places on a map and mark them with points.

3. Connect all the points using a ruler.

4. Display your map on the bulletin board under your Travel Mate's picture.

5. Create a hypermedia screen for your Travel Mate. If your Travel Mate has not returned, design a screen to commemorate him or her.

From *Hypermedia As a Student Tool.* © 1995. Teacher Ideas Press. (800) 237-6124.

Pioneers

Level: Elementary

Curriculum Connections:

Social studies, problem solving, mathematics, language arts

Purpose:

Teams of students will create a pioneer family and trace their journey west, creating a set of events that are historically probable.

Content Goals:

- Differentiating between established eastern communities and the pioneer settlements of the west.
- Mapping a journey from an eastern community to a settlement in the west
- Including appropriate activities and methods of completing tasks during the time period of 1800–1860.
- Sequencing the events in the story in a historically probable and interesting manner.
- Determining the distance traveled by this fictional family and estimating the amount of time required for such a journey.

Planning Forms:

Pioneer Project Sheet

Pioneer Unit Planning Sheet

Screen Planning Form (see appendix B)

Students Experiences:

- Students read and are read books about the western movement in the United States. Examples are: *Addie Across the Prairie* (A. Whitman 1986), the Laura Ingalls Wilder *Little House* books, *Magical Melons* (Macmillan Child Group 1990).
- use a computer simulation program such as *Oregon Trail*.
- use a map to plot the travels of the family in the simulation game.
- are given experiences in pioneer crafts: candle making, quilting, cooking, dyeing, building a log cabin using Lincoln Logs, and so on.
- use a commercial text (if available) to study the pioneer era.
- visit local re-creations of pioneer villages or other pioneer exhibits (if available).

Hypermedia Skills Needed for This Project:

The "Software Support Materials" section of this book contains handouts appropriate to the hypertext program being used by the class, covering the following areas:

- Starting up
- Creating a stack
- Adding a border (optional)
- Adding a transition (optional)
- Using Paint tools
- Using the Text tool

- Importing or creating graphics (optional)
- Creating buttons:
    1. To display text (optional)
    2. To link to screen or card
    3. To add sound (optional)
    4. To link to stack
- Saving the work

Social Skills Emphasized in This Project:
1. Working in small groups.
2. Planning and executing a plan within a time framework.
3. Peer editing and evaluation.

Suggested Time-Frame:
Three or four classroom sessions for planning, story writing, and editing. Three or four computer lab sessions, 40 minutes each.

Description of Sessions:
Sessions 1–3 (classroom session): The student groups use the Pioneer Unit Planning Sheet and the Pioneer Project Sheet to help them create the characters and plan their routes and activities. The students develop the written materials necessary for the project and use the Screen Planning Forms to plan their stack.

Sessions 4–7 (computer session): Students create the screens or cards necessary to their stack and link them according to the planning sheet.

Assessment:
- Peer assessment: Midway through the project, student groups each display to the class the screens they have created and tell what remains to be created. They should ask the class for feedback and questions. The teacher may help direct this assessment.

- Final assessment: A checklist of the project objectives and the criteria for a successful hypermedia program is given to students in another classroom, as well as to other students and teachers who participated in this project.

- Self-evaluation: It would be appropriate for group members to evaluate their own work.

Extensions:
A project similar to this one would be appropriate for units on family history or the history of a particular city or area of the country. Students could take on the personae of an immigrant family settling in the area, and tell their stories.

Pioneer Unit Planning Sheet

Name: _____

Members of this group: _____

1. Names of the family members, approximate ages, and professions or skills:

   _____

   _____

   _____

   _____

2. Where does their journey begin?

3. Where are they heading?

4. Trace their route on a map.

5. Choose as many "markers" along the way as there are members in your group. Mark them on your map and have one group member develop a short story for each of these points. All members of the group must agree to these points and the basic story line. A final marker (not included in this group) should be placed at the end of the journey.

   Marker # 1:

   Marker # 2:

   Marker # 3:

   Marker # 4:

6. Work together on your family's story. Develop a short presentation that you can share with the class. You may use costumes and props. You should use a map to trace the journey for the class.

Pioneer Project Sheet

Names of people in this "family" and their pioneer names:

_____

_____

_____

_____

Screen A: Introduce the family.

Screen B: Map the journey (use buttons to link to each of the markers).

Screen C (1–4): Markers (one for each member of the group). These should be linked linearly so that a user can follow the journey, and they should be linked nonlinearly to the map screen. Each group member should develop one marker screen and tell its story from the perspective of his or her pioneer character.

Be sure to include a button on the last screen which will link to another stack.

1. Date:_____ All planning sheets should be complete.

2. Date:_____ Linking diagram should be complete.

3. Date:_____ Introduction screen should be complete.

4. Date:_____ Map screen should be complete.

5. Date:_____ Marker screens should be complete.

6. Date:_____ Entire stack should be ready.

The States Project

Level: Elementary

Curriculum Connections:
Social studies, research skills

Purpose:
Students acquire knowledge of one of the 50 states through independent research. Then, working with a group, they develop a hypermedia presentation for the class.

Content Goals:
- Using community resources for information.
- Knowledge and use of maps.
- Gathering information regarding the history, physical landmarks, political system, famous people, unique sights, flora, and fauna of a particular state.

Planning Forms:
States Project Guidelines

Individual Research-Writing Planning Form

Screen Planning Form (see appendix B)

Navigation Planning Form (see appendix C)

Student Experiences:
- Writing to state tourist agencies for information.
- Conducting research in libraries.
- Working with maps in groups.

Hypermedia Skills Needed for This Project:
The "Software Support Materials" section of this book contains handouts appropriate to the hypertext program being used by the class, covering the following areas:
- Starting up
- Creating a stack
- Adding a border (optional)
- Using the Text tool
- Importing or creating graphics
- Using Paint tools
- Adding transitions (optional)
- Creating buttons:
  1. To display text
  2. To link to screens or cards
  3. To link to stacks
- Saving the work

Social Skills Emphasized in This Project:

1. Working in groups.
2. Planning and executing a plan within a time framework.
3. Sharing equipment and time.
4. Peer coaching.
5. Peer editing and evaluation.
6. Group assessment.

Suggested Time-Frame:

Six to ten 40-minute sessions following the initial research and presentation of the project in its original form.

Description of Sessions:

Sessions 1–3 (classroom sessions): Students work in groups using the Navigation Planning Form to map their stacks. The first screen or card will have the state's name and a button for each topic covered, or the first card may be connected to a table of contents card, which would then link to each topic. (See the example for this stack in appendix B, "Generic Planning Sheets.")

Sessions 4–10 (computer sessions): Students will work on creating the stack that they have planned. It should incorporate the information gathered during the individual classroom states project. It may incorporate scanned graphics, video discs, or videos.

Assessment:

- Peer assessment. Midway through the project, student pairs each display to the class the screens they have created and tell what remains to be created. They should ask the class for feedback and questions. The teacher may help direct this assessment.

- Final assessment: A checklist of the project objectives and the criteria for a successful hypermedia program is given to students in another classroom, as well as to other students and teachers who participated in this project.

- Self-evaluation: It would be appropriate for group members to evaluate their own work.

Additional Notes:

This project involves editing and revising information gathered for a previous project and then representing it in a hypermedia format. The teacher may decide to have the hypermedia project be the final presentation to the class. Both presentation methods work effectively.

Extensions:

This type of presentation of material allows the student to become the resource person after having done research and writing. It is adaptable to any long-term classroom research project, regardless of subject matter.

Individual Research-Writing Planning Form

Name: _____

Topic: _____

After reading about your topic, write questions that you will answer in your report. Record your questions below:

Question # 1 _____

_____

Question # 2 _____

_____

Question # 3 _____

_____

Question # 4 _____

_____

List any resources that you will use to research and write your reports:

1. Title: _____

   Author(s): _____

2. Title: _____

   Author(s): _____

3. Title: _____

   Author(s): _____

4. Title:_____

   Author(s): _____

The City

Level: Middle School

Curriculum Connections:
Social studies, science, fine arts

Purpose:
Students cooperatively research a topic related to a part of their city. Included in the research will be the effect of this topic upon the environment.

Content Goals:
- Defining major topics related to a city.
- Defining the subtopics related to a major topic.
- Researching a subtopic.
- Defining positive and negative effects of the subtopic on the environment

Planning Forms:
City Project Research Assignment Sheet

The City Topic and Subtopic Planning Sheet

The City Interview Form

The City Interview Permission

Peer Evaluation Form (see appendix A)

Student Experiences:
Each pair of students collaboratively creates a web of topics related to the city. Students may choose topics to investigate based on personal interest or curiosity. The main topic is placed in the center of the second web sheet, and subtopics related to this topic are then entered. The topic will determine whether students use a science, social studies, or fine arts approach.

- Research—The resource center: Students use the card catalog or online catalog to find sources of information that relate to their topic.

- Research—Interviews: Students use the interview form to plan questions. They interview a person with information or knowledge on their chosen topic.

- Research—Onsite visit: Students visit the area of the city associated with their topic, gathering firsthand information in the form of pamphlets, notes, and sketches. If possible, they may take photographs.

Hypermedia Skills Needed for This Project:
The "Software Support Materials" section of this book contains handouts appropriate to the hypertext program being used by the class, covering the following areas:
- Creating a stack
- Creating a new stack or folder
- Creating an opening screen

- Choosing or creating a background:
  1. Using Paint tools
  2. Importing or creating graphics
- Choosing appropriate font(s)
- Creating buttons:
  1. To display text
  2. To add sounds
  3. To link to another screen
  4. To link to another stack
- Saving the work

Social Skills Emphasized in This Project:
- Working in collaborative groups.
- Interviewing techniques.
- Peer evaluation.

Suggested Time-Frame:
Five 40-minute sessions each week for four weeks. The hypermedia project begins at the conclusion of the research, which takes three to five class periods.

Description of Classroom Sessions:
The entire class will brainstorm a list of city topics and put the topics on a web using an overhead or the chalkboard. Each group will select their first two choices to research. If two groups want the same topic, the class will reach a consensus to assign topics to groups.

Session 1 (web of the city): Students work collaboratively in teams of two or three. Each activity will guide students in the planning of the project.

Teams create a web of all the topics related to a city. They discuss among themselves the merits of each topic, deciding which would be their first and second choices to research further. See appendix B for the Topic Web Form.

Session 2 (topic web): The teams build a web for their topic. This may develop into the need for a third web (example: city=museums=specific museum).

Session 3 (research): Teams will research their topic based on the elements of their second or third web. They use materials in the classroom and have access to the resource center. Students should also remember to research the environmental impact of their topic. Bibliographic information should be noted.

Sessions 4–6 (planning and creating the hypermedia project): Teams design the major screens for their project. Using research notes they will decide how the information is related and in how many different ways. This will help students decide how the buttons will connect screens. Students design and create the stack screens and create or import graphics.

Assessment:

- Peer assessment: Using the Peer Evaluation Form, each group is responsible for evaluating two other projects. Groups should be allowed to edit their projects before a final class evaluation.

Additional Notes:

This project can become very involved and it may be necessary to carefully limit student project goals. For example, it would be too much for one project to try to completely research all the city's sports. However, it would be feasible for a group to choose a specific sports venue, such as an arena where hockey, ice skating competitions, and basketball games are held. A student group that concentrates on a particular sport team will have more than enough information to complete the project. The environmental effects of sports include traffic congestion and pollution and the refuse generated by fans. Students may want to interview a city planner to learn about the overall results of having a recognized team as part of the city.

Extensions:

Implementing a thematic approach in a traditional setting:

- Social Studies—relationships within a city.
- Science—environmental impact.
- Language Arts—short stories of people in the city; biographies of people who made a difference to the city, both historically and present day.
- Art—perspective.
- Music—sounds of the city.

City Project Research: Student Directions

Purpose

To learn how to use reference materials to gain an understanding of the environmental impact of the life of a city. To use hypermedia to share the results of this research.

Content

The research project will include, but not be limited to, the following sections:

1. An overview description of the city.

2. A detailed description of the selected subtopic of the city.

3. Biographical information concerning person(s) related to this topic and why they are important to the subtopic.

4. Description of the effects (positive and negative) the subtopic has on the environment.

Resources

Learning center resources on the topic and subtopic, including reference books, vertical file, magazines, and newspapers if the subtopic is of current importance.

The City Topic and Subtopic Planning Sheet

I. The City
   As a class, decide on which city to research—a nearby large city, a smaller city, or their hometown.

II. Team planning
   • List as many large topics as you can think of that are related to this city.

   a._____   e._____

   b._____   f._____

   c._____   g._____

   d._____   h._____

   • On the Topic Web Form, place the city's name in the center. Put the topics from your list in as many of the boxes as you need.

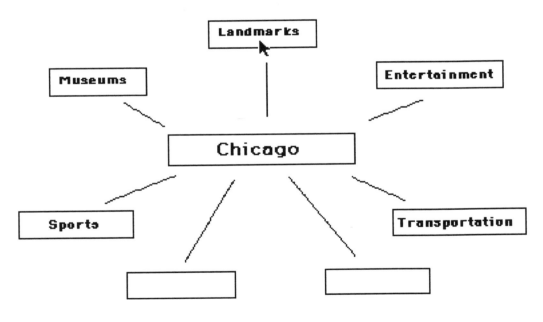

Web of a city.

   • As a team, decide first and second choices to research.

III. Class Web
- As a class, make a web of all the topics teams have listed.
- Teams take turns starting their first research choice.
- Come to a consensus if there are conflicts.
- Teams are assigned their topics.

IV. Topic Web
- Put the topic in the center.
- Put related subtopics in as many boxes as needed.
- Discuss the topic and subtopics.
- Make a team decision as to whether a subtopic has enough research material available.
- Place your subtopic on the class web to inform everyone of your decision.
- Make a subtopic web.

V. Research

A. Collecting Information
   1. Put each element of the subtopic web on an index card.
   2. Divide the cards among team members.
   3. Use the resource center and classroom materials to find information on subjects listed on the cards, including:
      a. Description
      b. Impact on the environment
      c. People of interest
      d. Bibliographic information on sources used now

B. Interview
   1. Pick up a copy of The City Interview Form.
   2. Write your questions on the form.
   3. Make an appointment with the person or persons you will interview.
   4. Record their answers on the form.
   5. Add this information to your data cards

C. Firsthand Accounts
   1. Plan a visit to the location of your topic.
   2. Collect any literature available (pamphlets, postcards).
   3. Write down any information about your visit, including the date.
   4. Make sketches or take pictures if possible.
   5. Add this information to your data cards.

Handout continues on page 74.

VI. Planning the Hypermedia Project

    A. Sorting the Information
1. Circle the topic of each card (these are the subtopics related to your main topic).
2. Sort the cards by subtopic, putting aside those you won't need.
3. Number each of the cards that will be used, starting with the number 3 (notes from the visit and the interview should be on cards).

    B. Layout
1. Sketch a proposed title screen on a card; number it 1.
2. Sketch out a menu card; number it 2. The menu card will list all the subtopics.
3. Place all cards on a sheet of 12-x-24-inch poster paper.
4. Arrange together cards that have related information.
5. After cards are fastened to the paper, draw lines between cards that should be connected.
6. First cards of subtopics should be connected to the menu card.
7. Some cards may have more than one connection.
8. The connections will become buttons when you create the screens.
9. Mark each card with the number of buttons it will have.

VII. The Hypermedia Project
Refer to the Start Up handout for your software to help you create your project. Follow the steps to create the screens.

The City Interview Form

Name: _____

Interview a knowledgeable person who can tell you facts about your subject. The goal is to find out as much as you can about your topic so you can share the most relevant information in your hypermedia project.

Choose a person who you consider knowledgeable about your topic.

1. Ask permission to set up a time for an interview.

2. Prepare your questions wisely. You want to know why this person knows about the topic of your research, what the person does, how this person feels about your topic, and if they know how your topic affects the environment.

3. What is your feeling about this person's expertise? Does this person know more than you do? Can they explain it so that you understand?

4. Write up what you have discovered:

    1. Name of the source of information. _____

    _____

    _____

    2. Describe how this person is involved with your topic._____

    _____

    _____

    _____

    3. Give a summary of what you learned. _____

    _____

    _____

    _____

    4. What is your feeling about this person's knowledge? _____

    _____

    _____

    _____

Use this information to help you complete your screens. Remember to give credit to the person you interviewed as part of your bibliography.

From *Hypermedia As a Student Tool.* © 1995. Teacher Ideas Press. (800) 237-6124.

The City Interview Permission Form

I, _____, give

permission to be interviewed for a class assignment by _____

_____. I have knowledge of

_____ because of my

position as _____.

Signature: _____

Date: _____

The '60s

Level: Middle School

Curriculum Connections:
Social studies, art, music, language arts

Purpose:
Students learn about many aspects of the 1960s in American history. They research events and the biographies of people who dominated the news during this decade. They use their notes to complete a hypermedia document that relates the events or people to the dates, adding their conclusions as to the effects of the event or person.

Content Goals:
- Understanding how people and events create history.
- Understanding how social order can be changed.
- Using biographical references.

Planning Forms:
1960s Research Assignment Sheet

1960s Topic Form

Concept Map Planning Sheet (see appendix C)

1960s Hypermedia Project Planning Sheet

Evaluation Form for Hypermedia Projects

Student Experiences:
- Researching an area of interest related to the '60s in cooperative groups.
- Concept mapping, to create a web of information (e.g., people's names, events, social issues, places, and other ideas that relate to their topic)
- Using biographical references to research the people having a dominant influence on their topic. This information should include names, age (if important), places, contribution to the topic, and any other relevant information.
- Searching *Dominos*, a videodisc, for relevant visuals that corroborate the chosen topic. Students make notes of the frame(s) and number(s).

Hypermedia Skills Needed for This Project:
The "Software Support Materials" section of this book contains handouts appropriate to the hypertext program being used by the class, covering the following areas:
- Creating a stack
- Creating an opening screen:
  1. Creating a background or a border
  2. Using fonts
  3. Importing or creating graphics

- Creating buttons:
  1. To link to a new screen or a stack
  2. To display text
  3. To add sound
- Using Edit to cut, copy, paste
- Using Paint tools
- Saving the work

Social Skills Emphasized in This Project:
- Collaborative learning.
- Presentation skills.
- Peer assessment.

Suggested Time-Frame:
Five 40-minute lab sessions each week for three weeks. The hypermedia project begins after the research is complete.

Description of Sessions:
Session 1: Topics from the 1960s are brainstormed by the whole class (e.g., rock music, the Vietnam War, peace demonstration, the Civil Rights movement, communes). Groups of two to four students form around one topic. Each student must be part of a group. The groups use a concept-map planning sheet to fill in all the information connected to their topic. Reference books should be made available.

Session 2: Student groups continue their research to fill out their concept map and to make reference cards of information. Students use biographical reference sources to research the people who influenced their topic. This information should include names, age (if important), places, and contribution to the topic (and any other relevant information). Events can also be researched in history books related to the period, almanacs, and encyclopedias, both print and online media.

Session 3: Research continues. Each group should have a minimum of 10 cards. These include the description of the topic, persons, events, dates, and consequences of particular actions.

Session 4: Give a demonstration for the class on how to use a videodisc (*Dominos, An Uncensored Journey Through the Sixties*) to access information and images. The teacher should be aware of what information is available on the disc. Students can refer to the table of contents to decide if there is information available on the disc for their topic. Students should write down the frame numbers that correspond to any single frames or sequences of frames they wish to use.

Session 5: Students plan their hypermedia project by using the 1960s Hypermedia Project Planning Sheet and their reference cards. The concept map will help students decide which cards should be connected, and in which order. Laying out the cards, numbering them, and noting which cards must be connected to one another before using the computer is a good planning strategy. All projects should have a title screen, a menu screen, a bibliography screen, and screens that cover the topic.

Session 6–10: Students take their project outlines and create their hypermedia stacks, including text, graphics, and buttons. At the conclusion of the project, students do peer evaluations of each other's projects. After a final edit to incorporate peer suggestions, students share their projects with the whole class.

Assessment:

- Peer assessment: Each group of students evaluates the stack created by another group, using a Peer Evaluation Form. Editing can take place before total class viewing of all projects.

Additional Notes:

Middle-grade students are fascinated by the 1960s. This is a period for which there are many images that students are familiar with and can use in their projects. Often, their parents will have some memorabilia from the '60s, which makes history very much alive for the students.

Students might engage in debates over some of the social issues that occurred and still affect us today.

1960s Research Assignment Sheet

Purpose

The purpose of this research is to learn about the '60s. Narrow the topic to cover one aspect, such as politics, music, education, or the Vietnam War.

Content

Your research should include, but not be limited to, the following sections:

1. An overview of the chosen topic.

2. Dates that are applicable to the topic.

3. Biographical information on people who had a major part in the topic.

4. Bibliographic information showing resources used.

5. Pictures of events related to the topic.

6. A sequence of the event from the *Dominos* videodisc that can be referenced during your oral report.

7. Your opinion about the topic and its effect on history or social consciousness.

Resources

Vertical file

Biographical references

Books

History of the '60s references

Videodisc: *Dominos, An Uncensored Journey Through the Sixties*

1960s Topic Form

Fill in the information as you conduct your research.

Topic:_____

    Description: _____

_____

Dates important to the topic: _____

People involved:

    Name:_____

    Notes:_____

_____

    Name:_____

    Notes:_____

_____

    Name:_____

    Notes:_____

_____

    Name:_____

    Notes:_____

_____

References

_____

_____

Videodisc Frame Numbers:

    Beginning: _____ Ending: _____
    Beginning: _____ Ending: _____

Notes:

1960s Hypermedia Project Planning Sheet

Check the blank when the step is completed.

_____ 1. Obtain a data disk and start the hypermedia program.

_____ 2. Create a new stack and name based on your team's topic
(e.g. rock music of the '60s).

3. For your topic:

_____ Create an opening screen. This title page and byline should include, text, a
graphic, and color.

_____ Add one button with a graphic to link to the next screen.

_____ Name the new screen based on the topic event.

4. Goal 1: Create a screen to illustrate and describe the event. The screen
should have:

A graphic
A button to display text
A button to connect to another screen

_____ Go to the screen named for the event.

_____ Design how this screen should look.

_____ Add a graphic.

_____ Add a button(s) to display text giving information on traits.

_____ Add a link to the screen button (for a new screen named after the
people described); include a graphic.

5. Goal 2: Create a screen to tell about people who were connected to the topic.

_____ Go to the people screen.

_____ Design this screen.

_____ Add text.

_____ Add a graphic.

_____ Add a link to Next Screen button (for a new screen named for "causes" related
to the topic); include a graphic.

6. Goal 3: Create a screen to tell about causes related to your topic. The screen
should have:

A graphic
Three buttons (could be Sound, Display Text, Link to Screen with a graphic
or more text)

From *Hypermedia As a Student Tool.* © 1995. Teacher Ideas Press. (800) 237-6124.

A button to connect to another screen

_____ Go to screen and select the "causes" screen.

_____ Design how this screen should look.

_____ Add a graphic or text or both, about '60s causes. Use your research.

_____ Add buttons to give information, sound, and to bring up other screens.

_____ Add a link to the screen button; include a graphic.

_____ Think about the possibilities for connections!

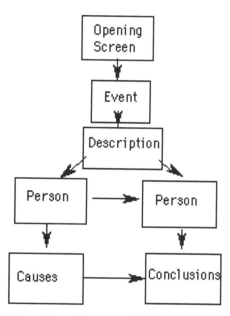

Map showing possible connections.

7. Goal 4: Your stack should include a screen about your group's reaction to or conclusions about this topic, which should include a concluding statement that summarizes your reactions.

8. Goal 5: Your stack should include a menu screen and a final screen.

_____ The final screen should include a bibliography of books and other materials used for your research.

The menu screen should include:

_____ A title.

_____ Main entries of the stack, such as topic and description, events, people, and conclusions.

_____ A button on each entry that connects to that screen.

_____ A change information button on screens so they connect to the menu.

_____ A button for returning to the title screen.

Chinese Lunar Calendar

Level: Middle School

Curriculum Connections:
Social studies, art, music, language arts

Purpose:
Students learn about the Chinese calendar. They research biographies of people born under one of the signs of the Chinese calendar, and complete a hypermedia project that compares the lives of the people to the beliefs held by the Chinese for a person born under that sign.

Content Goals:
- Learning about the beliefs of another culture.
- Learning about the celebrations held by another culture.
- Using biographical references.

Planning Forms:
Chinese Lunar Calendar Research assignment sheet

Chinese Lunar Calendar Topic Form

Chinese Lunar Calendar Hypermedia Project Planning Sheet

A Peer Evaluation Form (see appendix A)

Student Experiences:
- Researching the symbolic meaning of the sign animals.
- Students will research people and important events that occurred during the different years represented by the sign animals.
- Researching people born under a particular sign to see if there are relationships between the people's life and the characteristics associated with the Chinese sign.
- Using a variety of reference sources in research.

Hypermedia Skills Needed for This Project:
The "Software Support Materials" section of this book contains handouts appropriate to the hypertext program being used by the class, covering the following areas:
- Creating a stack
- Creating an opening screen:
  1. Adding background or a border
  2. Using the Text tool
  3. Importing clip art or creating graphics
- Creating buttons:
  1. To link to screen or stack
  2. To display text
  3. To play sound
- Using Edit to cut, copy, paste
- Using Paint tools
- Saving the work

Social Skills Emphasized in This Project:
1. Collaborative learning.
2. Presentation skills.
3. Peer assessment.

Suggested Time-Frame:
Five 40-minute lab sessions each week for three weeks. The hypermedia project begins after the research is complete.

Description of Sessions:
Session 1 (the calendar): Students are divided into 12 teams. The class discusses the Chinese lunar calendar. Each team is assigned one of the signs from the calendar. Each team draws their sign's animal and place it on the class calendar.

Session 2 (research): The teams use calendars and January newspapers to determine which years in the last century have been under the sign of their animal. Using the *Book of Facts*, teams find an important event that happened during each of those years. Each team finds between one and five people born during any of their sign animal's years.

Session 3 (research): Students continue to search for information relating to events and people born in the years of their sign animal.

Session 4 (biographical references): Students use biographical references to research the people born during their sign animal's years. This information should include names, date of birth, place of birth, contribution to society, and other interesting information.

Session 5 (Chinese-custom research): Teams use the vertical file on the Chinese lunar calendar, books on China and its customs, and newspaper and magazine articles (January editions) to find out the symbol that represents the animal and what personality traits are connected to people born under that sign. What kind of people are born under that sign? The students write descriptions of the people they researched and of the sign. What are the relationships between the people and the meaning of the sign?

Session 6 (Chinese-custom research): Teams continue to gather information on worksheet and notecards. Teams arrange their notecards in order, by year. There should be cards representing:

   a. The animal name and picture
   b. Chinese symbol for the animal
   c. Chinese meaning of the symbol
   d. Events
   e. People born under the sign and information about these people (one to five cards).

Session 7 (personal research): Each student prepares a card on him- or herself. This card should contain their birthday, the sign animal of the year they were born, what the year represents, and how this information relates to the student.

Session 8 (reports): Students create their hypermedia reports. Refer to the Chinese Lunar Calendar Hypermedia Project Planning Sheet for instructions.

Assessment:

Teams use the Chinese Lunar Calendar Topic Form to evaluate their progress. Peer Evaluation Forms should be used to evaluate the hypermedia projects. Teams should be given time to edit their projects before final class evaluations.

Extensions:

Implement a thematic approach in a traditional setting:

- Social Studies cultures of other countries
- Art experience related to Chinese art and nature
- Music and instruments of Chinese and other countries
- Math, the Chinese abacus
- Language arts; myths and fables

Chinese Lunar Calendar Research

Purpose

The purpose of this research is to find out about one of the animals of the Chinese lunar calendar and about people born under the sign of that animal.

Content

Your research should include, but not be limited to, the following sections:

1. A graphic representation of the sign animal.

2. Information on the meaning of this animal.

3. Details of people born during any of the years that have this animal as their sign.

4. Biographical information that shows relationships between people's lives who were born under that sign and the beliefs of the Chinese about that sign.

5. Conclusions drawn from these relationships.

6. The sign animal for the year you were born.

7. Biographical information that shows relationships between your life and the beliefs of the Chinese about your sign.

Resources

Vertical file

Biographical references

Books

Interviews

Newspaper articles

Chinese Lunar Topic Form

Fill in the information as you conduct your research.

Animal: _____

Source of graphic: _____

Years: _____

People born under this sign

    Name: _____

    Notes: _____

    _____

    Name: _____

    Notes: _____

    _____

    Name: _____

    Notes: _____

    _____

References used:

_____

_____

_____

Facts about my partner and me

    Birthdate: _____Sign: _____

    Birthdate: _____Sign: _____

    How Our Lives Compare to Chinese Belief:

    _____

    _____

    _____

Notes:

Chinese Lunar Calendar Hypermedia Project Planning Sheet

Check off each step when completed.

____ 1. Obtain a data disk and start the hypermedia software.

____ 2. Create a new stack and name it based on your team's sign animal.

    3. For your topic:

       ____a) Create an opening screen. This title page and byline should include, a text, graphic, and color.

       ____b) Add one button with a graphic to link to the next screen.

       ____c) Name the new screen based on the sign animal.

    4. Goal: Create a screen to illustrate the kind of person born in that year. The screen should have:

    ____ A graphic.

    ____ A button to display text.

    ____ A button to connect to another screen.

    ____ Go to the screen named for the sign.

    ____ Design how this screen should look.

    ____ Add a graphic.

    ____ Add a button(s) to display text giving information on traits.

    ____ Add a link to screen button (for a new screen named after events occurring during your sign animal's years) with a graphic.

    5. Goal: Create a screen to tell about events that occurred in a year of your sign animal.

    ____ Go to the event screen.

    ____ Design this screen.

    ____ Add text.

    ____ Add a graphic.

    ____ Add a link to Next Screen button (for a new screen named for people); include a graphic.

    6. Goal: Create a screen to tell about people born during one of the years you are studying. The screen should have:

    ____ A graphic.

    ____ Three buttons (could be Sound, Display Text, Link to Screen with a graphic or more text).

    ____ A button to connect to another screen.

    ____ Go to Screen button and select the "people" screen.

    ____ Design how this screen should look.

Handout continues on page 90.

_____ Add a graphic or text or both, about people born during the year of your sign animal. Use your research.

_____ Add buttons to give information, sound, and bring up other screens.

_____ Add a link to the screen button; include a graphic

_____ Think about the possibilities for connections!

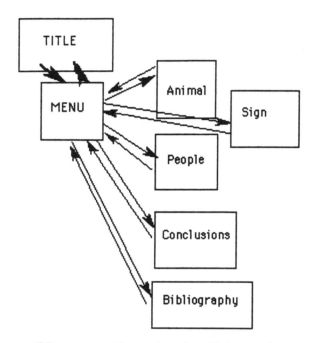

Map of possible connections for the Chinese lunar calendar.

7. Goal: Your stack should include a screen about the team that includes:

    _____ Team members' birthdays.

    _____ Team members' lunar year sign (animal).

    _____ A concluding statement that summarizes whether the members' signs and meanings are compatible with the sign that your stack describes.

8. Goal: Your stack should include a menu screen and a final screen.

    _____ The final screen should include a bibliography of books and other materials used for your research.

    The menu screen should include:

    _____ A title.

    _____ Main entries of the stack, such as the sign animal's name, the symbol, people, and events.

    _____ A button on each entry that connects to that screen.

    _____ A change information button on screens so they connect to the menu.

    _____ A button for returning to the title screen.

6
Visual Literacy

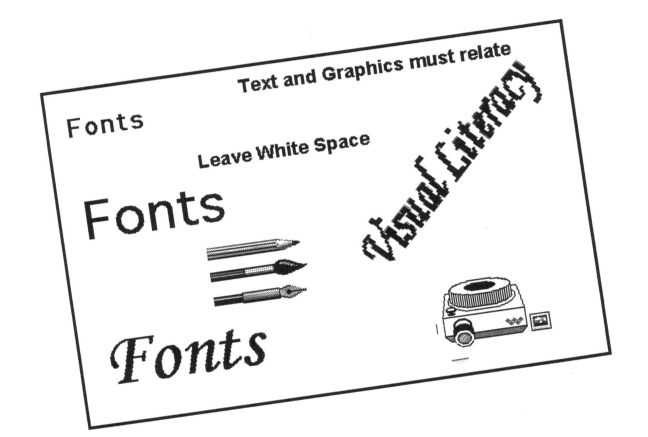

Looking at Software:
Developing a Sense of Screen Design

Level: Elementary, Middle School

Curriculum Connections:
Visual literacy

Purpose:
Students analyze a piece of software to develop an awareness of screen design concepts. They present and discuss their findings.

Content Goals:
- Developing observation skills.
- Becoming aware of design issues.

Planning Forms:
- Software Evaluation Form

Student Experiences:
- Analyzing software by looking at it from an observer's point of view, not a users'.

Hypermedia Skills Needed for This Project:
- None

Social Skills Emphasized in This Project:
1. Working in partnerships.
2. Observing, discussing, and making decisions within a time framework.
3. Sharing equipment.
4. Group assessment.

Description of Sessions:
Session 1 (classroom): The teacher presents pieces of software on a large screen. Starting with the title screen, a discussion takes place concerning the elements of the screen that are numbered on the Software Evaluation Form. These are text (font style and size), arrangements of elements, color, and directions given for use of the software. This modeling should take place before student analysis.

Sessions 2–3 (computer sessions): Students in small groups look carefully at a piece of software, and using the Software Evaluation Form, discuss and note their reactions to the questions.

Session 4 (classroom session): Students use the large screen to present an example screen from their software and discuss their findings with the whole class. The class adds to the discussion, making relevant comments that will further students' knowledge of good screen design.

Assessment:

- Students list elements of good screen design.

- Using different software, the class uses their checklist to analyze the software as a class project.

Additional Notes:

This project helps students become more observant of what makes software easier to use and more pleasing to the eye. Students who completed this project became aware of the value of larger font size and styles that were easier to read. They discovered that the use of too many colors was disconcerting. Screens that were too crowded with many font styles and sizes and too many graphics were confusing and detracted from the purpose of the software. This project helps students to understand the elements that make better screens in their hypermedia projects. Even if the software directions don't help them, they know to use the correct buttons when they create their own projects.

Resources for the teacher that give helpful information on screen design are publications from the International Society for Technology in Education.

McCain, T. (1993). *Teaching graphic design in all subjects*. Eugene, OR: ISTE.

McCain, T. (1992). *Designing for communication*. Eugene, OR: ISTE.

Parker, R. (1993). *One minute designer*. Eugene, OR: ISTE.

Software Evaluation Form

Names of Group Members: _____

Name of Software Being Evaluated: _____

The Screen: How Do You Relate to It?

Spend several minutes looking at the screen. In your group, discuss what appeals to you about the screen. Make comments concerning the following suggested questions.

1. Text on the screen:
   Describe the size and shape of the letters.

   Font-style concerns—What differences do you notice? How many different styles are on the screen?

   Proportional kerning means that space between letters has been adjusted. How does the kerning look for the particular fonts used on the screen?

   Is punctuation used? What could have been done more effectively?

2. Arrangement of information of the screen:
   Describe how items on the screen are arranged.

   Why do you think it was done this way?

   How would you have done it?

   Do you notice any balance? Explain.

3. Color:
   Impressions? What do you think about the use of color.

   Usually there is a background color and one or more foreground colors. Does anything unusual happen to you when you look at the screen?

   Is color important? Is it used effectively? Explain.

4. Directions:
   How easily is it to get into the program?

   What do you need to know to use the program?

   What do you have to do before you can run the program?

5. What other information can your group share about this software?

From *Hypermedia As a Student Tool.* © 1995. Teacher Ideas Press. (800) 237-6124.

Thinking About Screen Design

Level: Elementary

Curriculum Connections:
Visual literacy

Purpose:
Students create hypermedia screens or cards to illustrate good and bad screen design. They then discuss these screen design issues.

Content Goals:
- Developing observation skills.
- Becoming aware of audience viewpoint.
- Becoming aware of design issues.

Planning Forms:
- Screen Planning Form (see appendix B)

Student Experiences:
- Creating hypermedia cards.

Hypermedia Skills Needed for This Project:
The "Software Support Materials" section of this book contains handouts appropriate to the hypermedia program being used, covering the following areas:
- Starting up
- Creating a stack
- Adding a border (optional)
- Using the Text tool
- Importing or creating graphics
- Using Paint tools
- Adding transitions (optional)
- Creating buttons:
    1. To display text
    2. To link to screens
    3. To link to stacks
- Saving the work

Social Skills Emphasized in This Project:
1. Working in partnerships.
2. Planning and executing a plan within a time framework.
3. Sharing equipment and time.
4. Peer coaching.
5. Peer editing and evaluation.
6. Group assessment.

Suggested Time-Frame:
Two or three 40-minute sessions.

Description of Sessions:
Session 1 (classroom session): Students plan a screen to illustrate either a good or a bad design technique. They should perhaps view an old stack and discuss the elements of design: text, readability, spacing, use of color, connections between graphics and text, ease of use, and so on.

Sessions 2–3 (computer sessions): Students create the screens following their planning forms. When the screens are complete, each group presents their screen to the class, asks for comments, and finally, discusses which design issues they had in mind in when they created the screen.

Assessment:
If further assessment is desired, students should create their own checklists for examining the screens. Teacher-created checklists would also be appropriate.

Additional Notes:
This project evolved from class discussions during mid-project evaluations of hyper-media projects. The students thought that it would be fun to create screens or cards that were purposely bad. The discussions brought up subjects that might not have been addressed otherwise; for example, the use of colored lettering and its readability due to the mixing of text and background colors, the relationship between text and graphics, and placement of navigational buttons and icons.

Software Support
Materials

7
HyperScreen
Support Materials

Exploring HyperScreen: A First Visit for Elementary Grades

Name: _____

Today you will explore HyperScreen for the first time. There are several sample *stacks* but today we will look closely at two of them. We will look at U.S. States and at The Human Body. If you finish the questions for these two, you may search through the other sample stacks.

Exploring the stacks means you will be clicking on *buttons* to move through them. Sometimes the buttons look like arrows of other *icons*, sometimes they are invisible. You will have to explore carefully to find the answers to the following questions.

U.S. States

1. What date is on the timeline where Illinois is shown as a new state? New states are shown in red. When they are red, special information about them is available. Can you figure out how to find that information?

2. Move the timeline to 1830. Look at the states that border Illinois. How many were new states in 1830? _____ How many were partly settled? _____ How many were older states? _____ (Do not count Illinois). Use the legend to answer these questions.

3. What date is on the timeline where Alaska is shown as a new state? What year did Alaska legally become a state?

The Human Body

1. How many bones are in the skull?

2. When you take a closer look at the heart, what color are the arrows?

3. What two *icons* are on the skeleton *screen* of The Human Body *stack*?

4. How do you return to the *home card* (or *menu screen*) when you are through answering the questions about The Human Body *stack*?

Starting Up HyperScreen Using Two 3-½" disks

These directions will help you to start up HyperScreen if you are using a computer with a 3-½"disk drive. If you are using a 5-¼" disk drive, you will need a different set of directions.

If you have two 3-½" disks, you can begin to use HyperScreen. Look at the two disks. One of them should be the HyperScreen program disk. The other is a HyperScreen stack disk.

1. Place disk 1 (the program disk) into the drive. Be sure you are holding the labeled end as you place the disk into the drive.

2. If the computer is off, turn the computer and the monitor on, hold down the Open Apple (OA) key and the Control (CNTRL) key and at the same time press the Reset key at the top of the keyboard. Let go of the Reset key and then the other two keys. The computer will load the program.

3. When you see the Homescreen (white background) on the monitor, press the Escape (ESC) key.

4. Remove the program disk and place the stack disk into the drive.

5. Go to the File menu and double click on Open Stack.

6. Double click on the stack you want to open (e.g., Exploring5).

7. If you want to work on a specific screen, click Open Screen and then select the screen (e.g., Quilttext). If you want to work on a new screen, click New Screen, then choose the Graphic or Text screen. Graphic screens use more space, but allow pictures or drawings. At times, the program will ask you to change from your stack disk to your program disk. Just remove the disk that is in the drive, put in the disk that is named on the screen, and press Return.

8. When you have finished your work:

    Press the Escape key.

    Pull down the File menu.

    Select Save Screen.

    Delete the "Untitled" and type in a screen name. (Do this by pressing the delete key and then typing in the name.)

    Press Return (**very important**).

    The message "Saving the screen" should appear on the monitor.

9. Remove the stack disk from the 3-½" drive.

Starting Up HyperScreen Using Two 5-¼" Disks

These directions will help you start up HyperScreen if you are using a computer that has two 5-¼" disk drives and you have three 5-¼" disks. If your teacher has given you two 3-½" disks, or one 5-¼" disk and one 3-½" disk, you will need a different set of directions. The three disks include the program disk (double-sided), the background and clip art disk (double-sided), and a stack disk.

1. Place the program disk into drive 1. Be sure you are holding the labeled end as you place the disk into the drive.

2. If the computer is already on, hold down the Open Apple (OA) key and the Control (CNTRL) key and at the same time press the Reset key at the top of the keyboard. Let go of the Reset key and then the other two keys. The computer will load the program.
    If the computer is off, turn the computer and the monitor on. You will see the red light on the disk drive go on as the program is loaded into the computer.

3. When you see the Home Screen (white background) on the monitor, press the escape (ESC) key.

4. Insert your files disk into drive 2. The stack disk is your files disk.

5. Go to the File menu and double click on Open Stack.

6. Be sure the computer is reading drive 2. You may have to select Tab to make this happen.

7. Double click on the stack you want to open (e.g., Exploring5).

8. If your want to work on a specific screen, click Open Screen and then select the screen (e.g., Quilttext).If you want to work on a new screen, click New Screen, then choose Graphic or Text screen. Graphic screens take more space when they are stored on the disk but allow for pictures or drawing.

9. When you are finished with your work:

    Press Escape.

    Pull down the File menu and select Save Screen.

    Delete the "Untitled" and type in a screen name. (Do this by pressing the delete key and then typing in the name.)

    Press Return (**very important**) and watch for "Saving the screen" message.

10. Remove the stack disk from drive 2. Remove the program disk from drive 1.

From *Hypermedia As a Student Tool.* © 1995. Teacher Ideas Press. (800) 237-6124.

Starting Up HyperScreen
Using One 3-½" disk and One 5-¼" Disk

These directions will help you start up HyperScreen if you are using a computer that has one 5-¼" disk drive and one 3-½" disk drive. If your teacher has given you two 3-½" disks, or three 5-¼" disks, you will need a different set of directions.

1. Place your 3-½" program disk into the smaller drive. Be sure you are holding the labeled end as you place the disk into the drive.

Program disk.

Stack disk.

2. If the computer is already on, hold down the Open Apple (OA) key and the Control (CNTRL) key and at the same time press the Reset key at the top of the keyboard. Let go of the Reset key and then the other two keys. The computer will load the program.

    If the computer if off, turn the computer and the monitor on. You will see the red light on the disk drive go on as the program is loaded into the computer.

3. When you see the Home Screen (white background) on the monitor, press the Escape (ESC) key.

4. Insert your files disk (the stack disk) into the larger drive.

5. Go to the File menu and double click on Open Stack.

6. Be sure the computer is reading the large drive. You may have to select (click on) Tab or Drive to make this happen.

7. Double click on the stack you want to open (e.g., Exploring5).

8. If your want to work on a specific screen, click Open Screen and then select the screen (e.g., Quilttext). If you want to work on a new screen, click New Screen, then choose Graphic or Text screen. Graphic screens take more space when they are stored on the disk but allow for pictures or drawing.

9. When you are finished with your work:

    Press Escape.

    Pull down the File menu and select Save Screen.

    Delete the "Untitled" and type in a screen name. (Do this by pressing the delete key and then typing in the name.)

    Press Return (**very important**) and watch for "Saving the Screen" message.

10. Remove the stack disk from the larger drive. Remove the program disk from the smaller drive.

From *Hypermedia As a Student Tool.* © 1995. Teacher Ideas Press. (800) 237-6124.

Creating Your First Stack in HyperScreen

Be sure that you have a formatted stack disk before you begin.

To begin your first stack, go to the opening HyperScreen screen and press the Escape key. Using either the mouse or the arrow key, move to the File menu on the Menu Bar. Insert your stack disk now. If you have one disk drive, replace the HyperScreen program with the stack disk. If you have two drives, place the stack disk into the second drive. All the HyperScreen menus can be found at the end of this section.

1. Select New stack from the menu; a dialog box comes up on the screen. Notice that the name of the disk (Stacks) appears in the dialog box. Most dialog boxes show you the name of the disk you are using. That will show you which disk is in the disk drive at any time. If the name of the disk is HS, you need to press Tab to go to the other drive, or replace the HyperScreen disk with the stack disk.

2. You will need to name your stack. This first time, type the name PracticeStack where it asks you to name your stack. You will create new screens in this stack as you learn new ways to use HyperScreen.

3. As soon as you name the stack and press Return, a new dialog box appears. It asks you to select the kind of screen you are going to work on. There are two different kinds of screens, Text and Graphic screens. The most important difference is that you cannot place graphics on Text screens. This first time, select a Graphic screen.

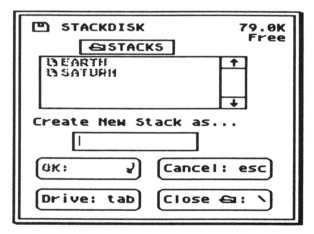

Naming a stack.

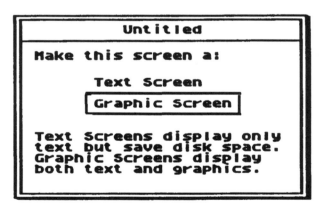

Selecting a graphic screen.

As you press return, the first screen opens, and it is waiting for you to go to work!

You are going to create a border, enter text, and place a graphic on this screen. But first you need to know how to save the screen on which you are working. If you do not save your screen each time you update it, you will lose your work. It is important to know where you save the screen and the stack. They must be in a folder on your stack disk. If you are not careful about where you are saving files, you may not be able to find your screen the next time you want to use it.

From *Hypermedia As a Student Tool.* © 1995. Teacher Ideas Press. (800) 237-6124.

First you are going to save this screen. This time your screen is named HomeScreen. Do not change the name of this screen. When the dialog box says "HomeScreen," press Return to save it that way. After you have completed your work on the HomeScreen, you should save it before you begin work on any other screens. The HyperScreen program will remind you that your work has not been saved, but get into the habit of saving it often. When you create the next screen, you will give it a different name. After you have saved your work, you can open the stack again and practice so that you will not have a problem saving screens and finding your work later.

Saving a Screen

1. Select Save Screen from the File menu.
2. Now reverse what you did before. Remove the HS disk.
3. Place your stack disk into the drive and press Tab.
4. The first screen in your stack is always named HomeScreen.
5. Select OK or press Return. Watch while it says "Saving the screen."
6. The screen returns with the File menu open.
7. Go on with your work, or use the Browse tool to view what you have already created.

The next time you work on your stack, open HyperScreen, go to the File menu, and select Open Stack. You will need the disk named Stack Disk in one drive. To be certain you have the correct disk, look for the name Stack Disk in the upper left corner of the dialog box. If you do not see it, click on the button that says "Drive" and then Tab until you do see Stack Disk in that corner. Once you see it, you are ready to click on the folder Stacks folder. If you have done this correctly, you will see an open folder and the word "Stacks" above the list of stack names. Select the name of the stack you want to work on, and open that stack.

As you work in HyperScreen, you will use all the following menus. This figure will help you know which menu item you need to open. Refer to it until you are sure where the tools you need are located.

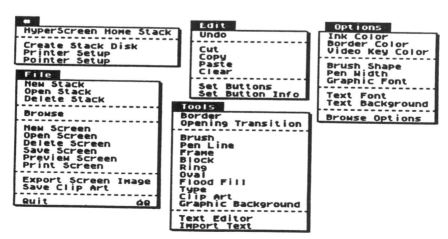

All the HyperScreen menus.

From *Hypermedia As a Student Tool.* © 1995. Teacher Ideas Press. (800) 237-6124.

Creating a Border in HyperScreen

When you create a border, you have two choices to make. You need to choose the type of border for your screen. You also need to choose what color you want the border to be.

1. Move to the Tools menu and choose Border. Check your HyperScreen menus on page 105.

2. From the next dialog box choose Change Border.

3. A new dialog box opens that lists the files on the disk. Notice that there is a picture of a disk in the corner. It has the name of the disk that is in the drive. It probably says "Stack Disk".

If you only have one 3-½" drive, you need to remove that disk and put your HyperScreen disk into the drive. If you are using 5-¼" drives, you need to make sure that you have the correct disk in the drive. The name of the disk in the picture didn't change.

1. Click on the button that says Drive and press the Tab key. Now the name of the disk has changed to HS. HS appears in the box above the list of files as well. In front of each filename, you should see an icon of a folder. That means that there are more files inside each of the folders.

2. Click on the Borders folder. Now the name of the disk is still HS, but the name in the box above the list of borders is the name of the folder, Borders. Select a name that sounds interesting to you and press Enter. The new border is now on your screen and you can decide whether to keep it or try another border.

3. To try another border, select Change Border.

4. When you have found the border you want to use, press the Escape key.

Creating a Text Item in HyperScreen

When you start a new screen, you have to choose text screen or graphic screen. Selecting a text screen means you cannot have any graphics on the screen. Selecting a graphic screen means you can have text and graphics. You can also write something in your word processor, save it as a text file, and import the file onto the screen.

A Text Screen

Choosing a text screen means you can only put words on it, no graphics.

1. Open your practice stack.

2. Select New Screen from the File menu and choose Text Screen.

3. You should add a border to this screen. Put the flip side of the Background & Clip Art disk into drive 2 if you have two 5-¼" drives. Choose Border. Make your choice as to what border you would like.

4. Select Text Font from the Options menu. Select a font; there are eight to choose from. System Large is a good-sized font that can be clearly read.

5. Put the cursor where you want to start typing. Use the Delete key to erase. Press the Escape (ESC) key when you are finished. Press Escape again to make another choice from the menus.

6. Put your stack disk into the drive and select Save Screen from the File menu.

A Graphic Screen

With a graphic screen you can add text and graphics.

1. Select New Screen from the File menu and select Graphic Screen.

2. Select Graphic Font from the Options menu. If you are using 5-¼" disks, put the Fonts disk into the disk drive. Font choices are on the flip side of the Background/Clip Art disk. There are 10 choices of fonts. Orpheum 24 is a large, clearly readable font.

3. Select Type from the Tools menu and put the cursor where you want your text. Click and type. Use the Delete key to erase. Press the Escape key when you are finished.

4. Put your stack disk into the drive and select Save Screen from the File menu.

From *Hypermedia As a Student Tool.* © 1995. Teacher Ideas Press. (800) 237-6124.

Creating a Button in HyperScreen

Linking to a New Screen

1. Be sure you know which screen you want your button to take you to.

2. If the button needs to go around a graphic or words (see graphic below), be sure to place the graphic or type the words before you set the button.

3. Go to the Edit menu. Select Set Button. Put your cursor where the button box should begin. Hold the mouse button down while you draw the box. When you have made a good size box, let go of the mouse button.

4. Go to the Edit menu again. Select Set Button Info. If you have any other buttons, they will show as dotted-line button frames with the number of the button in the corner. Click on the button you want to set the information for. Now another box will open that looks like this:

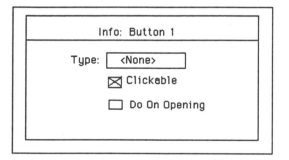

Set Info Button dialog box.

Click on None. The Button Type window appears. Click on Link to Screen.

The Link to Screen menu is the next to appear. Click on A New Screen and then either press the Return key or click on the OK box. You have returned to the dialog box where you selected Link to Screen. All that is left to do is to name the new screen. In this example, the new screen is named Screen2.

When you have completed this screen, be sure to save it before going to the newly created screen.

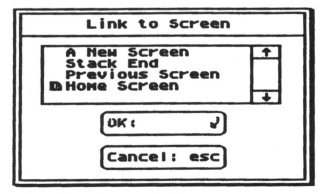

Showing where to link a new screen.

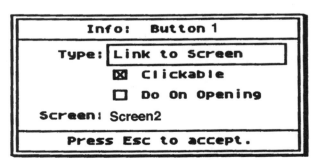

Returning to Info Window.

5. Go to the File menu and choose Open Screen. Select Screen2. Notice that the icon is empty. It does not look filled the way your other pages do. That is because you have never worked on the screen. Once you select Screen2, you will need to decide if it is to be a graphic or a text screen. You are on your way now! Have fun.

Linking to a New Screen On Opening

1. Go to the Edit menu. Select Set Button. Put your cursor where the button box should begin. In the box above, you can see an X at a good place for you to start. Hold the mouse button down while you draw the box. Create the button on an empty section of screen. Don't worry about the size of the button. Once you have created the button and set the information, it will not show on the screen.

2. Go to the Edit menu again and select Set Button Info. If you have any other buttons, they will show as dotted-line button frames with the number of the button in the corner. Click on the button you just created. Now another box has opened that looks like this. Click on None. You will see a box with button choices. Click on Link to Screen just as you did before. Then click in the box next to the work Clickable. Now neither of the boxes are selected. Click in the box in front of Do On Opening.

   Now move down to the choice next to Screen and click on None. The Link to Screen menu is the next to appear. Click on PageTwo (or the name of the page that you want to link to the new button) and then either press the Return key or click on the OK box. You have returned to the dialog box where you clicked on Link to Screen.

   When you have completed creating all the information you need for the button, be sure to save it before you go on with your project.

3. Go to the File menu and choose Browse. Watch as your screen moves, automatically, to the screen that you chose when you selected Button Info.

Creating a Button to Display Text

1. Select Set Buttons from the Edit menu.

2. Draw a box around the graphic on the screen. The number in the corner shows the number of this button. If this is your first button, its number will be 1.

3. Press Escape. Open the Edit menu again. Now select Set Button Info.

4. Click on the outline of the button. The Info dialog box appears. It lists the number of the active button.

5. Click on None in the Type box.

6. You are going to create a Pop-up Text button. Click on Pop-up Text.

7. In the Pop-up Text box, enter the text you have planned.

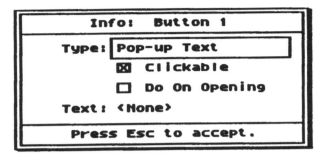

The Pop-up Text button is selected.

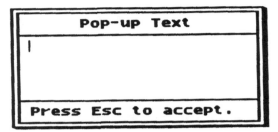

Ready to enter text for a Pop-up Text button.

8. Press the Escape key to accept the text. Press Escape to exit the Info box. Press Escape one more time to return to the main Menu Bar.

9. You must save your screen before you can try it.

Importing a Graphic into HyperScreen

HyperScreen Graphics

HyperScreen has two different types of graphics:

- Graphic backgrounds
- Clip art

Both of these files are on the 3-½" HyperScreen disk. If you are using HyperScreen on 5-¼" disks, the graphic backgrounds files are on side A of the second disk and the clip art files are on side B of the same disk.

Choosing a Graphic Background

When you are ready to add a background to the first screen in your stack, you should have opened your stack from your stack disk. The HyperScreen Menu Bar should be visible at the top of the screen.

1. Select Tools from the menu.

2. The Graphic Backgrounds disk should replace your stack disk if you are using a 5-¼" disk. Do not replace any disks if the HyperScreen software is on a 3-½" disk.

3. Select Graphic Backgrounds.

4. Select Backgrounds.

5. Select a background from the list. The selected background appears.

6. If you want to explore all the background selections, press the Escape (ESC) key once and then make another choice. Continue to explore the selections until you are ready to make a final decision.

7. Press the Escape key twice to accept your final choice. Your final choice will fill the screen. You may want to add clip art graphics to this screen and text (to do this use the following directions).

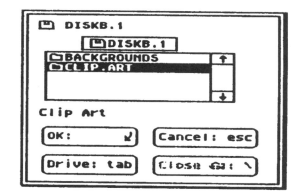

Menu showing choice of Backgrounds or Clip Art.

Selecting Clip Art Graphics

Adding graphics or pictures to your screen is easily done with graphics from the Backgrounds/ClipArt 5-¼" disk or from the files on the 3-½" HyperScreen disk. Obtain a hardcopy of the available pictures from your teacher. Look over your choices. Be sure to remember the filename of the graphic you wish to use.

1. Select Tools on menu.
2. Be sure to use side B of the Backgrounds/ClipArt disk if you are using a 5-¼" drive, or the HyperScreen Program disk if you are using a 3-½" drive.
3. Select ClipArt from the Tools menu.
4. Select the name of the ClipArt file where the graphic of your choice is located.
5. Select your graphic from the list.

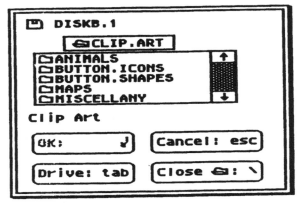

ClipArt Menu.

> If the graphic that appears is not what you expected, press the Escape key to cancel it. The list of available files will appear again and you can select another. When you find the appropriate graphic and it appears on the screen, move the mouse until you have positioned the graphic where you want it. Then click the mouse to place your graphic on the screen.

To place a second copy of your graphic on the screen, move the mouse to relocate and then click the mouse button to get another copy.

6. Complete the selection process by pressing the Escape key.

When you press the Escape key, it tells the computer that you have finished selecting a graphic. Then the main menu bar appears, and you can go on to the next step in your stack.

Selecting Clip Art Graphics from Another Graphic Disk

There are other sources of graphics that may be available to you, such as *Graphics at Your Fingertips* by Victoria League (see "Software Resources"). There are other commercial graphics programs that will work with HyperScreen. Perhaps your school already has some. In choosing a graphic from another source, look at printouts of the available graphics. Choose one graphic that you would like to import for your stack.

1. Select Tools from the menu.
2. Place the Backgrounds/ClipArt disk or the HyperScreen Program 3-½" disk in the drive.
3. Select ClipArt.
4. Put the disk with your graphic choice into a drive.
5. Select Drive or press the Tab key. A list of the graphics on the disk you selected appears. (It may be necessary for you to press the Tab key more than once depending on the number of drives connected to your computer.)
6. Select the name of the graphic you wish to use. The graphic selected appears.
7. Move the mouse to place the cursor where you want the graphic located.
8. Click the mouse button to place the graphic.
9. Press the Escape key to let the computer know you have finished selecting your graphic.

Creating a Background in HyperScreen

Using HyperScreen, you can create a graphic that can be used as a background template. A template is like a rubber stamp. It allows you to "stamp" the same graphic over and over again. This can be a useful feature if you want a button or clip art to appear in the same place on every screen.

This is also useful when you want several screens in your stack to have the same background. You can add items to this background as you go. You can add the items to your screen and save it again with a different name. You can also write, draw, or add buttons to each of the screens just as you have been doing.

Creating the Background

1. Select New Screen from the File menu. Make sure you select a Graphic screen.

2. Press the Escape (ESC) key to begin designing your screen.

3. After you have finished designing the background template, select Save Screen from the File menu.

4. Go to the File menu again. This time select Export Screen Image. When the dialog box opens, enter the name that you want to call your screen. It might be a good idea to title the screen after what the background looks like (e.g., "Paw Border.").

5. Remember to click on OK to save your screen.

Using the Background

You are now ready to use your background template.

1. Select new screen from the File menu to create a new screen.

2. Make this a Graphics screen.

3. Select a Graphic background from the Tools menu. A dialog box will open on the screen.

4. Make sure you are on your stack disk. If not, press Tab until your stack disk appears. Scroll down through the names until you see the name you gave your background. As soon as you select the background name, your background will be placed on your graphics screen.

5. You are now ready to add buttons, clip art, or text to this screen.

From *Hypermedia As a Student Tool.* © 1995. Teacher Ideas Press. (800) 237-6124.

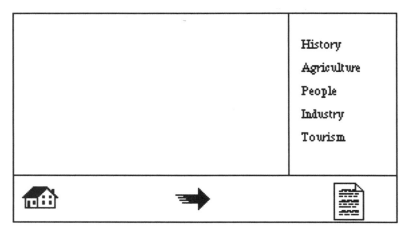

An example of a completed background.

Below are two modified backgrounds. Notice that each started out looking just like the background above. After background 1 was created, a box was added around the word "people." The difference is that Background 2 has a box added around the word "history." The first card tells us we are in the section of the stack about people. The second card tells us that we are in a section about history.

If this were a real stack, it might be one that a student was developing about a country or a state. Each student would have the important button icons in the same place. This makes a stack easier for the user to read.

Background 1   **Background 2**

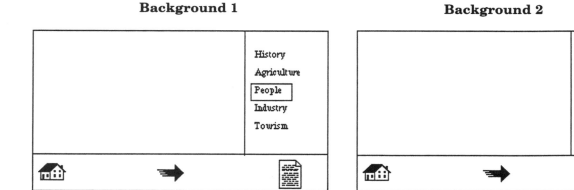

Two different modifications of the background.

The buttons at the bottom of the card all do the same job on each card. The house icon returns the user to the stack's table of contents. The arrow goes to the next stack in the series. The paper icon with the turned-down section links to the reference section of the particular stack.

8
HyperStudio IIGS
Support Materials

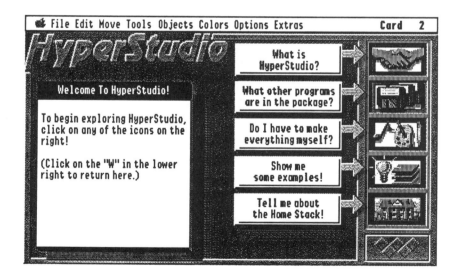

Exploring HyperStudio on the Apple IIGS: A First Visit

Name: _____

Today you will explore HyperStudio on the Apple IIGS for the first time. There are sample *Stacks* and you will have a chance to explore several of them. That will give you an opportunity to see the kinds of buttons, graphics, and text items that you will be able to create with HyperStudio.

Exploring means you will be clicking on *buttons* to move through the stack. Sometimes the buttons look like arrows or other *icons*; sometimes they are placed on top of words or pictures and are invisible. You will have to explore carefully to find the answers to the questions that follow.

The first screen you see is called the Home Card. From this card you can go to many different places. Today we will examine just one of the places. Click on Show Me Some Examples! button. It is a gray button and is right next to the words "Show Me Some Examples!" The button has pictures of a light bulb and a stack of disks.

Clicking on the button has taken you to a new page. There are two choices for you on this page, a Pencil and a Chair. Click on the Pencil. It has the word "School" printed under it. For some of the questions that follow you will need to look at the Animal Book stack, the Space History stack, and the Whales stack. To look at the Animal Book Stack, click on the More button. Now you have five icons and another arrow that says "More". There are 16 choices all together. After answering the questions about the three stacks just named, you are welcome to explore any the others. They can each give you good ideas.

Animal Book Questions

1. What is the largest animal in Africa?

   _____

   _____

2. What picture is an example of a primate?

   _____

   _____

Click on one or two of the animals. You can hear how they sound. Were you surprised that clicking on a button can cause a sound to be played? The buttons on each of the animals are invisible and soon you will learn how to make buttons like this.

Space History Questions

Find the icon of a house. Click on it. This has returned you to the Animal Book icon. Click on the arrow pointing left. Find the Space History icon and click on it. The buttons on this card do some special actions. As soon as the title card appears, Sara Cook reads to you. Sara has put a large invisible button over the title card. Did you notice the animation? Click anywhere on the screen to go to the second card. Click near the moon and see what happens.

Now can you find the answer to another question?

3. What did Galileo discover about Jupiter?

_____

_____

To find this answer you had to click on the arrow in the bottom right corner of the box where the text is printed. That box is called a text item, or a text field. The bar at the side is called a scroll bar; when the bar shows up in this manner, the field is called a *scrolling* text field. Text items can be created with or without scroll bars. You can click on the arrow at the top of the scroll bar to move up through the information, or click on the arrow at the bottom to move down. Clicking on the shaded section in the middle moves you down one full page at a time. Sometimes you see a field where the middle section of the scrolling field bar is not shaded. This means that you are looking at all of the information in that field.

Whales Questions

Now, can you click on the buttons that will take you to the card where you can click on Whales. Can you find the button that lets you listen to humpback whales sing?

5. What did you click on to hear the whale sing?

_____

_____

6. How much fish can a humpback whale eat in one day?

_____

_____

7. Where besides the oceans can you find killer whales?

_____

_____

When you are through, click on the Home icon. Then click on the arrows to return to the first card. Click on the W at the bottom of the left side. This returns you to the main menu, or Home Card of HyperStudio. Click on the File menu and choose Quit HyperStudio if you are finished exploring.

From *Hypermedia As a Student Tool.* © 1995. Teacher Ideas Press. (800) 237-6124.

Creating a Stack in HyperStudio for the Apple IIGS

Before you begin, make sure that you have a formatted data disk on which you can save your work. Boot the HyperStudio disk. The HyperStudio Home Card is the first screen that you see. Go to the File menu and select New Stack. Follow the screen directions for putting the proper disks into the drive. You may have to put in the systems disk first and then the HyperStudio program disk.

Look at the menu bar on your new stack. Does it say "Card 1"? If it doesn't, open the Apple menu and select Preferences Select Show in menu bar. Using this function allows you to know which card you are working on at all times.

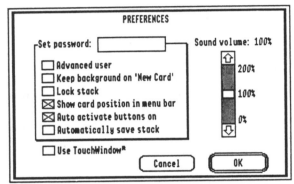

Preferences dialog box.

It is a good idea to save your stack to your data disk before you begin. Go to the File menu and select Save. A dialog box comes up to help you find the right place to save your stack. Click on Volumes. In the next box that opens, find the name of your data disk. Select it and click on Open. Now is the time to enter the name of your first stack. Name it *PracticeStack.Your Initials*. Enter the name of your stack in the box under the request "Please Name This Stack". Click on Save.

A blank card is the first card of your stack. Remember, you are creating a stack that may consist of many cards (or screens) before you complete it. This means that when you are ready to create the next card, you open the Edit menu and select New Card. Do not make the mistake of returning to the File menu and beginning a New Stack. Many students make that error when they first start to create stacks. You will know that you have made the right selection if when you look at the title bar it says "Card 2".

It may help you to think of your stack as a file folder. A file folder helps you keep track of the different papers that you place inside it. The cards in your stack are just like those pieces of paper. They belong inside the stack.

Edit menu.

Before you leave HyperStudio, remember to save your work. To save your stack to your data disk, be sure to select Save Stack As from the File menu. This allows you to select Volumes before you name your stack so you can be sure that you are saving it where you want. Click on Volumes and the names all of the places you can save your work appear in the window. Select the name of your data disk. Click on Open. Highlight the rectangle where you will type the name of the stack you have just created (or just click Save if you have already named your stack). After you have entered the name of the stack, click on the Save button.

From *Hypermedia As a Student Tool*. © 1995. Teacher Ideas Press. (800) 237-6124.

Creating a Border in HyperStudio for the Apple IIGS

HyperStudio does not have a special Border command or a Border tool in any of its menus. That means that you can select tools to help you create a border from the Tools menu in the menu bar. The steps for creating a border in your first stack are the same for creating a border in any stack.

1. Open the File menu and select Open Stack. You have already created your Practice stack. Highlight that stack name and click on Open.

2. Open the Apple menu and select Preferences from the Apple menu. The Preferences dialog box opens. You can see the Preferences menu on page 118.

3. Select Show card position in menu bar. The right corner of the menu bar should say "Card #" with the number representing the number of the card. This allows you to know just where you are in the stack at all times.

4. Select Keep Background on "New Card." This is an important capability, and you may be going into the Preferences menu to change that mark frequently. If there is an X in front of Advanced User, click on it to remove the X; then you can click on Keep Background. The card is blank and you are about to begin.

Getting the Tools

To create your border, you will be selecting several different tools from the Tools menu. So it is a good idea to be able to get to them as easily as you can. You can "tear off" the tools menu from the menu bar and place it on the screen by dragging it with the mouse. To create the borders, it would be useful to have your Tools and Color menus in the middle of the screen, at least for now. Follow these steps to move the menus:

1. Using the mouse, click on Tools from the menu bar. Do not let go of the mouse button.

2. Drag the menu by moving your mouse to the middle of the card. As you drag the cursor along, you will see a dotted box outline. When that dotted box outline is where you want the menu, release the mouse button. You should have the Tools menu in the middle of the screen. Follow the same steps to place the Colors menu next to it.

Tools menu.

Creating a Border

To start your border, follow these steps:

1. Choose the solid color you want for your lines from the Colors menu. Click on that color and a box forms around it to show that it has been selected.

2. Select the Rectangle tool to the right of the Spray Can tool in the middle column of the Tools menu. When you click on the rectangle, that box in the Tools menu will darken so you will know it has been selected. Move the cursor around the screen. It has changed to a new shape and looks like a cross-hair symbol.

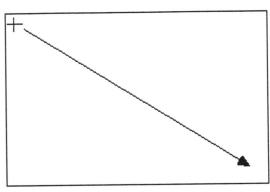

Getting ready to draw the first rectangle.

3. Place the cursor in the upper left-hand corner of the card. Drag the cursor to the lower right-hand corner. This will draw a rectangle across the whole card. That box will be the outside of your border.

4. Draw the inside edge of the border. Place the cross-hair cursor about 1 inch from the edge of the upper left-hand corner.

Drag it the same distance from the lower right-hand corner and release the mouse button. Your border outline is in place.

Look at the four border pictures at the end of the section. Your screen should be similar to the first border picture.

5. Choose a pattern from the Colors menu. HyperStudio also works on computers that do not have color. Your patterns will show in black and white and you can still use them to fill your border.

6. Select the Paint Can tool from the Tools menu. It is located just below the Spray Can tool.

7. Place the cursor, which now looks like the paint can, *inside* the border. Click the mouse. Watch the pattern fill your border. Your screen should be similar to the second border picture.

Another Way to Create a Border

Try using these steps to create the effect of an inner border.

1. Open the Options menu and select Draw Filled. Click on the Rectangle tool from the Tools menu. When you draw a rectangle, it will be a filled shape.

2. Use the same pattern you used before.

3. Place the cross-hair cursor about 1-½ inches from the upper left-hand corner of your border and drag it the same distance from the lower right-hand corner. A rectangle appears on the screen filled with the color or pattern you selected. Notice how the rectangle drew behind the Tools and Colors menus. If you do not like the color, go to

the Edit menu and select Undo. You can select another color or pattern and replace the rectangle. If you are satisfied with the rectangle, move to step 4. You can close the menus by clicking in the Close box in the upper left-hand corner. Look at the third border picture. Your screen should be similar.

4. Open the Colors menu and select the white box.

5. Select the rectangle tool and draw a white-filled rectangle on top of the first filled rectangle. Your screen should look very much like the fourth border picture.

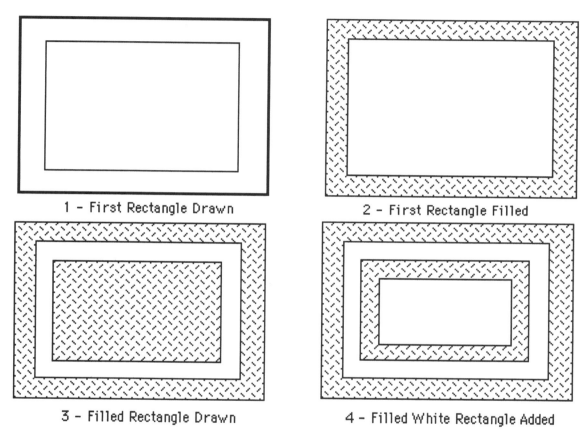

1 – First Rectangle Drawn

2 – First Rectangle Filled

3 – Filled Rectangle Drawn

4 – Filled White Rectangle Added

All the steps in creating a double border.

You have nearly completed this first card. It appears as though you have added three bands to the card, but you have really added one filled border and created a border-like appearance using two filled rectangles. These are techniques you will use many times in the future.

Before you leave HyperStudio, remember to save your work. To save your stack to your data disk, be sure to select Save Stack As from the File menu. This allows you to select Desktop or Disk before you name your stack, so it will be saved where you want it.

Creating a Text Item in HyperStudio for the Apple IIGS

Selecting Add a Text Item from the Objects menu is the first step to placing a text field on your card. You can place this text field anywhere on the card, and it can have a scroll bar that allows you to put as much information as you wish in that field. The important thing to know is that you are not using graphic text the way that you did when you selected the Text tool from the Tools menu. Entering text into a text field is like using a word processor.

As a matter of fact, with HyperStudio you can write in your word processor and place the information into the text field. Your teacher will have to show you how to save your writing as a text file (sometimes called an ASCII file), then you can put your story, poem, or report into your HyperStudio stack. We will try that technique later using a sample that comes with HyperStudio.

Creating a Text Field

Start by making a field where you enter the text.

1. Open your practice stack.

2. Create a new card.

3. Pull down the Objects menu and select Add a Text Item.

4. Use the cursor to position the text field where you would like it on the screen. Place the arrow inside the dotted-line frame when you move the field. Place the arrow along any edge of the frame to change its size. Don't forget to hold the mouse button down when you move the field or change its size.

The Objects Menu.

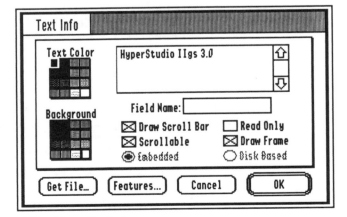

The Text Info box.

5. Click outside of the field to set the position of the text field.

6. The Text Info box allows you to choose the color of the text, the style of the text, and the color of the background. It even shows you a sample of how the text will look. Explore these choices until you have a combination that you like.

From *Hypermedia As a Student Tool.* © 1995. Teacher Ideas Press. (800) 237-6124.

7. Name your field. This is a good habit to develop. It helps you remember the special reason you had for creating your objects.

8. If you are going to include a lot of information, it might be important to have a Scroll Bar on the side. Click in the box in front of Draw scroll bar. Click OK.

Moving the Text Field and Editing the Text

You are back on the card, the cursor is blinking, and you are ready to enter text into the screen. When you have finished typing, you can still make the text field larger or smaller, even change its location on the card and change how the text looks. Try that now.

1. Open the Tools menu and select the Field tool. It looks like a piece of paper.

2. Click *once* on the text field. The dotted outline is back. Now you can change the size and placement of the field.

3. Clicking *twice* on the text field brings up the Info box, so you can change the background color of the field and some other features of the field.

4. Open the Tools menu and select the Browse tool. It looks like a hand. Notice that the cursor is at the start of the text in the field. Select all, or part, of the text the way you would if you were using a word processor. That is, hold down the mouse button and pull (drag) the cursor across the text you want to select. That text should now be highlighted.

5. Open the Options menu. Choose Set Text Color to select a different color for your text. Open the Options menu and select Text Style to change the font, style, and size. Click outside the field or outside the selected text. You have now changed the color of the text.

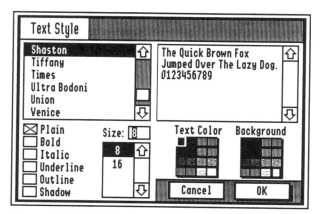

Text Style Drag Dialog Box.

Creating a Button in HyperStudio for the Apple IIGS

You have now created two cards. The first could be a title screen for your stack. The second card may have a graphic or other information about your stack. Now you need to create a button, or link, that will help the person who is reading your stack go from the first card to the second card.

Until you create your button, you need to have another way to move between cards. Select Move from the menu bar. This method is so easy that you may choose to use it even when there are buttons available.

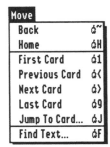 **The Move menu.**

Now create the first button. Open the Objects menu and select Add a Button. This first dialog box provides many choices as the button is created.

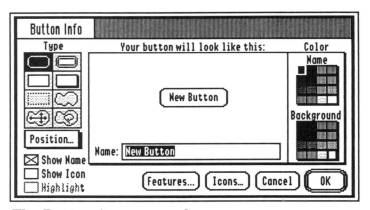

The Button Appearance box.

1. It is always a good idea to give your button a name. You can decide later if you want the name of the button to show. Name your button Next Screen by typing the name into the box next to Name. There is a box in the lower left-hand corner that says "Show Name". If you want the name to show, be sure there is an X in that box.

2. Choose the type of button that you will use. Click in any of the four frames at the top of the button appearance choices. Select the one you want to use.

3. Select background and text colors. Experiment by clicking on the different colors in each section. When you find a combination that you like, select it.

From *Hypermedia As a Student Tool.* © 1995. Teacher Ideas Press. (800) 237-6124.

4. Place your button: Click on Position. The dotted-line frame around the button signals that you can move the button to where you want it. Place it in the lower right-hand corner of the card, then click outside the box. Click OK in the button dialog box.

5. Select the Button Actions: On the left-hand side are the choices for Connections; Actions are on the right. If you click in the Another Card check box on the Connections side, a new dialog box appears. Use the right arrow to move to the next card. If you do not have another card, go to the Edit menu and select New Card, or hold down the Apple Key and press N to create a new card. The dialog box is now on "Card 2". Click on OK. Click OK again and the Transitions menu appears.

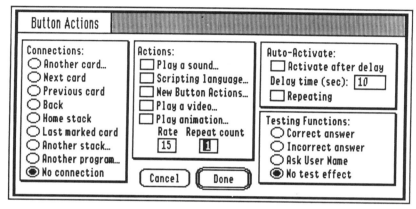

Moving to another card dialog box.

Did you wonder why we didn't just choose Next card? What would happen if you created a new card after your first card but before your second card? Your "Card 2" would say "Card 3" and would not be the next card anymore. By always using Another Card, you can be sure your buttons go to the right place.

6. Setting the visual effect. There are a lot of different looks you can provide for users as they move from one card to another. Try some of them out. Click on Right to Left, choose Medium Speed, and click on Try. Now try Rain and Dissolve, at different speeds. When you find one you like, click on OK.

Try your button now. Can you create a button to take you back to the first card? Try it. Here are some things to think about as you make this second button:

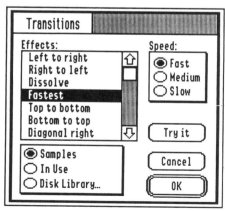

- In which direction should your arrow point?

- In which corner of the screen will you place your button?

Remember to think about your audience when you place these buttons.

Transitions menu.

Editing a Button in HyperStudio for the Apple IIGS

Sometimes you change your mind about where a button should be placed or how it should look. These are easy things to change in HyperStudio. Go back to the button you created on the second page of the practice stack. Let's change how it looks.

1. Open the Tools menu. Select the Button icon with the B on it. Now you have activated the Button tool.

2. Click once on the button and the dotted outline appears. If all you want to do is move the object, hold down the mouse button and drag. If you want to make other changes, go on to the next steps.

3. Open the Objects menu and select Button Info. If you know you want to go to this menu from the start, you can double click on the original button. The Button Info dialog box appears and you can make your changes.

Objects	
Button info...	⌂I
Card Info...	
Background Info...	
Stack Info...	
Bring Closer	⌂+
Send Farther	⌂-
Add a Button...	⌂B
Add a Graphic...	⌂G
Add a Text Item...	⌂T
Add a Video...	⌂L

The Objects Menu.

4. When you have finished, go back to the Tools menu and select the Browse tool (the hand icon) to try out your changed button.

Using Graphics in HyperStudio for the Apple IIGS

To place a graphic on your card, select Add a Graphic Item from the Objects menu. You can place this graphic anywhere on the card. Use Clip Art from HyperStudio, Pict, Tiff, or EPS files, or any paint program that you have access to. This method for adding graphics to your stack is for when you want a graphic on a single card, not as part of the background. To add a graphic, open your practice stack, create a new card, and follow these directions.

1. Pull down the Objects menu and select Add a Graphic Item.
2. Select the Clip Art file you want to use from the HS.Art disk.
3. Select a picture file and click OK after selecting it. A frame appears.
4. Use the hand (Browse tool) to move the pictures around. Whether there are several pictures in the file or only one, the one you want must be selected by moving the image to the upper left-hand corner of the frame. You can adjust the size of the frame by dragging its corners. The frame must appear around the graphic you want.
5. Click outside the frame and the Graphic dialog box appears. Name your graphic and choose frame color and width. If you don't want a frame, hold down the arrow until it disappears. Click OK or press the Return key when finished.
6. Drag picture into position with mouse. When satisfied with position, click outside picture.

When you are adding a graphic by this method, you can edit it by choosing the Graphic tool from the Tools menu. It is a square with a G in the center. Click on the Graphic tool, then click on your graphic. The dotted-line frame tells you that it is selected. Now you can move the frame to a new location. By adjusting the frame, you can make the graphic larger or smaller. Click outside the graphic when you are done. Go back to the Browse tool.

Adding a Graphic to the Background

If you want a special graphic to be the background of every card in a stack or in a group of cards, use Add Clip Art from the File menu. Remember, this graphic will be on every card until you choose Erase Background.

1. Go to File menu and select Add Clip Art.
2. Select the Clip Art File you wish to use and select the Picture file.
3. Use the lasso (Select tool) to draw around the picture you want to place on the background of each card. Click on OK.
4. The picture is now on your card; move it to its location and click outside the picture.

To edit this type of graphic, use Graphic tool from Tool menu. After putting dotted-line box around graphic, move it to a new location and change size. Click outside the graphic when satisfied. If you used Load Background to get your graphic, use the same files to select picture; however, to edit, it is necessary to use Select tool. When dotted-line frame is around the graphic, it can be moved and resized, or part of it can be selected and cut out by using Cut Background from the Edit menu. Remember, this graphic will now be on every card in your stack. When you are ready to change to a new graphic as a background, go to the Edit menu, choose Erase Background, go to Preferences, and remove the X from Keep Background on "New Card."

Creating a Background in HyperStudio for the Apple IIGS

It is not unusual to want the same border, background color, or graphic to appear on several cards in your stack. What if you wanted to have arrow buttons, a help button, and a button to return to the home stack on each card? You could create a basic card that looks the way you want them all to look and add invisible buttons later! It might look like this:

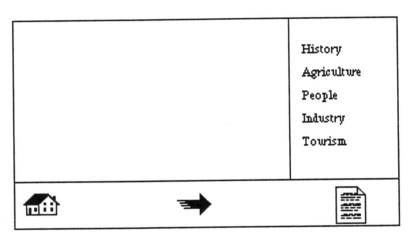

Sample background card.

Or, you simply might want to have the same background color and graphic on each card in your program. When you want this to happen, you create a background and it appears on every new card you create. Be certain that Keep Background on "New Card" under the Preference menu has an X in front of it.

1. Pull down the File menu and select New Stack.

2. Create a background that would work for several cards. Select Erase Background from the Edit menu and then select Set Background Color from the Options menu: a new color fills the screen. Create a border or add clip art. If you want the graphic to show on the background, you must select Add Clip Art from the File menu. Remember, clip art becomes a part of the background but graphic items are placed only on a single card.

3. Add text to a background if you want it to appear on each card of this stack. Use the Text tool to add this kind of text.

9
HyperCard Support Materials

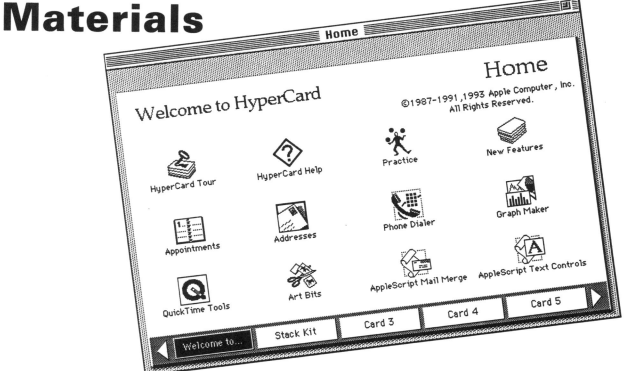

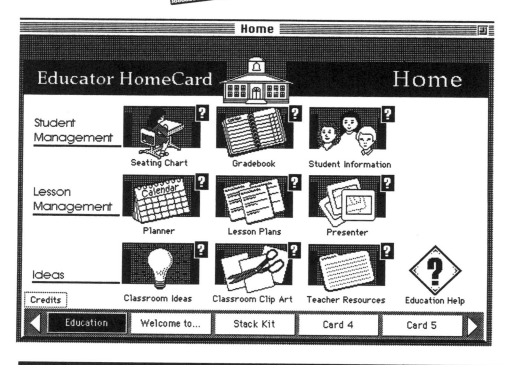

Exploring HyperCard

TO THE TEACHER:

The stacks used in this introduction to HyperCard are part of a larger group of stacks developed by Apple Computer, Inc. in 1990. The Educator Home Card is described as a set of HyperCard 2.0 stacks that will demonstrate the power of HyperCard and provide a set of useful tools. It includes HyperCard, the Education Home Card, a Seating Chart stack, a Gradebook, a Planner, Lesson Plans, Classroom Ideas, Classroom Clip Art, and other stacks.

The section used for this activity was designed to demonstrate how HyperCard can be used for different curricular areas and at different grade levels. It also provides an opportunity for your students to learn about HyperCard and to become familiar with ways of navigating through the stacks.

The Educator Home Card set is available from Intellimation. The address can be found in the Reference section of this book.

This is meant to be a model of how students can first explore the HyperCard program. If you have other stacks available that would be fun for students to explore, create your own Exploring HyperCard First Visit. You are free to use any of the text in this example and create questions that would be appropriate for the stacks that you are going to use.

Exploring HyperCard: A First Visit

Name: _____

Today you will explore HyperCard for the first time. On the Home Card from the Educator Home Card set there is an icon called Classroom Ideas. All you need to do is click on that icon. If you have a different Home Card, move the mouse to the File menu and click on Open Stack. When the dialog window opens, highlight Classroom Ideas and double click.

Looking at the stacks in this section will give you an opportunity to see the kinds of buttons, graphics, and text items that you will be able to create.

Exploring means you will be clicking on *buttons* to move through the stack. Sometimes the buttons look like arrows or other *icons*; sometimes they appear on top of words or pictures and are invisible. You will have to explorer carefully to find the answers to the following questions.

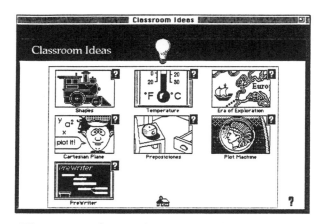

These are the options available in Classroom Ideas.

Shapes Station Card.

- Click on Shapes. Notice that you have to click on Start before you can explore the train and see what buttons are on the card.

What happens when you click on Start? What if you do something else? Click in other places to see what happens. This is a fun way to explore HyperCard stacks; just click somewhere and see what happens. Soon you will be creating your stacks, but for now let's continue exploring.

You have already found out some interesting things about HyperCard:

1. Buttons can be invisible. (Like the ones over the different shapes.)
2. Clicking on a button can make a sound play or text appear on the screen.
3. Clicking on a button can make more than one thing happen. Remember when you clicked a right answer? You saw an animated graphic of smoke, but when you clicked on an incorrect answer, you had a different response.

From *Hypermedia As a Student Tool.* © 1995. Teacher Ideas Press. (800) 237-6124.

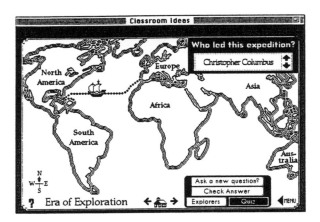

Card showing one activity in the Era of Exploration.

Now click on Menu to go back to the Classroom Ideas card. This time select Era of Exploration. There are more buttons to choose from here. In this game, you answer questions and get information about explorers. Make a list of the different examples of what can happen when you click different boxes. Remember that each of those boxes is a button.

Be ready to share the things you found out about using HyperCard with your classmates. You will be learning some interesting facts about explorers as well.

I found out that HyperCard buttons can:

_____

_____

_____

_____

_____

When you have finished your list, you are ready to try another activity. Go back to the Classroom Ideas menu card. If you don't remember how, reread this lesson until you find the information you need. You will be receiving more sheets like this one. They are meant to give you the information you will need as you work on your own or with a partner.

Our last activity is called Plot Machine. Here you will have a chance to write a story as you learn new things about HyperCard. First of all, how will you put the token in the slot? If you hold down the mouse button when you are over the coin, you can drag it to the coin slot and let go. Look what happened! If you don't like the elements in your story, you can put the coin back and try again.

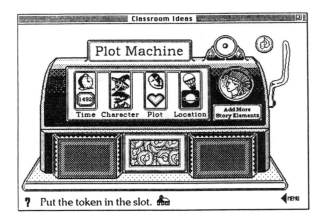

The Plot Machine card as it first appears.

Some other new choices have appeared as well. This could mean that you have moved to another card. There are new buttons along the bottom of the screen. You can select Start Writing or Print Card. Print Card will print a copy of the screen. You might use this if you wanted to write at your desk and not at the computer. Click on Start Writing and see what happens. You have the list of items presented in a new way to help you start writing. Why not write for just a few minutes? When you have written a paragraph or two, you will be ready to continue.

You have two more items to explore on this screen. What happens when you click on Add Story Elements? What would you guess is the difference between Print Story and Print Card? (Print Story gives you a copy of the paragraphs you have just finished writing.) Now try Add More Story Elements. Again, the button you clicked on opened a new window on the screen and will let you add to the program.

Once again, list the new things you found out that a HyperCard button do and be ready to discuss them with a friend.

I found out that HyperCard buttons can:

_____

_____

_____

_____

_____

Creating a Stack in HyperCard

Open the folder that has HyperCard and the Home file in it. The dialog box on your computer may not look exactly like the one in the following figure, but you will find the Home file and HyperCard on your screen. Click on Home.

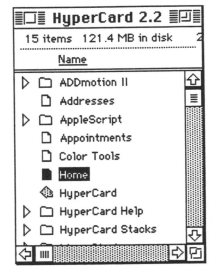

Dialog box for opening HyperCard or Home Card.

The Home Card should now be on the screen. Pull down the File menu and select New Stack.

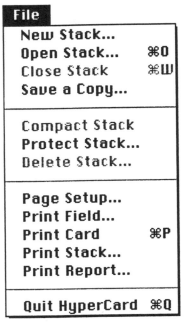

File menu in HyperCard.

When you release the mouse button, a new dialog box will come up and ask you to name the new stack. It is a good idea to use a name that will remind you what is in the stack. It is also a good idea to place a period (.) at the end of the title and then add your initials. This way, a classmate working on a similar project will not name a stack with the name you chose, and it will also help your teacher, or you, when you link a group of stacks together. A stack title might be *OpenHouse.MH*.

A blank card appears, and you have opened your new stack and are ready to begin. Remember, you are creating a stack that may have consist of cards before you complete it. This means that when you are ready to create the next card, you pull down the Edit menu and select New Card. Do not make the mistake of returning to the File menu and beginning a New Stack. Many students make that error when they first start to create stacks.

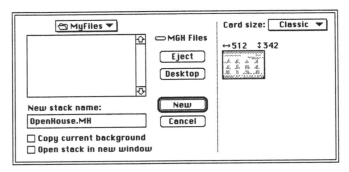

Dialog box for naming a stack.

It may help you to think of your stack as a file folder. A file folder helps you to keep track of the different papers that you place inside it. The cards in your stack are just like those pieces of paper. They belong inside the stack.

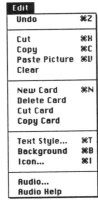

The Edit menu.

Creating a Border in HyperCard

HyperCard does not have a special Border command or a Border tool in any of its menus. That means that you can select tools to help you create a border from all of those available to you in the Tools menu in the main menu bar. The steps for creating a border in your first stack are the same for creating a border in any stack.

In HyperCard, elements such as text, painted items, and buttons, fields, or graphics can be placed either on the card level or on the background level. For this project, you are going to place the border on the card level. This means when you create a new card, the border from the previous card will not be on the new card. Later, you will learn how to create a border that can appear on as many cards as you would like.

You have already created your stack. The menu bar is at the top of the screen and you can see the name of your stack in the select bar. The card looks like a fresh piece of paper and you are about to begin.

To create your border, you will be selecting several different tools from the Tools menu. It is a good idea to be able to get to them as easily as you can. You can tear off the Tools menu from the menu bar and place it anywhere on the screen. To create the borders, it would be a good idea to have your Tools menu in the middle of the card, at least for now. Follow the steps below to move the menu to the middle and draw rectangles for your border frame.

1. Using the mouse, click on Tools on the menu bar. Do not let go of the mouse button.

2. Drag the menu by moving your mouse to the middle of the card. As you drag it along, you will see a dotted box outline. When that dotted box outline is where you want it, remove your finger from the mouse button. You should have a menu right in the middle of the card that looks like this:

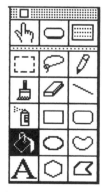

The Tools menu with the Paint Bucket tool selected.

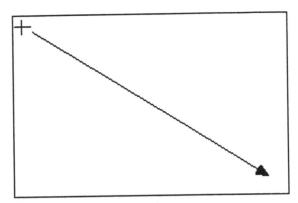

Getting ready to draw the first rectangle.

3. Select the Rectangle tool on the Tools menu by clicking your mouse on the rectangle. The rectangle symbol is to the right of the Spray Can tool in the middle column of Tools. When you click on the rectangle, that box in the Tools menu will darken, which shows that you have selected that tool. Move the cursor around the screen. The cursor has changed to a new shape. It looks like a cross-hair symbol.

4. Place the cursor in the upper left-hand corner of the card. Holding the mouse button down, drag the cursor to the lower right-hand corner. This will draw a rectangular box across the whole card. This box will be the outside of your border.

5. Draw the inside edge of the border. Place the cross-hair cursor about 2 inches from the edge of the upper left-hand corner. Drag the cursor to the same distance from the lower right-hand corner and release the mouse button. Your border outline is in place. Look at the first of the four rectangles at the end of this section.

6. To fill in the space between your border outlines, select Color from the menu bar. Or, if your HyperCard does not have color, you can fill it in with a pattern. To have an interesting border, you may want to select a pattern from the Patterns menu on the main menu bar. This is a good time to mention that the menu bar does not always have the same choices available to you, but as long as you are working in the Tools menu, the Patterns menu will be ready for you to use. Click on the Patterns menu and select the pattern you want to use to fill your border.

7. Select the Paint Can from the Tools menu. It is located just below the Spray can.

8. Place the cursor, which now looks like the paint can, inside the border. Click the mouse and watch the pattern fill your border. It should look like the second of the four rectangles at the end of this section.

Another Way to Create a Border

Follow the steps below to create an inner border.

1. Double click on the Rectangle from the Tools menu. Double click means to click twice, very quickly. If you have double clicked correctly, the blank rectangle will turn into a filled rectangle. When you draw a rectangle now, it will be a filled shape. (If you were unable to double click, there is another way to accomplish this: Select the Options menu and then select Draw Filled. When you release the mouse, your Tools menu will show the shapes ready to draw filled.)

2. Place the cross-hair cursor about 2-½ inches from the upper left-hand corner of your border and drag the cursor to that distance from the lower right-hand corner. A rectangle appears on the screen filled with the pattern you had previously selected. If you do not like the pattern, go up to the Edit menu and select Undo. You can select another pattern and replace the rectangle. When you are satisfied with the rectangle, move to step three. It should look like the third rectangle.

3. Open the Patterns menu. Select the white box.

4. Select the Rectangle tool. Draw a box on top of the filled rectangle 1 inch from its upper left-hand corner. Your rectangle should look like the fourth rectangle.

You are almost through with this first card. It appears as though you have added three bands to the card. Really you have added one filled border and created a border-like appearance using two filled rectangles. These are tools you will use many times in the future.

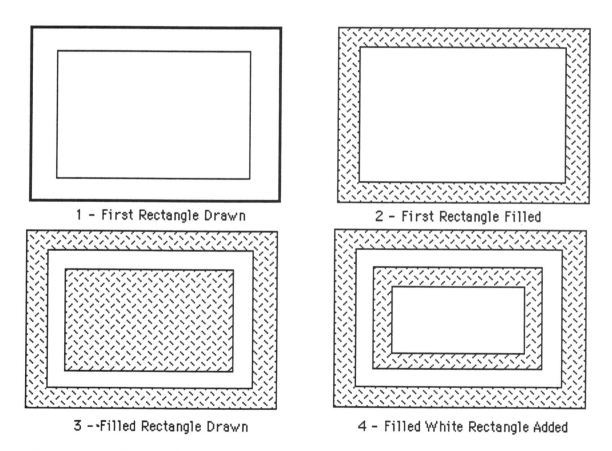

1 – First Rectangle Drawn

2 – First Rectangle Filled

3 – Filled Rectangle Drawn

4 – Filled White Rectangle Added

All the steps in creating a double border.

Creating a Text Item in HyperCard

Selecting New Field from the Objects menu is the first step to place a text field on your card. You can place this text field anywhere on the card and it can have a scroll bar that allows you to put as much information as you wish in that field. The important thing to know is that you are not using graphic text the way that you did when you selected the Text tool from the Tools menu. Entering text into a text field is like using a word processor.

As a matter of fact, with HyperCard you can write in your word processor and place the information into the text field. You will have to learn how to save your writing as a text file, then you can put your story, poem, or report into your HyperCard stack.

Creating a Text Field

Start by making a field where you enter the text.

1. Open your practice stack.
2. Create a new card.
3. Pull down the Objects menu and select New Field.
4. Use the cursor to position the text field where you would like it on the screen. Place the arrow inside the dotted-line frame when you move the field. Place the arrow along any edge of the frame to change its size. Don't forget to hold the mouse button down when you move the field or change its size.
5. Click outside the field to set the position of the text field.
6. Double click inside the text field to go to the Field Info window. You can also get to this window clicking inside the field and then selecting Text Info from the Objects menu.

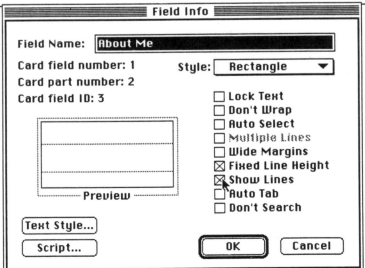

Field Info window.

From *Hypermedia As a Student Tool.* © 1995. Teacher Ideas Press. (800) 237-6124.

7. Select Text Style and choose a font, style, and size. Notice that the lines in the Preview of the text field change when you change the size. Close the window when you are finished.

8. Select the Browse tool from the Tools menu, the one that looks like a Hand.

9. Put the cursor where you want to start typing. Use the Delete key to erase. When you are finished, click outside the text field.

Moving and Editing the Text Field

After you have finished typing, you may decide to make some changes:

- Open the Tools menu and select the Field tool. It looks like a piece of paper. It's in the upper right-hand corner.

- Click once on the text field. The dotted-line frame is back. Now you can change the size or placement of the field.

- Clicking twice on the text field brings up the Text Info box so you can change the name and other features of the field.

- Open the Tools menu and choose the Browse tool. It looks like a hand. Notice that the cursor is at the start of the text in the field. Select all, or part, of the text the way you would if you were using a word processor. That is, hold down the mouse button and pull (drag) the cursor across the text you want to select. The text should now be highlighted.

- Make the changes you want in font, style, and size. Click outside the field when finished.

Creating Text with the Graphic Tool in HyperCard

The first card in your About Me Stack should be on the computer screen. You are going to be adding the title to this card. Click on the Tools menu and select the box that contains the letter A, the symbol for the Text tool. There is a white area in the middle of the card where you should enter the text "About Me."

Click inside the white box and enter that text. It could look better, don't you think? Select Undo from the Edit menu to go about finding some better looking text. Under the Edit menu, select Text Style; or, if you have "torn off" your Tools menu, double click on the A (the text graphic tool).

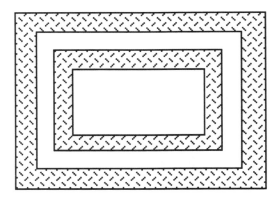

Card ready to accept paint text.

You can try out different fonts while this dialog box is open by clicking on the name of a font, such as Chicago, Courier, or Helvetica. All of these may not be in your computer, so choose from the ones you have. You can try out different styles as well. They will appear in the box in the lower right-hand corner just the way they will look on the screen. Once you have found the style you want to use, click on the OK box and you will be ready to enter the text onto your card.

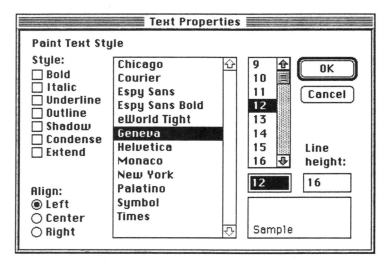

The Paint Text Style dialog box.

Remember, you are writing with Paint Text, which means that the Delete key will not erase this text. Only the Eraser tool on the Tools menu will work. Try it out. This will help you understand the differences of Paint text.

Creating a Button in HyperCard

You have now created two cards. The first is the title screen for your stack. The second card has information about your stack. Now you need to create a button, or link, that will help the person who is reading your stack go from the first card to the second card.

- Be sure you know which card you want to add a button to.
- If the button is to go on top of a graphic or words, like the one below, be sure to place the graphic or type the words before you create the button.
- If you want to move from card to card before you create a button, you do so by using the right and left arrow keys, or by going to the Move menu and select First or Next.

1. Go to the Objects menu and select New Button. You will see a button named New Button in the middle of the screen. Notice the dotted line around the button that seems to be moving. Those moving dotted lines are called "marching ants." When you see the marching ants it means that whatever is inside them has been selected and can be worked with it in some way.

2. Place the arrow cursor inside the button. Hold the mouse button down and move the mouse. You can move the button anywhere on the card. Place the button where you want it to be. (Just remember, if you change your mind you can move the button at any time.)

3. Click on the Objects menu.

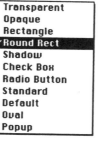

The Objects menu.

Select Button Info. A dialog box appears on the card. You can type in any name that you want for the button. Sometimes, the name of the button should be visible. This is one of those times. The blue in the background means that you can start typing immediately. Type in the name "Next Card."

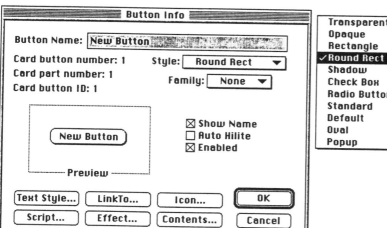

Notice that the Show Name box has an X in it. If you did not want the name to show, you would click on the box again so there is no X in it.

The Button Info window.

From *Hypermedia As a Student Tool.* © 1995. Teacher Ideas Press. (800) 237-6124.

4. Choose a shape from Style.

5. Choosing Effect will let you select a visual effect, the way the card reacts when the button is clicked. You can select Dissolve or Right to Left, for example. When finished, select OK.

6. The Link To dialog box appears on the screen after you click OK.

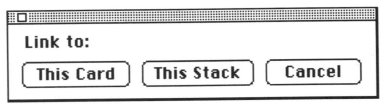

Link To dialog box.

DO NOT click on any buttons yet. First press the right-arrow key once. Now you are on the second card that you created. Click on This Card. As soon as you click you return to the first card.

7. Try out the button to see if it works. Open the Tools menu. The Button tool is currently selected.

Tools

 **The Tools menu with the Button tool selected.**

You want to change to the Browse tool, the one that looks like a hand. Click on the hand now.

 **The Tools menu with the Browse tool selected.**

Now the Browse tool is selected. When the menu has closed, click on the Next Card button. If you have followed all the steps, you are now on the second card in your stack.

Challenge 1: Can you create a button named Return to take you back to your first card? If you can, then you know that you understand how to create a button that links one card to another. There are many other things that buttons can do, which you will learn about as you continue to work with HyperCard.

Challenge 2: Sometimes you might want to place a button on top of a graphic or words on the screen. Can you create a button placed on top of a graphic that would go to another card?

Editing a Button in HyperCard

Sometimes you change your mind about where a button should be placed or how it should look. These are easy things to change in HyperCard. Go back to the button you created on the second page of the practice stack. Follow the steps below to change how it looks.

1. Open the Tools menu. Select the Button icon with the B on it. Now you have activated the Button tool.

2. Click once on the button and the dotted-line frame appears. If all you want to do is move the button, you can do that now. If you want to make other changes, go on to the next steps.

3. Open the Object menu and select Button Info. If you know you want to go to this menu from the start, you can double click on the original button. The Button Info window appears and you can make your changes. Change the shape under Style or choose an icon that could mean Return. If you select Effect, you can choose the way the screen moves when the button is clicked.

4. When you have finished, go back to the Tools menu and select the Browse tool (the hand icon) to try out your changed button.

Importing a Graphic into HyperCard

Graphics can be imported into Hyper-Card several different ways. You can copy pictures from the Scrapbook and paste them into a HyperCard stack; you can copy HyperCard clip art and paste it into a stack; or you can import graphics from the paint format into HyperCard using the Import Paint command. Whichever method you use, your card will look the same.

A completed card after bringing in a graphic from the Scrapbook.

Using the Scrapbook

1. You can find the Scrapbook under the Apple menu on the left-hand side of the screen. Open the Apple menu and select Scrapbook.

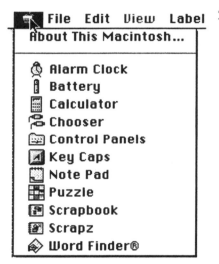

Selecting the Scrapbook from the Apple menu.

2. By clicking along the scroll bar at the bottom of the Scrapbook, you can select the graphic that you want. This time select the image of the two children reading.

Finding a graphic in the Scrapbook.

3. When the graphic is displayed, open the Edit menu and select Copy (or press Command [⌘]-C). Click on the Close button in the upper left-hand corner of the scrapbook graphic window.

---

4. You are back in your practice stack, and your card has its frame and is ready for the graphic to be placed. Open the Edit menu and select Paste Picture, or you can press the Command (⌘)-V to paste the graphic on the card. The graphic appears on the card surrounded by a dotted-line frame.

5. As you move your cursor onto the graphic, it turns into an arrow. That means that you can grab the graphic with a mouse click and place it anywhere on the card.

6. When you have placed the graphic, add text using the Text tool from the Tools menu. Remember that when that tool is selected you can select Text style from the Edit menu to choose the font and style you want to use.

Using Graphics in HyperCard

HyperCard graphics are available from many sources. With the right software, you can create them yourself by scanning a picture. Some come in a stack (Art Bits) included with HyperCard. The ones in these examples come from classroom clip art in The Educators Home Card. Your teacher may have these graphics for you to use. If not, there will be others available that you can try.

1. Open your practice stack and go to a card with a background border.

2. Create a New Card (or press ⌘-N).

3. Open the File menu and select Open Stack (or press ⌘-O).

In this window you would select Classroom Clip Art and then click on Open. When you find the stack you will use, click on Open.

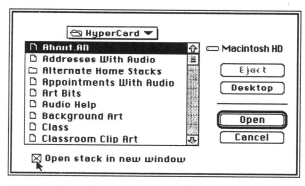

Dialog box to open a stack in a new window.

4. Select the graphic you want to use. For this example, select the two children reading.

5. Open the Tools menu and select the Lasso tool. It will let you draw around the object you want to select. When you are through drawing, a dotted-line frame will surround the selected object.

Graphic selected using the Lasso tool.

---

6. Once the dotted-line frame appears, open the Edit menu and select Copy Picture (press ⌘-C).

7. Click in the Close box in the upper left-hand corner of the stack. This closed the second stack that you opened, and you are now back in the practice stack.

8. To place the graphic on this card open the Edit menu and select Paste Picture (or press ⌘-V). Move the cursor into the graphic. When you see the arrow, drag the graphic where you want it and click outside the graphic.

9. Select the Text tool from the Tools menu and type an appropriate message onto your card.

Importing a Paint Graphic

As you have seen, graphics can be found in several different formats. This time, the file you are going to import will be in a paint format. Once again, your teacher will tell you where to find the paint file, but the steps you follow will be the same.

1. Open your practice stack and go to a card that has a background border.

2. Create a New Card or press ⌘-N.

3. Open the Tools menu and select any graphic tool. A graphic tool must be selected to import a paint file into HyperCard.

4. Open the File menu and select Import Paint. A new dialog box will appear on the screen. It asks you to find the paint graphic. In this example, the graphic is called "Two Children Reading."

5. Highlight the file name of your graphic and click on Open. The graphic will appear on your card. It probably covers the whole card, in which case you won't be able to see your border.

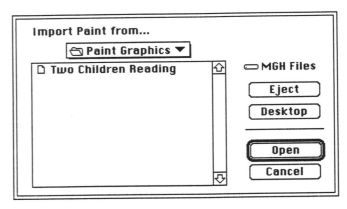

Selecting the file from the Import Paint dialog box.

6. Open the Paint menu and select Transparent. Now your graphic is surrounded, once again, by the border.

You have now placed graphics in your HyperCard stack in three different ways. Remember to refer back to these handouts when you need to place graphics into other stacks.

Creating a Background in HyperCard

You have already learned how to create a border in HyperCard. But what if you wanted that same border to appear on more than one card? And what if you didn't want to make it over again for each card? In HyperCard you can do just that. It is called creating a background.

Open your practice stack and create a New Card. Now you can begin.

1. Open the Edit menu and select Background. Look at the menu bar; it is surrounded by dotted-line frame, which is a sure way to tell if you are on the background. If the lines are not dotted, you are not on the background. You can also go the background by pressing ⌘-B.

2. Create a border that you like in the same way that you did in an earlier activity. Leave most of the center open.

3. Select Background from the **Edit menu** (or press ⌘-B). Now you are leaving the background and the dotted-line frame is gone.

4. Using either the pencil or the paintbrush, type "This is the story" in the middle of the card. If you chose a pattern for your border, be sure to go back and pick a solid fill.

5. Create a new card. Notice that your words are not there (but the border is). You can now finish the story on this card.

Each time you make a new card, it will have the same background until you create a new one. It is always a good idea to give your background a name. It helps you remember what you have done.

- Open the Objects menu.
- Select Background Info and type the name you want to give this background. "Border" might be a good choice this time.

You do not need to have the same background for every card in your stack. To create a new background, open the Objects menu and select New Background. Remember to give it a name.

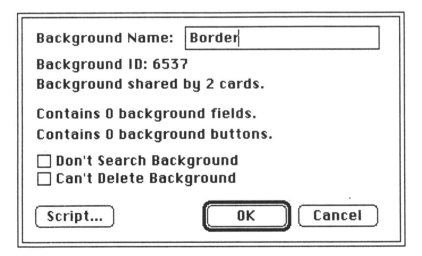

Background Name: |Border|

Background ID: 6537
Background shared by 2 cards.

Contains 0 background fields.
Contains 0 background buttons.

☐ Don't Search Background
☐ Can't Delete Background

[Script...]   ((OK))   [Cancel]

Background Info dialog box.

Hint: Don't get confused if you don't see the Objects menu right away. Have you been using your paint tools? When you are using the graphics tools, the Objects menu does not show.

From *Hypermedia As a Student Tool*. © 1995. Teacher Ideas Press. (800) 237-6124.

Background with Menu Information

Another reason to develop a background is to create a menu to help users navigate through your stack. You can place the important pieces of the menu on the background and then add to it on the card level.

1. Create a card with the important layout and information about the stack.

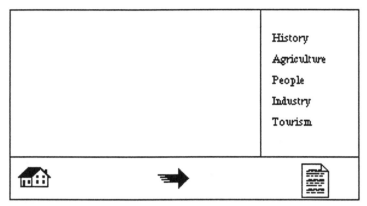

Creating background card.

2. Now you can add to the background on the card level to show the user where he or she is in the stack.

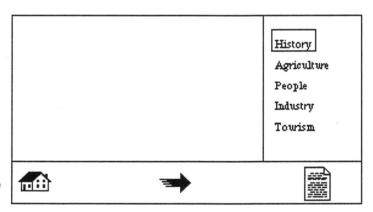

Showing the user where he or she is in the stack.

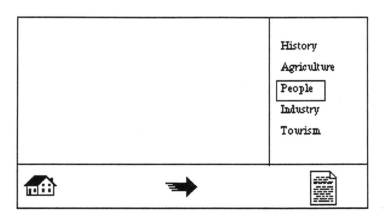

Another option for the user.

From *Hypermedia As a Student Tool.* © 1995. Teacher Ideas Press. (800) 237-6124.

Linking Stacks in HyperCard

One of the important things to learn is how to link stacks. There are several situations when you will want to do this:

- The first is when you create a menu for a group of stacks and want the user to be able to choose how they navigate through the stacks. Look at the Creating a Menu Stack worksheet (see appendix C) to better understand how to do this.

- Another important time to link stacks is when a stack can be used in more than one hypermedia program. For example, if you were to create a program about different groups in your school and one of the smaller stacks was about one of the sports teams, that stack could also be used in a hypermedia program about sports in general.

It is very easy to link stacks in HyperCard. In fact, you can link to any card in any stack from any card in another stack. Most often, though, you will probably be linking the first card of one stack to the first card of another stack.

Let's see how it is done.

Creating the First Stack

1. Open the Home stack in HyperCard.

2. Go to the File menu and select New Stack.

3. Name your stack "Stack One."

4. "Tear off" the Tools menu and drag it to the center of the screen.

5. Select the Rectangle tool and draw a border around the first card.

6. Select the Text tool (T) and type "This is the first card of stack one" near the top of the card.

7. From the Edit menu, select New Card (or press ⌘-N).

8. Select the Rectangle tool and draw a border around the second card.

9. Select the Text tool (T) and type "This is the second card of stack one" near the top of the card.

Creating the Second Stack

1. Go to the File menu and select New Stack.

2. Name your stack "Stack Two."

3. Tear off the Tools menu and drag it to the center of the screen.

4. Select the Rectangle tool and draw a border around the first card.

5. Select the Text tool (T) and type "This is the first card of stack two" near the top of the card.

6. From the Edit menu, select New Card (or press ⌘-N).

7. Select the Rectangle tool and draw a border around the second card.

8. Select the Text tool (T) and type "This is the second card of stack two" near the top of the card.

Linking the Two Stacks

Select the Browse tool. Open Stack One and you are ready to link your two stacks.

1. Go to the Objects menu and select New Button. The new button, encircled by a dotted-line frame, is on your screen. With the arrow cursor that appears when you enter the button using the mouse, position the button directly under the sentence that you typed.

2. Double click on the button; the Button dialog box appears. Type "to Stack Two." The name now appears on your button.

3. Click on the Link To button. This places you back on the card with the Link To dialog box visible.

4. Open the File menu and select Open Stack. Click in Open stack in new window box.

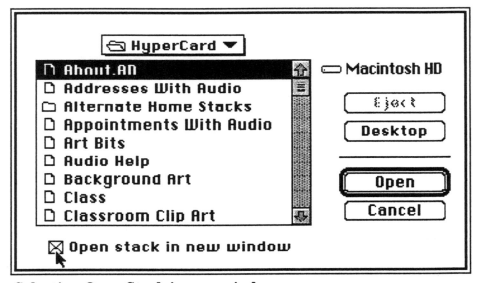

Selecting Open Stack in new window.

From *Hypermedia As a Student Tool.* © 1995. Teacher Ideas Press. (800) 237-6124.

5. Select Stack Two and click on Open. The Link To dialog box still shows, and you are in Stack Two.

6. Click on the This Stack button in the dialog box. You are now back in Stack One, and there is a dotted-line frame around the button to Stack Two.

7. Open the Tools menu and select the Browse tool. The dotted-line frame is gone, and you can try out your new button by clicking on it. There you are—on the first card of Stack Two.

Now what if you want to go back to Stack One, Card Two? The idea of linking is very much the same. Only a few of the steps are different.

1. Go to the Objects menu and select New Button. The new button, encircled by a dotted-line frame, appears on your screen. With the arrow cursor that appears when you enter the button using the mouse, position the button directly under the sentence that you typed.

2. Double click on the button and the Button dialog box appears. Type "to Stack One, Card Two." The name now appears on your button.

3. Click on the Link To button. This places you back on the card with the Link to dialog box visible.

4. Open Stack One. The Link To dialog box still shows, and you are in Stack One. You can see that you are on Card One of Stack One. Press the right arrow key just once. Now you are on Card Two of Stack One. (This is the step that may surprise you.) Click on the This Card button in the Link To dialog box.

5. Do just what you did the last time. Select the Browse tool from the Tools menu. Click the button. There you are—right where you wanted to be, Card Two of Stack One.

Keep this sheet handy when you work. You will be able to link between stacks, and between cards in different stacks, whenever you need to.

10
HyperStudio 3.0
Support Materials

Exploring HyperStudio 3.0 on the Macintosh: A First Visit

Name: _____

Today you will explore HyperStudio 3.0 on the Macintosh for the first time. There are sample *stacks,* and you will have a chance to explore several of them. That will give you an opportunity to see the kinds of buttons, graphics, and text items that you will use with HyperStudio 3.0.

Exploring means you will be clicking on *buttons* to move through the stack. Sometimes the buttons look like arrows or other *icons*; sometimes they will be on top of words or pictures and are invisible. You will have to explorer carefully to find the answers to the questions that follow. If you are using the HyperStudio 3.0 CD it should be in your CD player now.

The first screen you see is called the Home Card. From this card you can go to many different places. Today you will examine just one of the places. Click on the Sample Projects button. It is in the upper left next to the Show Me How button.

Clicking on the button takes you to a new page. There are more choices for you on this page. Click on the At School button. You will explore some of the stacks in this section. Click on the mouse icon to see all the titles here. For the first questions in this handout, you will look at the Rwanda stack and the Saturn stack. Look at the Rwanda stack and then click on the Home icon to scroll down to the Saturn stack.

Rwanda Stack Questions

1. In what special place in Rwanda do the mountain gorillas live?

   _____

   _____

   _____

   _____

2. What can you find out about the soil and plant growth in Rwanda?

   _____

   _____

   _____

   _____

Find the icon, or picture, of a house on the card. Click on it. This icon returns you to the At School list. Click on Saturn. The buttons on this card do some special actions. Stephanie has put a large invisible button over her picture and the directions "Hear My Voice!" Click on the words or the picture and see what happens.

Notice the icon of a piece of film on the graphic in the lower left-hand corner. Click on it. How did you like that? Now click on the words "See My Movie." You can see the film as many times as you would like by clicking on that button. Now see if you can find the answer to another question.

2. What myth was Galileo reminded of when he first saw the rings of the planet Saturn?

_____

_____

_____

_____

To find this answer, you had to click on the arrow in the bottom right-hand corner of the box where the text is printed. That box is called a text item, or a text field. The bar at the side is called a scroll bar; when the bar shows up in this manner, the field is called a *scrolling* text field. Text Items can be created with or without scroll bars. You can click on the arrow at the top to move up through the information; clicking on the arrow at the bottom moves you down. Clicking on the shaded section in the middle moves you down one full page at a time. Sometimes you see a field where the middle section of the scrolling field bar is not shaded. This means that all of the information in that field is displayed on the screen.

When you were exploring the Rwanda stack, did you read the information about the authors? If you did, the information you read about Roger Arndt and Kristen Garnett was in a Text Item that did not have a scroll bar.

Now, click on the Home icon that will take you to the list where you can select Whale Tales. Can you find the button that lets you listen to humpback whales sing?

3. What icon did you select to hear the whales sing?

_____

_____

_____

_____

4. What kind of whale is the humpback?

_____

_____

_____

_____

5. How fast can killer whales travel?

_____

_____

_____

_____

Find Brown is Brown in the list. Click on it.

6. What did Travis Fossati write a poem about?

_____

_____

_____

_____

Search for the stack Bobcats.

7. What are some of the things that bobcats eat?

_____

_____

_____

_____

When you are through, click on the Home icon then click Sample Projects. Click on Home at the bottom of the screen. This returns you to the main menu, or Home Card, of HyperStudio 3.0. Click on the Quit Program button if you are finished exploring.

Creating a Stack in HyperStudio 3.0 for the Macintosh

Before you begin, make sure that you have a formatted data disk to save your work. From the desktop, open the folder that has HyperStudio 3.0 and the Home Card in it. The HyperStudio 3.0 Home card is the first screen that you see. Go to the File menu and select New Stack. A dialog box on the screen tells you that this is the beginning of a new stack and tells you some of the tools you can use as you create your stack.

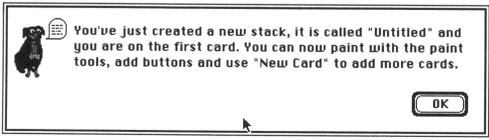

You've just created a new stack, it is called "Untitled" and you are on the first card. You can now paint with the paint tools, add buttons and use "New Card" to add more cards.

OK

The dialog box for starting a new stack in HyperStudio 3.0.

If a different dialog box appears, the Preferences menu (under the Edit menu) is set for experienced users. When you are an experienced user, every time you start a new stack you will be asked to select how many colors you want to use. If you are not using a color monitor, select "black and white." If you are using a color monitor, select "16 colors," so that a set of patterns will be included in the Colors menu. If you select "256 colors," many more colors appear in the Colors menu, but there are no patterns for you to use.

Look at the menu bar on your new stack. Does it say "Untitled - Card 1"? If it only says "Untitled," open the Edit menu, select Preferences, and put an X in the box in front of select Show card number with stack name. This way you always know which card you are working on.

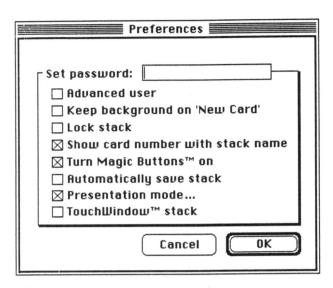

The Preferences dialog box.

It is a good idea to save your stack to your data disk before you begin. Go to the File menu and select Save Stack. A dialog box comes up to help you find the right place to save your stack. Click on Disk or Desktop (one of these choices will be in your dialog box). In the next box that opens, find the name of your data disk. Select it and click on Open. Now you name your first stack. Name it *PracticeStack.Your Initials*. Enter the name of your stack in the box under the request "Please Name This Stack." Click on Save.

A blank card is the first card of your stack. Remember, you are creating a stack that may consist of many cards (or screens) before you complete it. This means that when you are ready to create the next card, open the Edit menu and select New Card. Do not make the mistake of returning to the File menu and beginning a New Stack. Many students make this error when they first start to create stacks. If you have made the right selection, the title bar will say *"PracticeStack.Your Initials - Card 2."* It may help you to think of your stack as a file folder. A file folder helps you keep track of the different papers that you place inside it. The cards in your stack are just like those pieces of paper; they belong inside the stack.

Before you leave HyperStudio 3.0, remember to save your work. To save your stack to your data disk, be sure to select Save Stack As from the File menu. This allows you to select Desktop or Disk before you name your stack, so you can be sure you are saving it where you want. Select Desktop or Disk, and the names of all the places you can save your work will appear on the screen. Select the name of your data disk. Click on Open. When you have entered the name of the stack, click on the Save button (or just select Save if you have already named your stack). If you are saving your work directly to the HyperStudio 3.0 folder on your hard drive, select Save Stack from the File menu.

Creating a Border in HyperStudio 3.0 for Macintosh

HyperStudio 3.0 does not have a special Border command or a Border tool in any of its menus. That means that you can select tools to help you create a border from the Tools menu in the main menu bar. The steps for creating a border in your first stack are the same for creating a border in any stack.

1. Open the File menu and select Open Stack. You have already created your Practice stack. Highlight that stack name and click on Open. The name of the stack appears in the title bar.

2. Open the Apple menu and select Preferences from the Edit menu. The Preferences dialog box opens.

3. Select the box in front of Show card position in menu. The bar at the top of your stack should say "Card #," with the number representing the number of the card. This allows you to know just where you are in the stack at all times. You can return to Preferences at any time to change your selection.

4. Select Keep Background on "New Card." This is an important capability, and you may be going into the Preferences menu to change that mark frequently. If there is an X in front of Advanced User, click on it to remove the X, then you can click on Keep Background. The card is blank and you are about to begin.

Getting the Tools and Creating a Border

To create your border, you will be selecting several different tools from the Tools menu, so it is a good idea to be able to get to them as easily as you can. You can "tear off" the Tools menu from the menu bar and place it anywhere on the screen by dragging it with the mouse. To create the borders, it would be useful to have your Tools and Colors menu in the middle of the card, at least for now. Follow these steps to move the menus:

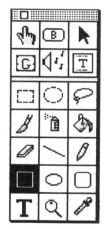

1. Using the mouse, click on Tools from the menu bar. Do not let go of the mouse button.

2. Drag the menu by moving your mouse to the middle of the card. As you drag the cursor along, you will see a dotted box outline. When that dotted box outline is where you want the menu, release the mouse button. You should have a menu in the middle of your card that looks like the following figure.

The Tools menu in HyperStudio 3.0.

Follow the same steps to place the Colors menu next to the Tools menu.

3. Choose the solid color you want for your lines from the Colors menu. Click on that color and a box forms around it to show that it has been selected.

4. Select the Rectangle tool under the eraser tool in the left column of the Tools menu. When you click on the rectangle, that box in the tools menu will darken so you will know it has been selected. Move the cursor around the screen. It has changed to a new shape and looks like a cross-hair symbol.

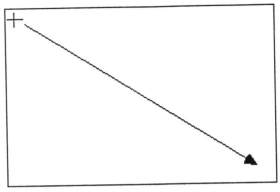

Getting ready to draw the first rectangle.

5. Place the cursor in the upper left-hand corner of the card. Drag the cursor to the lower right-hand corner. This will draw a rectangle across the whole card. That box will be the outside of your border.

6. Draw the inside edge of the border. Place the cross-hair cursor about 1 inch from the edge of the upper left-hand corner. There are four rectangles pictured on the next page. Your border should look similar to the first rectangle. Drag the cursor to the same distance from the lower right-hand corner and release the mouse button. Your border outline is now in place.

7. Choose a pattern from the Colors menu. HyperStudio 3.0 also works on computers that do not have color. Your patterns will show in black and white and you can still use them to fill your border.

8. Select the Paint Can tool from the Tools menu. It is located just below the lasso icon.

9. Place the cursor, which now looks like the paint can, inside the border. Click the mouse. Watch the pattern fill your border. Look at the second rectangle; yours should look almost like it.

Another Way to Create a Border

Try using these steps to create an inner border.

1. Double click on the Rectangle tool from the Tools menu. Double click means to click twice, very quickly. The blank rectangle will turn into a filled rectangle if you have double clicked correctly. When you draw a rectangle now, it will be a filled shape. (If you were unable to double-click, select Draw Filled from the Options menu. When you release the mouse, your Tools menu will show the shapes ready to draw filled.)

2. Use the same pattern you used before.

3. Place the cross-hair cursor about 1-½ from the upper left-hand corner of your border and drag it to that distance from the lower right-hand corner. A rectangle appears on the screen filled with the color or pattern you selected. Notice how the rectangle drew behind the Tools and Colors menus. If you do not like the color, go to the Edit menu and select Undo. You can select another color or pattern and replace the rectangle. If

you are satisfied with the rectangle, move to step 4. You can close the menus by clicking in the Close box in the upper left-hand corner. Your border should look similar to the third rectangle.

4. Open the Colors menu and select the white box.

5. Select the Rectangle tool and draw a white-filled rectangle on top of the first filled rectangle. Look at the fourth rectangle. Yours should look similar to the way it appears.

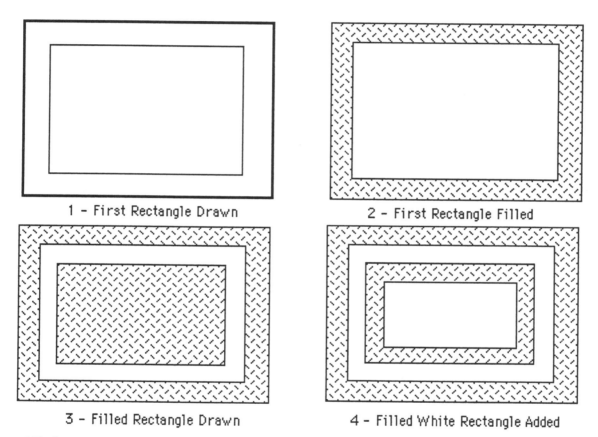

All the steps in completing a double border.

You have nearly completed this first card. It appears as though you have added three bands to the card, but you have really added one filled border and created a border-like appearance using two filled rectangles. These are techniques you will use many times in the future.

Before you leave HyperStudio 3.0, remember to save your work. To save your stack to your data disk, be sure to select Save Stack As from the File menu. This allows you to select your disk before you name or re-save your stack, so that you are saving it to your data disk.

Creating a Background in HyperStudio 3.0 for the Macintosh

It is not unusual to want the same border, background color, or graphic to appear on several cards in your stack. What if you wanted to have arrow buttons, a help icon, and a house icon to return to the home stack on each card? You could create a basic card that looks the way you want them all to look and add invisible buttons later! It might look like this:

Or, you simply might want to have the same background color and graphic on each card in your program. When you want this to happen, you create a background and it appears on every new card you create. There are two ways to create backgrounds in HyperStudio 3.0. In this exercise, you will have a chance to try them both. You can come back to this handout when you create other stacks to choose the way that will work best for you.

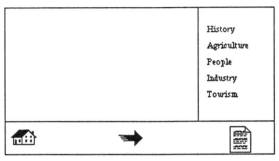

Sample background card.

Using Ready Made Cards in the Edit Menu to Create a Background

1. Pull down the File menu and select New Stack.

2. Create a background that would work for several cards. First choose a background color from the Colors menu, then select the Paint Can tool from the Tools menu and click anywhere on the card. Create a border or add some clip art. If you want the graphic to show on the background, you must select Add Clip Art from the File menu. Remember: Clip art becomes a part of the background but graphic objects are placed only on a single card.

3. Add text to a background if you want it to appear on each card of this stack. Use the Text tool to add this kind of text.

4. Now you are ready to test your background. Pull down the Edit menu. Select Ready Made Cards. Another floating menu appears next to it. Select Same Background. You are now on the second card

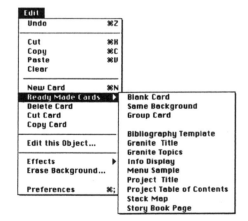

Selecting Ready Made Cards from the Edit menu.

of your stack. Did you notice that you could have selected Blank Card? When you are ready to start a different card or create a second background, that is the selection you will make.

Using Import Background in the File Menu to Create a Background

1. Pull down the File Menu and select Input background.

Creating Graphic Text in HyperStudio 3.0 for the Macintosh

When you were creating the border for your first stack, you were using the Rectangle tool from the Paint tools. These are special tools that let you create your own artwork. You should try each tool and find out what it does.

When you are creating a stack, there are many times that you might like to paint a large word or type a very small word. Suppose you were doing a map of a state or of your room and you wanted to label places or things. This would be a time to use graphic text. Look at the Tools menu. Find the letter T. That is the Text graphic tool.

Try the Text tool. Open your Practice stack and follow these directions:

1. Open a new card.

2. Click on the Tools menu and drag it onto the screen.

3. Select the Circle tool and draw 3 different-sized circles on the new card.

4. Select the T (Text graphic tool).

5. Click on the Options menu.

6. Select Text Style.

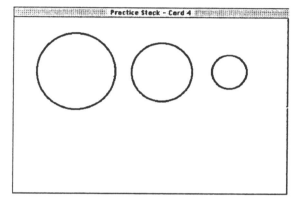

Three different circles.

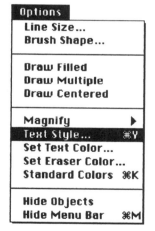

The Options menu with Text Style selected.

You will be able to select the font, style, and size for the letters you want to type. A preview window lets you see how the letters will appear.

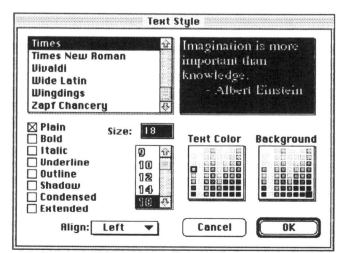

The Text Style window.

7. Label the circles with the words "Large," "Middle Sized," and "Small." If you want to write the words in color, choose Text Color under the Options menu before you type.

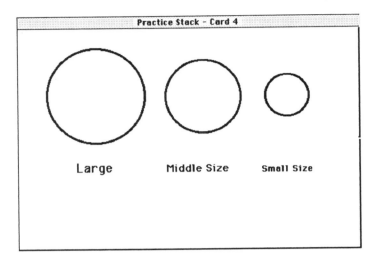

Labeled circles.

You can change sizes, styles, and colors, even in the middle of a word. Here are precautions you need to think about.

- Text graphics are painted.
- To erase you must immediately press the Delete key, use the Eraser tool from the Tools menu, or select the word with the Select tool (dotted-line rectangle) and press the Delete key.
- You can move a word by selecting it with the Select tool, putting the cursor into the box, pressing the mouse, and dragging the word to a new place.
- If you select a word, you can use the Scale, Rotate, and Flip actions from the Edit menu.
- Don't forget to save your stack.

Think of text graphics as another way to write about your ideas.

Creating Text Objects in HyperStudio 3.0 for the Macintosh

Selecting Add a Text Object from the Objects menu is the first step in placing a text field on your card. You can place this text field anywhere on the card and it can have a scroll bar that allows you to put as much information into that field as you wish. The important thing to know is that you are not using graphic text the way that you did when you selected the Text tool from the Tools menu. Entering text into a text field is like using a word processor.

As a matter of fact, with HyperStudio 3.0 you can write in your word processor and place the information into the text field. You will need to learn how to save your writing as a text file (sometimes called an ASCII file); then you can put your story, poem, or report into your HyperStudio 3.0 stack. You will try that technique later on with a sample from the HyperStudio software.

Creating a Text Field

Follow the steps below to make a field where you can enter the text.

1. Open your Practice stack.

2. Create a new card.

3. Pull down the Objects menu and select Add a Text Object.

4. Use the cursor to position the text field where you would like it to appear on the screen. Place the arrow inside the dotted-line frame when you move the field. Place the arrow along any edge of the frame to change its size. Don't forget to hold the mouse button down when you move the field or change its size.

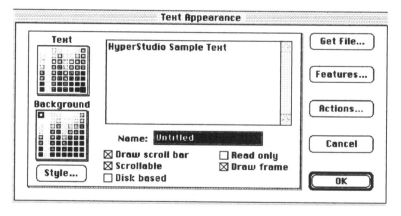

The Text Appearance box.

5. Click outside the field to set the position of the text field.

6. The Text Appearance box allows you to choose the color of the text, the style of the text, and the color of the background. Click on Style to choose the font, size, and alignment of the words. It even shows you a sample of how the text will look. Explore these choices until you have a combination you like. Look back at page 161.

7. Name your field. This is a good habit to develop. It helps you remember the special reason you had for creating your objects.

8. If you are going to include a lot of information, it might be important to have a scroll bar on the side. Click in the box in front of Draw Scroll Bar. Click OK.

Moving the Text Field and Editing the Text

You are back on the card, the cursor is blinking, and you are ready to enter text onto the screen. When you have finished typing, you can still make the text field larger or smaller, and even change its location on the card and how the text looks. Try this now by following the steps below.

1. Open the Tools menu and select the Field tool. It has the letter T on it.

2. Click *once* on the text field. The dotted-line frame is back. Now you can change the size and placement of the field.

3. Clicking *twice* on the text field brings up the Text Appearance box, so you can change the background color of the field and some other features of the field. Click on Style to make changes on the text you have written.

4. Open the Tools menu and select the Browse tool. It looks like a hand. Notice that the cursor is positioned where the text begins. Select all, or part, of the text the way you would if you were using a word processor. That is, hold down the mouse button and pull (drag) the cursor across the text you want to select. That text should now be highlighted.

5. Open the Colors menu. Choose the color you want to use for the selected text. Click outside the field or outside the selected text. You have now changed the color of the text.

Importing a File into a Text Field

There is one last thing to try before you are through creating Text Objects. You are going to select a file and bring it into a text field.

1. Create a new card.

2. Pull down the Objects menu and select Add a Text Object.

3. Position the text field on the screen and click outside the field.

4. Click on Get File.

5. Open the HS Text folder.

6. Select Addy's Poem and click on Open. You can see the text in the sample box of the Text Appearance window. If you want to change the color of the text or the background, you can do so now. When you are ready, click OK.

7. Click on the scroll bar to read the poem about Addy.

Now you have practiced two ways to create Text Objects. You can reread these directions whenever you need a reminder.

Creating a Button in HyperStudio 3.0 for the Macintosh

You have now created two cards. The first could be a title screen for your stack. The second card may have a graphic or other information about your stack. Now you need to create a button, or link, that will help the person who is reading your stack go from the first card to the second card.

Until you create your button, you need to have another way to move between cards. Select Move from the main menu bar. This method is so easy that you may choose to use it even when there are buttons available.

Move	
Back	⌘~
Home	⌘H
First Card	⌘1
Previous Card	⌘<
Next Card	⌘>
Last Card	⌘9
Jump To Card...	⌘J
Find Text...	⌘F

The Move menu.

Now create the first button: Open the Objects menu and select Add a Button. This first dialog box provides many choices as the button is created.

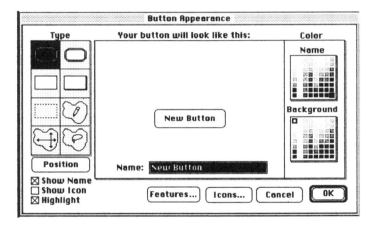

The Button Appearance dialog box.

1. It is always a good idea to give your button a name. You can decide later if you want the name of the button to be visible. There is a box in the lower left-hand corner that says "Show Name." If you want the name to show, be sure there is an X in the box. Name your button "Next Screen" by typing the name into the box next to Name:.

2. Choose the type of button that you will use. Click in any of the four frames at the top of the button style choices. The other choices are special kinds of buttons and you will learn about them later. Select which one of the four you want to use.

3. Select background and text colors. Experiment by clicking on the different colors in each section. When you find a combination that you like, select it.

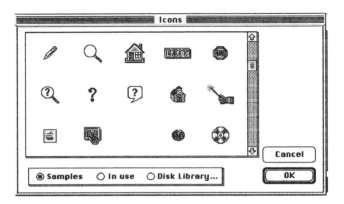

Choosing an Icon for a Button.

4. Click on Icons. Click on the scroll bar to view the various icons available for you to use. Clicking on the arrow you want to use will select it. Click on OK. Select an icon that points to the right. Notice that the icon and the name are both visible.

5. Place your button. Click on Position. The dotted-line frame around the button signals that you can move the button where you want it. Place it in the lower right-hand corner of the card, then click outside the box and the Actions window appears.

6. Selecting the Actions. On the left-hand side are the choices for Places to Go; Things to Do are on the right. If you click in the Another Card check box on the Places to Go side, a new dialog box appears. Use the right arrow to move to the next card. If you do not have another card, go to the Edit menu and select New Card (press Command-N) to create a new card. The dialog box is now on "Card 2." Click on OK. Click OK again and the Transition menu appears.

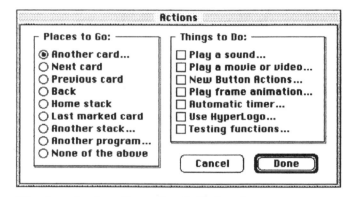

Moving to Another Card dialog box.

Did you wonder why you couldn't just choose Next card? What would happen if you created a new card after your first card but before your second card? Your "Card 2" would say "Card 3" and would not be the next card anymore. By always using Another Card you can be certain your buttons go to the right place.

7. Setting the transition. There are a lot of different visual effects you can provide for users as they move from one card to another: Try some of them now. Click on Right to Left, choose medium speed, and click on Try. Now try Rain and Dissolve, at different speeds. When you find the one you like, click on OK. Now click Done.

Try your button now. Can you create a button to take you back to the first card? Try it. Here are some things to think about as you make this second button.

- In which direction should your arrow point?

- In which corner of the screen will you place your button?

Remember to think about your audience when you place these buttons.

From *Hypermedia As a Student Tool.* © 1995. Teacher Ideas Press. (800) 237-6124.

Editing a Button in HyperStudio 3.0 for the Macintosh

Sometimes you change your mind about where a button should be placed or how it should look. These are easy things to change in HyperStudio 3.0. Go back to the button you created on the second page of the practice stack. Let's change how it looks.

1. Open the Tools menu. Select the Button icon with the B on it. Now you have activated the Button tool.

2. Click once on the button and the dotted-line frame appears. If all you want to do is move the button, you can do that now. If you want to make other changes, go on to step 3.

3. If you know you want to edit from the start, double click on the original button. The Button Appearance dialog box appears and you can make the changes that you want. If you click on the Actions button, you will go to that dialog box, and if you want to change the icon, click on Icons. You may want to change the Show Name and Highlight boxes to see what difference that makes.

4. When you have finished, go back to the Tools menu and select the Browse tool (the hand icon) and try out your changed button.

Using Graphics in HyperStudio 3.0 for the Macintosh

To place a graphic on your card, first select Add a Graphic Object from the Objects menu. You can place this graphic anywhere on the card. You can use the Clip Art files that come with HyperStudio 3.0, clip art from Pict, Tiff, or EPS files, or clip art from any paint program.

To learn how to add a graphic, open your practice stack, create a new card, and follow these directions.

1. Pull down the Objects menu and select Add a Graphic Object.

2. Select the Clip Art file you want to use.

3. Select a picture file and click OK after selecting it. For practice, select Addy.

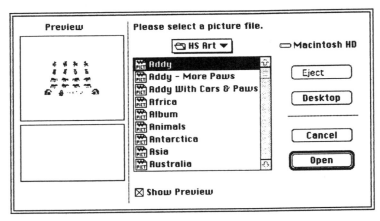

Selecting a picture file.

Choosing the picture.

4. Use the Frame or the Lasso tool to draw a box or circle around the picture you wish to move to your card. Whether there are several pictures in the file or only one, the one you want must be selected with one of these tools. After clicking OK, and the image is moved to your card, you can select Get Another Picture and choose again.

5. Drag the picture into position with the mouse. When the picture is where you want it, click outside the picture. While in the Graphic Appearance window you can add a frame.

When you are adding a graphic by this method, you can edit it by choosing the Graphic tool. It is a square with a G in the center. Click on the Graphic tool, then click on your graphic. The dotted-line frame tells you that it is selected. Now you can move the frame to a new location. By adjusting the frame, pushing and pulling with the mouse, you can make the graphic larger or smaller. Click outside the graphic when you are done. Go back to the Browse tool.

Putting a QuickTime Movie in HyperStudio 3.0 for the Macintosh

The first step in placing a QuickTime movie into your stack is to open the Objects menu and select Add a Button. Follow the steps below to create and place a button.

1. Name the button "Play Movie."

2. Click on Position and place the button where you want it. The lower left-hand corner might be a good place. Click outside the button. When the button is placed and you click OK in the Button Appearance window, the Button Action window opens. Under Things to Do, click on the box in front of a movie or video.

3. A dialog box opens so that you can select the movie you are placing in your stack.

4. Open the QuickTime Movies Folder.

5. Select Saturn Movie and click on Open. The movie is placed on the card and is surrounded by a dotted-line frame. Use the mouse to move the movie window where you want it.

6. Clicking outside the movie window returns you to the QuickTime Movies window.

7. Choose how the QuickTime movie should appear.

8. Click on Done. You are now ready to try the button that will play your movie.

On your card is the button you have created, but you cannot see the movie. Click on the button. Now the movie plays. Each time you click on the button the movie will play. The movie will stay on the screen until you move to the next card. It will close automatically when you move to another card or create a new card.

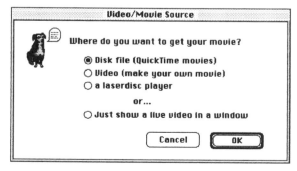

Video/Movie Source.

11
Digital Chisel
Support Materials

Exploring Digital Chisel on the Macintosh: A First Visit

Name: _____

Today you will explore Digital Chisel on the Macintosh for the first time. There are sample projects and you will have a chance to explore several of them. That will give you an opportunity to see the kinds of buttons, graphics, and text items that you will be able to create with Digital Chisel.

Exploring means you will be clicking on *buttons* to move through the project. Sometimes the buttons look like arrows or other *icons*; sometimes they will be on top of words or pictures and are invisible. You will need to explorer carefully to find the answers to the questions that follow. Most of the ones you will click on look like jelly beans.

After you open the Digital Chisel folder from the hard drive menu, click on the Demo Project icon. Clicking on the icon has taken you to a new screen. There are 12 choices for you on this screen. You can learn about hypertext by clicking on the Text icon. There is a movie about John Fitzgerald Kennedy under the Movie icon and two types of Animation are shown under the animation icon. For some of the questions that follows you will need to look at the Questions, Interactive Lessons, Custom Presentations, Stories and Reports, and Customized Instruction. You can look at others, too, to learn some of the special things you can do with Digital Chisel.

Questions?

1. What is the capital of Maine? _____

2. What are two interesting facts about the Oregon Trail?

    _____

    _____

Now can you find the answer to another question?

3. Which wheeled item under Custom Presentations had the highest sales? Do you know how many sold? _____

4. Who are the characters in the Stories and Reports example? _____

Now, click on the buttons that will let you put the man back together. You will find him under Interactive Lessons. Can you find the button for the knee?

5. What happened when you clicked on the Terrestrial Ecosystem button? (Hint: Look under Customized Instruction.) _____

6. When you are through exploring, click on the Quit icon. This will take you out of Digital Chisel.

Creating a Project in Digital Chisel on the Macintosh

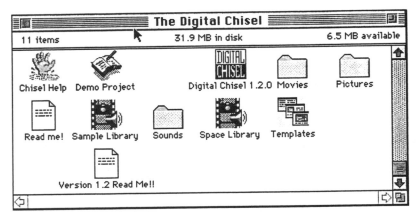

Digital Chisel folder files.

Before you begin, make sure that you have a formatted data disk for saving your work. From the desktop, open the Digital Chisel folder that has Digital Chisel in it.

The first screen that you see is a new window that gives you three choices. Click on Create a New Project.

You need to name your project:

1. Put your formatted data disk into the disk drive.
2. Click on Desktop and select your disk's name from the choices.
3. Click on Open.
4. Name the project (e.g., *Practice Your Initials* "PracticeIN").
5. Click on Save. A blank screen appears with *"Practice Your Initials"* at the top. Everything you do in your new project will automatically be saved to your data disk.

[Dialog box image:]

🖫 MYPROJ ▼		🖫 MYPROJ
▯ DCWNDO.TIF		Eject
▯ NMPRJTDC		Desktop
▯ NUPRJTDC.TIF		New 📁
Save project as:		Cancel
PRACTICEIN		Save

Naming a project to save on disk.

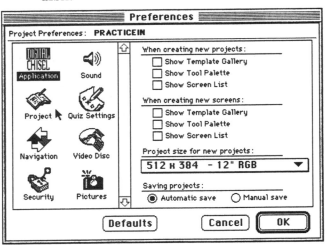

The Preferences window.

Before beginning, you need to change the preference level. For some of these activities, you should be working at the "advanced" level.

1. Choose Preferences from the File menu.
2. Click once on the Project icon.

3. Change the Author Skill Level to advanced by clicking on the circle in front of "advanced."

4. Click on OK.

It is a good idea to save your project frequently to your data disk. Go to the File menu and select Save. Your project will be saved automatically as you work on it, but it can't hurt (you might have accidentally selected Manual Save in the preferences window).

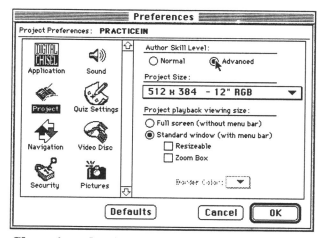

Changing the Author Skill Level.

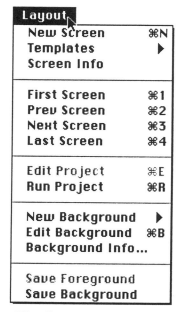

The Layout menu.

The first screen of your project is empty. Remember, you are creating a project that may consist of many screens before you complete it. This means that when you are ready to create the next screen, open the Layout menu and select New Screen. Do not make the mistake of returning to the File menu and beginning a New Project. Many students make that error when they first start to create projects.

It may help you to think of your project as a file folder. A file folder helps you keep track of the different papers that you place inside it. That screens in your project are just like those pieces of paper. They belong inside the project.

To help keep track of where you are, you should add a number to the first screen. Choose the Paint tools from the Tools menu and click on the letter A. This is the text Paint tool. Paint tools require that you draw a square to paint text in. The cursor changes to a cross. Draw a small square in the upper right-hand corner of the screen. Type "1" inside the square.

Go to the Layout menu and select New Screen. The screen that appears does not have any number on it. Add a box and type "2" in it (remember to select Paint tools and the letter A first). Then Save your project from the File menu.

Screen showing Paint tools and small number painted in the corner.

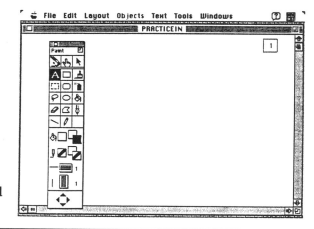

Creating a Border in Digital Chisel for the Macintosh

Digital Chisel does not have a special Border command or a Border tool in any of its menus. This means that you can select tools from all of those available to you in the Tools palette from the Windows menu in the menu bar. The steps to create a border in your first stack are the same for creating a border in any stack.

1. Click on the Digital Chisel icon in the Digital Chisel folder and click on Open a Project. Click on Desktop to access your data disk. You have already created your Practice project. Highlight the Project name and click on Open.

2. Open the File menu. Select Preferences, click on the Project icon, and change Author Skill Level to "advanced."

The card is blank except for the number you added; you are ready to begin.

Getting the Tools

To create your border, you will be selecting several different tools from the Tools palette.

1. Click on the Browse (hand) tool and then choose the Draw tool (the icon has a ruler and triangle).

2. Select the pattern you want by clicking once on the square next to the Pen tool. Choose "solid."

3. Select the color by clicking once on the third square next to the Pen tool and choosing your color from the color palette. To have an unfilled border, the square next to the Bucket tool must be white (no pattern, no color).

4. Select the Rectangle tool from the Draw menu. When you click on the rectangle, its box in the tools menu will darken and you will know that it has been selected. Move the cursor around the screen. The cursor has changed to a new shape. It looks like a cross-hair symbol.

5. Place the cursor in the upper left-hand corner of the card. Keeping the mouse button down, drag the cursor to the lower right-hand corner. This will draw a rectangle across the whole card. That box is the outside of your border.

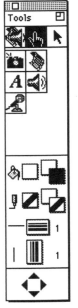 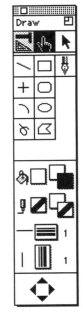

The Tools   **The Draw**
palette.   **tools.**

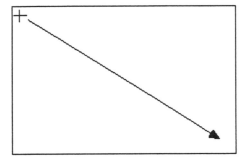

Getting ready to draw the first rectangle.

From *Hypermedia As a Student Tool.* © 1995. Teacher Ideas Press. (800) 237-6124.

6. Draw the inside edge of the border. Place the cross-hair cursor about 1 inch from the edge of the upper left-hand corner. Drag the cursor to the same distance from the lower right-hand corner and release the mouse button. Your border outline is in place.

7. To fill the area between the two rectangles, you must first select the outside rectangle by clicking on it. Small squares in the corners tell you when it has been selected. Choose a pattern by clicking once on the square next to the Bucket tool and selecting a pattern. The area between the borders will instantly fill with the pattern. See the figures below. Your rectangle should be similar to the second rectangle pictured.

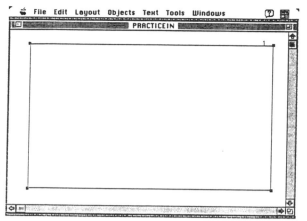

Border outline showing handles in corners and a painted screen number.

Another Way to Create a Border

Follow the steps below to create the effect of an inner border.

1. Click on the Rectangle in the Draw tools. When you draw a rectangle now, it will be a filled shape. This is because you selected a pattern from the Bucket Tool.

2. Place cross-hair cursor about 1-½ inches from upper left-hand corner of border and drag it to that distance from lower right-hand corner. A filled rectangle has appeared on the screen with the pattern or color you selected. If not satisfied with pattern or color, change to a new pattern by clicking the mouse on square next to Bucket tool; change color by clicking on the third square. As long as there are little squares in the corners of the rectangle, it will change as you make new selections. When satisfied with the rectangle, move to step 3. Your rectangle should look similar to the third rectangle pictured.

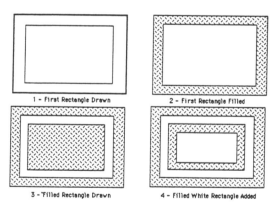

All the steps in creating a double border.

3. Click on the square next to the Bucket tool and the Patterns menu appears. Select the white box. Click on the third square and select the color white.

4. Select the Rectangle tool. Draw a white-filled rectangle on top of the first filled rectangle. Your rectangle should now look similar to the fourth rectangle.

You have nearly completed this first card. It appears as though you have added three bands to the card, but you have really added one filled border and created a border-like appearance using two filled rectangles. These are techniques you will use many times in the future.

Before leaving Digital Chisel, remember to save your work. Select Save from the File menu and your project will save to your data disk.

From *Hypermedia As a Student Tool.* © 1995. Teacher Ideas Press. (800) 237-6124.

Creating a Text Item in Digital Chisel for the Macintosh

Selecting Field tools from the Tools menu is the first step in placing a text field on your screen. You can place this text field anywhere on the screen. It can have a scroll bar, which allows you to put as much information as you wish into that field. The important thing to know now is that you are not using graphic text the way that you did when you selected the A tool from the Paint tools. Entering text into a text field is almost like using a word processor.

As a matter of fact, you can write in your word processor and place the information in a text field in Digital Chisel. You will need to learn how to save your writing as a text file (sometimes called an ASCII file) and then you can put your story, poem, or report into your Digital Chisel project. You will try that later with a sample from the Digital Chisel software.

Creating a Text Field

Start by making a field where you can enter text:

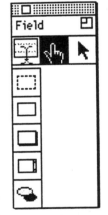

Selecting a text field.

1. With Digital Chisel open, select Open Existing Project and, after clicking on Desktop, open your disk and your Practice project.

2. Select New Screen from the Layout menu.

3. Open Tools palette menu and select Field tools.

4. Select the type of frame you want (transparent, shadowed, scrolling).

5. Position the cross-hair cursor in the upper left-hand corner where you'd like your text field to start. Click and hold the mouse button down as you drag the cursor to the right and down to size the text field.

6. Notice that the Objects menu is active because a text field is an object. Look at all the selections available! Whenever there are handles (small squares) in the corners of an Object, the object menu is available for selections.

7. To type, you must select the Browse (hand) tool from the Tools menu. Click inside the text field and type the words you want. The Text menu allows you to choose the color of the text, the style of the text, and the size of the letters. Explore these choices until you have a combination that you like. Select the text you want to change by dragging the mouse across it while pressing the mouse button.

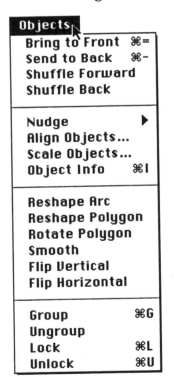

Objects menu selections.

From *Hypermedia As a Student Tool.* © 1995. Teacher Ideas Press. (800) 237-6124.

8. If you are going to describe your subject, it might be important to have a scroll bar on the side, but this time you don't need one.

Changing the Placement of the Text Field

You are back on the screen, the cursor is blinking, and you are ready to type something that you want to share about yourself. When you have finished typing, you can still make the text field larger or smaller or even change its location on the screen. Try that now.

1. Open the Tools Palette and select the Arrow tool. It is on the top right. You may also go to the Tools menu and select the Pointer tool.

2. Click once on the text field. The handles are back. Now you can change the size or placement of the field.

3. Select the Browse tool. It looks like a hand. Notice that the cursor is positioned at the start of the text in the field. Select all, or part, of the text the way you would if you were using a word processor. That is, hold down the mouse button and pull (drag) the cursor across the text you want to select. That text should now be highlighted.

4. Open Colors from the Text menu. Choose the color you want to use for the selected text. Click outside the field or outside the selected text. You have now changed the color of the text.

Putting a File into a Text Field

There is one more thing to try for creating text items. You are going to select a file and bring it into a text field.

1. Create a new screen.
2. Pull down the File menu and select Import.
3. Select Text.
4. Cancel the window that has opened.
5. Open the File menu and select Library, then select Open Library.

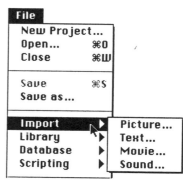

Importing text.

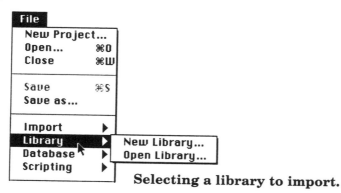

Selecting a library to import.

You may have to select Digital Chisel by clicking on Desktop to get to the libraries.

6. There are many files on the Digital Chisel Library. Click on the small arrow pointing down. The file names appear.

7. The only text files have an A in front of them. Open the Space Library and choose Space Race.

8. When the file appears, drag it onto the screen. Close the Library. The imported text will automatically be a scrolling field because the text may be a larger file than the field will hold. You can resize the field, so scrolling might or not be needed.

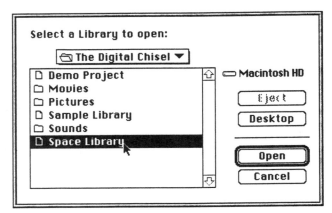

Selecting a text file to import.

9. Click in the scroll bar to read about the Space Race.

Now you have practiced two ways to create text items. You can reread these directions whenever you need a reminder.

Creating Hypertext

You have read about changing the font, size, and style of text, but there is one more thing you can do. It is possible to create hypertext, or "Hot Text", which is text with an invisible entry attached to it. When the text is selected, the invisible entry shows itself.

1. Create a new screen.
2. Place a text field on the screen.
3. Type "This is a story about me." into the text field.
4. With the Browse tool, highlight the word *me*.
5. Open the Edit menu and select Hot Link. A Hypertext field opens.
6. Type your name and age in a sentence into this field.
7. Select Done Hot Link from the Edit menu, or click Done on the smaller window. The text you selected is now in boldface and underlined.

You will have to select Run Project from the Layout menu to test your hot text! Remember that your project will automatically be saved.

From Hypermedia As a Student Tool. © 1995. Teacher Ideas Press. (800) 237-6124.

Using Graphics in Digital Chisel for the Macintosh

Selecting Import from the File menu is the first step in placing a graphic on your screen. You can place this graphic anywhere on the screen. You can use the pictures in the libraries that come with Digital Chisel or any clip art that is accessible to the Macintosh. If you have a CD-ROM drive with your computer system, you can get graphics from the CD-ROM disc that comes with your Digital Chisel software package.

Now you will learn how to add a graphic. Open Digital Chisel, open your existing project, and open your disk and your Practice stack. Create a new screen and follow these directions.

1. Open the File menu and select Import.

2. Select Picture.

3. Open the File menu and select Library.

4. Choose Open Library.

5. Click on the Desktop to access Digital Chisel's libraries.

6. Choose a library.

7. Select a picture.

Selecting a Picture file.

8. When the picture appears in its window you can scroll through the pictures using the right or left arrows, or you can click on the down arrow and a library list appears. Click on the picture you want and drag it to the screen.

9. Close the library file by clicking in the Close box.

10. Position and resize the picture.

11. If you change your mind, and if handles are in the corners, press the delete key and the picture will be deleted. If you think you will change your mind, do so before you close the library window so you don't have to open it again.

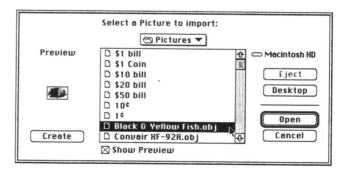

Selecting a picture.

When you are adding a graphic by this method, you can edit the graphic by clicking on it after selecting the Pointer tool from the Tools menu. Click on your graphic. The handles (squares in the corner) tell you that it has been selected. Now you can move it to a new location. By placing the cursor in a square in the corner you can make the graphic larger or smaller. Click outside the graphic when you are done. Go back to the Browse tool.

Adding a Graphic to the Background

If you want a special graphic to be on every screen in a project, or on a group of screens, select Edit Background from the Layout menu. Remember this graphic will be on every screen until you choose New Background.

1. Go to the Layout menu and select Edit Background.

2. Go to the File menu and select Import.

3. Select the Picture file.

4. Go to File and select Library, Open Library.

5. Select a library and the window will appear on the screen.

6. Scroll through the selections and drag the one you want onto the screen.

7. Close the library window.

8. Select Save Background.

Remember that this graphic will now be on every screen in your project. When you are ready to change to a new graphic for a background, go to the Layout menu and choose New Background.

Creating a Button in Digital Chisel for the Macintosh

You have now created two or more screens. The first could be a title screen for your project. The second screen may have a graphic or other information about your project. You need to create a button, or link, that will help the person who is reading your stack go from the first screen to the second screen. Until you create your button you need to know another way to move between cards. Select Layout from the menu bar and select Next Screen or Previous Screen or First Screen. You can also use the Command key and numbers 1, 2, and 3. Now you can see how easy it is for you to move between screens. You may use this method even when there are buttons already created.

If you want to create your own navigation icons, you must disable those set up in the program. Go to the Preferences in the File menu and click on Navigation. Remove the X in the boxes under the hand and arrow icons.

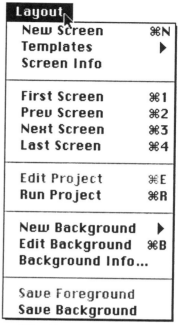

The Layout menu.

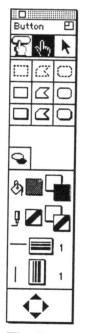

The Button tools.

Now create the first button: Open the Tools menu and select Button tools, or you can select the Tools palette from the Windows menu, and then select the Button tools. You can choose a transparent button or a regular or irregular shape. If you would like an arrow shape, hold the Command key down while you select the Polygon tool from the Draw tools. There are 21 polygons to choose from. You might choose the arrow that points to the right. Think about how you selected color. Put a transparent button over it.

1. Placing your button: The handles in the corners of the button signal that you can move the button where you want it. Place it in the lower right-hand corner of the screen. When you have placed the button, go to the Objects menu and select Objects Info. The Objects Info window appears. You can double click on the button and the same info window will appear. Name the button "Next."

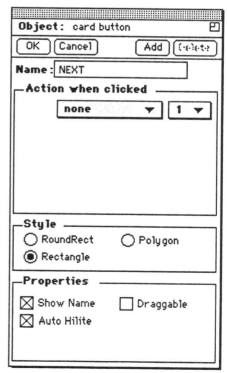

Object information.

2. Click on the arrow after "None." The selections that appear are all the actions you can have a button or any object do. Select Navigate.

3. Select Go to Next Card, or choose Link and choose the screen from the list.

4. Setting the transition: There are many different visual effects you can provide for users as they move from one card to another. Try some of them now. Click on Right to Left and choose fast speed, or try Rain or Dissolve at different speeds. Now click on Done.

Navigate selected.

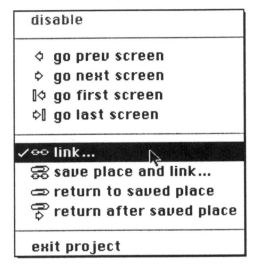

Selecting the screen to link to.

Try your button now. Can you create a button to take you back to the first screen? Try it. Here are some things to think about as you make this second button;

- Which direction should your arrow point?
- Which corner of the screen will you place your button?

Remember to think about your audience when you place these buttons.

Navigating with Objects

Any object, text field, picture, movie, sound, or paint or draw objects can be buttons. If you have such an object on your screen, use the Point tool and double click on the object. The Objects Info window will appear and you can choose many events for one object. A picture can cause a sound to play, a QuickTime movie to run, and then link to another screen with an inverse of colors as the transition event. There are lots of things to explore and try out as you work on your own projects.

Editing a Button in Digital Chisel for the Macintosh

Sometimes you change your mind about where a button should be placed or how it should look. These are easy things to change in Digital Chisel. Go back to the button you created on the second screen of the practice stack and change how it looks:

1. Open the Tools menu and select the Pointer tool.

2. Click once on the button and the handles appear. If all you want to do is move the button, you can do that now.

3. When you have finished, go back to the Tools menu, select the Browse tool, and try out your changed button.

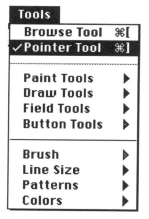

Selecting the Pointer tool from the Tools menu.

Creating a Background in Digital Chisel for the Macintosh

It is not unusual to want the same border, background color, or graphic to appear on several screens in your project. Think about it! What if you wanted to have a particular scene as the background on several screens. You could create the screen just the way you wanted it to look and add items in the foreground later.

A background is one of two parts of a screen. A foreground changes with each screen, but a background can be on each new screen in a project until you decide to change it.

You might want to have a background color and graphic on each screen in one section of your project. When you want this to happen, you create a background and it appears on each new screen you create if you follow the steps below. Note: You must be in the "advanced" skill level to work with backgrounds (see "Access Preferences Menu," *below*).

1. Put your Project Data Disk into the drive.

2. Open the Digital Chisel folder and double click on Digital Chisel.

3. Select Open Existing Project.

4. Click on Desktop.

5. Click on your Disk icon and open "Practice*YourInitials*."

Access Preferences Menu

1. Open the File menu and select Preferences.

2. Click once on Project icon.

3. Change the Author Skill Level to "advanced" by clicking on the circle in front of advanced.

4. Click on OK.

Creating a Background That Would Work for Several Screens

Edit Background Method

1. Open the Layout menu and select Edit Background.

2. Open the Tools palette from the Windows menu.

3. Use the Draw or Paint tools to create your own background, but Draw tools take up less memory. Memory is the space available in your computer to work with software. Painted objects take a great amount of space.

Do you remember how to select colors? Use Bucket tool square 1 for patterns. Use Bucket tool square 3 for colors.

4. To fill an area, draw the shape and it will be a filled shape.

There are design implications that will make your project easier for anyone to use. One of those design elements is consistency, another is to consider the user. You can do both of those by always placing the navigation aids in the same area of every screen. Across the lower part of the screen you can place arrows to let the user go to the next screen and to go back to the previous screen. Another icon can represent the home, or first, screen. When you begin a set of screens that will be about one topic, you could place a list of the other topics alongside, giving the user choices to select. Your screen might look like this:

Follow these steps to place arrows on the screen:

1. Select the Draw tools from the Tools palette.

2. Click on the Line tool and then draw a horizontal line 1 inch from the lower edge. Hold the shift key down as you drag the mouse and the line will stay straight.

3. Hold the Command key down while you select the Polygon tool. You will get a variety of shapes. Choose the arrow that points to the right.

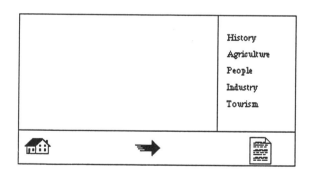

An example of a completed background.

4. Drag the arrow to the lower middle of the screen. When the handles (squares) are in the corners you can click in the center and place the arrow. You can click in the square and make the arrow larger or smaller.

5. If you choose to have a previous page icon, select the Polygon tool again and choose the arrow that points to the left. Drag and size it, placing it next to the first arrow.

6. For the Home icon, draw a house or choose clip art, if available.

From *Hypermedia As a Student Tool.* © 1995. Teacher Ideas Press. (800) 237-6124.

Each of these three icons (right, left, home) can be used to navigate (go to another screen) because they are objects. Selecting Object Info from the Objects menu gives you the chance to choose Navigate and tell the computer what should happen if an object is clicked. If you double click on an object, you will also get a list that includes "Navigate".

7. After you create your background, select Save Background from the Layout menu. You will be asked to name the background.

8. Select New Screen from the Layout menu. It should have the same background but will not have a number on it because you *painted* the number on the first two screens in your practice project.

Below are two different backgrounds. Notice that background 2 started out looking just like background 1. After it was created, a box was added around the word "people." The difference is that background 2 has a box around the word "history." The first screen tells us we are in the section of the project about people. The second screen tells us that we are in the section about history.

Background 1   **Background 2**

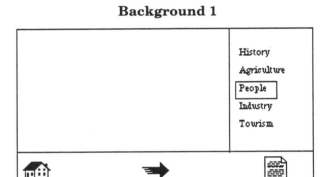
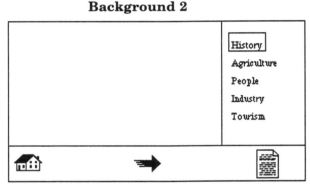

Two different modifications of the background.

If this were a real project, it might be one that a student was developing about a country or a state. Each student would have the important button icons in the same place. This makes a project easier for the user to read.

The buttons or objects at the bottom of the screen all do the same jobs. The House icon returns the user to the project's table of contents. The arrow goes to the next project in the series. The Paper icon with the folded-down section links to the reference section of this particular stack.

New Background Method

1. Get to the third screen of your project. New screens are added after the screen you are currently on. For example, you add a new screen when you are on screen 1, the new screen will become screen 2.

2. Select New Background, Other.

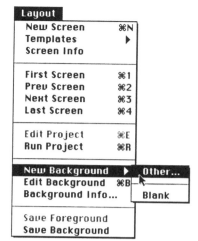

Choosing a new background file.

This file displays background templates that can be selected. You have choices of a blank, different continents, the USA, frames, notebooks, a stone tablet, among others. When you save a background, it becomes a template that you can use again.

3. Select the template you want to use.

4. If you add a text field to the background, the field travels with the background but the words do not. This lets you have a title box, ready for new text, on each screen.

5. Now test your background. Pull down the Layout menu. Select New Screen. Remember how you numbered the cards when you created your practice project. This new screen should not have a number. Do screens 1, 2, and 3 all have the same background? Do the next two screens have the background template you chose to use?

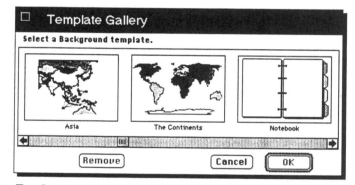

Background template choices.

6. Use the Layout menu to move to each screen (or press Command-1 for first screen, Command-3 for each "next" screen). Another way to see all the screens is to select Run Project from the Layout menu (or press Command-R).

7. You can add graphic objects, buttons, and text objects to any of the screens. They will only apply to the screen on which they are placed.

Remember: Your project will automatically be saved.

12
LinkWay Live! Support Materials

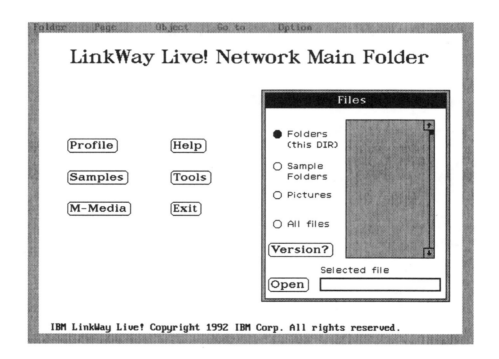

Exploring LinkWay Live!

Turn on your computer. At the c:\ prompt, type Llgo and press the Enter key, or click on the LinkWay Live! icon if you are running Windows on your computer. Now you are at the LinkWay Live! Main Folder page. It looks like the opening graphic of this section. Click on the Tools button. You can get help for a lot of different elements in LinkWay Live! For now, click on Tutorial in the LinkWay Tutorial rectangle. As you go through this tutorial, you will learn about many different things you can create in LinkWay Live!

Working through this tutorial can take a long time. You do not need to complete it in one session. Your place will be saved; then, in the next session, you can begin where you left off. Early in the tutorial, you will arrive at a page of some LinkWay examples. This shows you some specific examples of what you can create. When you click on Real Estate Manager, you see both pop-up text and pop-up graphics. You will be using pop-ups like these in your folders. Clicking on Animals Quiz shows you that color graphics can be used in your folders. Click on each of the animals to see what happens. What you see there is also pop-up text.

Continue through the pages. You will be learning the vocabulary of LinkWay as you explore folders, fields, objects, buttons, and much more. As you click on MyFolder, you will be creating pages, fields, and buttons, as well as practicing placing graphics on the pages in your Tutorial Folder. Trying out the editing tools in this tutorial will be of help to you when you create your own folders.

Continue along now until your teacher tells you it is time to stop. Remember, your place will be saved and you can continue where you left off the next time you use the computer.

Starting Up LinkWay Live!

These directions will help you start up LinkWay Live!, which has been installed on the c: drive of your computer. You will need a DOS-formatted 3-½" disk to save the folders that you create.

1. Turn on your computer. At the c:/ prompt, type LLgo and press the enter key. When the Main Menu appears, place your formatted 3-½" disk into the a: drive. If your computer also has a 5-¼" drive, put your disk into the b: drive. If you are running Windows, double click on the LinkWay Live! icon when Windows opens. Now you are at the LinkWay Live! Main Folder page. It looks just like the cover of this section. Along the top of the screen is the menu bar. By using these menus you will have access to all the tools you need to create your own folders.

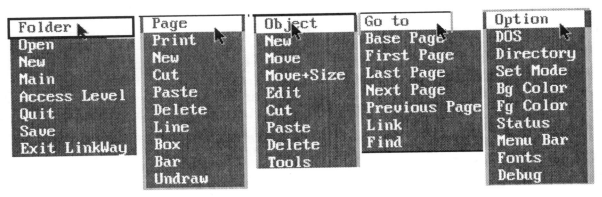

All the menus from the LinkWay Live! Menu Bar.

2. Click on the Option menu, highlight Set Mode, and click. When the Display Mode window appears, choose VGA. VGA gives you 16 colors to use, which is just the right amount for using LinkWay Live! When you have done that, click outside the window.

The Object menu.

Creating a Folder in LinkWay Live!

You have learned how to start up LinkWay Live! To begin your project, you will learn how to create a folder and add a page. Follow these steps:

1. Start up LinkWay Live!

2. Click on the Folder, highlight New, and Click. The New Folder Name window appears and provides a space for an eight-letter folder name. Choose a name that relates to your project. Remember to save two letters at the end for your initials, which you will capitalize (for example, AboutIN).

   > Look in the lower left-hand corner of the screen. You can see the name of your folder, the page that you are on (1), and the Identification number (ID) of that page (for example, AboutIN.1 ID=1).

3. You are ready to save this folder and the first page in it, so that you can work on them after you have planned your pages. Remember that the data disk to which you will save this folder is in the a: drive. You need to tell LinkWay Live! how to find that disk. Click on Option and select Directory. The window New Directory Name appears. Type in "a:" and press the enter key. Remember to check that the disk is not in the b: drive. Now click on Folder and select Save. The Save Folder As window appears and the name of your folder should appear in parentheses. Click in the Close box in the upper left-hand corner where you see a minus sign. Now your folder will be saved to the disk in the a: drive.

   > Before you finish this lesson, it is important to know how to add pages to your folder and how to find their ID number. You will need this information when you create buttons to link pages and folders. To add a page, click on the Page menu and select New. Do this several times and watch what happens in the lower left-hand corner.

4. Go to the Folder menu and select Quit.

Creating a Border in LinkWay Live!

There are two ways to place a border on your page. One is to use Bar from the Page menu, and the other is to use the LWPaint tool. You are going to create this border on a regular page and not on a Base page. You may want to have pages with different appearances, so it is not a good idea to put the border on the Base page.

Box Method

1. Open the Option menu and select Fg Color (Fg = foreground). A window of colors appears; click on the one you want for your border.

2. Open the Page menu and select Bar. A small rectangle appears. Without clicking, move the rectangle to the upper left-hand corner of the screen. Click once, let go of the button, and drag the mouse to the lower right-hand corner of the screen. Click a second time to place the rectangle. Repeat these directions to make a second rectangle about 1" smaller than the first. If the color does not look right or if you do not like the size of the rectangle you have drawn, go to the Page menu and select Undraw. Each time you select Undraw, one level of what you have placed on the screen disappears.

3. Save your work.

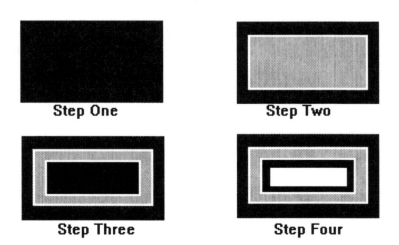

Step One   **Step Two**

Step Three   **Step Four**

All the steps for creating a border.

From *Hypermedia As a Student Tool*. © 1995. Teacher Ideas Press. (800) 237-6124.

LWPaint Method

1. Be sure that you are working from the c: drive, so that you can select the tools available in LinkWay Live!

2. LWPaint can be selected by clicking on the Object menu and selecting Tools. If you do not see LWPaint right away, click on the sidebar to move across the selection of tools until it does appear. Highlight LWPaint and then click outside the window. Another window appears and asks if you want to start the LWPaint program. Click on Yes. A new window and menu bar appear.

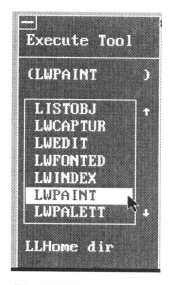
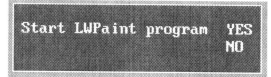

The LWPaint menu.

3. Click on Color. Select the color with which you would like to begin. Now click the Draw menu and select Bar. A rectangle appears; place it in the upper left-corner. Click on it once, pull it to the lower right-hand corner, and click again. This creates a box of the color you chose. Choose another color. Put the rectangle in the upper left-hand corner, about ½" to 1" from the box already drawn. Click, let go of the mouse button, and move the mouse to the lower right. Click the mouse button. Draw the Bars you need to finish your border. Look at steps 1 through 4 in the figure in the Bar Method.

4. To save the picture on your data disk, go to the Option menu, choose Directory, and type "a:". Go to the Picture menu and click on Save. Type in a name, such as "border1", and click outside the box.

5. Go to the Option menu, choose Directory, and type "c:". Go to the Picture menu and choose Exit Paint. The page you were working on appears. Return to the a: drive.

6. Go to the Object menu, choose New, and click on Picture. Move the small rectangle to the upper left-hand corner and click on it, then move the mouse to the lower right-hand corner and click. When the picture name window appears, type in the name of the picture. A picture file dialog box opens. Click on the picture name and it appears between the parentheses. Click on the name in the parentheses and click outside the box. The Adjust box appears. Click on FullPic if your border is placed correctly, otherwise use the adjust choices. The border is now placed.

The Adjust box.

7. Save it to your data disk.

Whenever you can it is better to use the Bar method within LinkWay Live! When you work in LWPaint, the graphic you create takes more space on your disk or hard drive.

Cut and Paste

But what happens if you want the border—in exactly the same way—on more than one page? There is a way you make this happen. You need to remember that, in LinkWay Live!, Cut (look under the Page menu to see it) really means Copy. These steps will let you create and then duplicate something exactly on as many pages as you wish.

When your border is complete, just the way you want it to look, follow these steps to see how it works:

1. Go to the Page menu and select Cut.
2. The Cut Page dialog box appears. Start to type. Perhaps you can call this "Border." Click outside the box and the Cut Completed dialog box appears on the screen. Click outside of the box.
3. Go to the Page menu again and select New.
4. When you are on the New page again, go to the Page menu and select Paste. The dialog box appears. Choose Border (or whatever you named your page when you Cut it). Notice that the name is now between the parentheses at the top of the screen. Click outside the box.

That's all there is to it. You can use these steps whenever you want to copy what you have put on one page to another page. Remember this when you create your menu pages.

From *Hypermedia As a Student Tool.* © 1995. Teacher Ideas Press. (800) 237-6124.

Creating Text in LinkWay Live!

When you create text in LinkWay Live! you can place your text anywhere on the screen, use different size fonts, and select the color you would like your text to be. All text is placed in a field that you create. You can have more than one text field on the screen.

1. Click on the Object menu, select New, then select Field, and click outside the box. A small dotted-line box appears.

2. Place the box in the upper left-hand corner of where you want to put your field. Click once. Drag the box to the lower right-hand corner of the text field you are creating. Make the box larger that you need it to be. You can always move and resize it later.

3. Choose the text size.

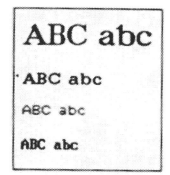 **Font choices.**

Click outside the font choice box and the Field Information window appears. Lastly, select the color.

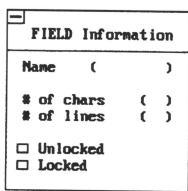 **The Field Information window.**

4. Double click in the upper left-hand corner of the field and begin typing. When you are through, click outside the field. Does it look just the way you want it to? If not, continue on to the next step.

5. Click on the field so that it is selected. Open the Go to menu and select Move + Size. Draw the box in the size and place you want it to be. Click outside the box and the text field is moved and resized for you.

From *Hypermedia As a Student Tool.* © 1995. Teacher Ideas Press. (800) 237-6124.

Creating a Button in LinkWay Live!

Creating a Button to Display Text

You can have a button that will display text on the screen when the button is clicked.

1. Select the Objects menu and highlight New. On the Object type, select Button.

2. Click where you want the button. Let go of the mouse button and move the cursor to create a button box the size you need for your text. Click the mouse button.

   • When Button Type dialog box appears, select Pop-Up.

   • Enter button's name where asked. Click outside box. A button icon window appears. Choose button icon that has the name you typed in. You do not always want to give the button a name. Sometimes you want to use an icon as the button. An icon is a small graphic. It can be an arrow or a picture. In the window where you selected your button there are arrows that look like this —->. Click on those arrows and select an icon from other windows of icons that appear. Try them out so that you know how they will look, then select button icon with name you entered.

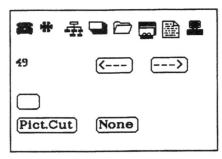

Button icon choices.

   • The text window appears, and this is where you enter your text. When you are finished typing the text, click outside the box. To try out the button, double click on the button name. When you finish reading the information, click outside the box to close it.

3. To edit the button: Click once on button to select it and the text field. Go to Objects menu and click on Move + Size. Place small rectangle where you want to relocate the button and draw a new box. The button will relocate. Double click to see if your text is how you want it.

4. Save your work to your data disk.

Creating A Link to Page Button

A button with an arrow icon should be added to your page to link to a new page.

1. At the Object menu, select New. On Object type, select Button.

2. Click where you want the button, let go of the mouse button, and move the mouse to create the button box the size you need for your text. Click the mouse button. When the Button Type dialog box appears, select Go. Type in Next for the name, or click outside the box and don't name it.

3. A button icon window appears. Choose the button icon that has an arrow pointing to the right. When window appears, choose Next. When finished, click outside the box.

4. Go to Page menu and select New. Notice the ID number is 2. This is the page the arrow button will link to. Use Go To menu to return to first page. Double click on arrow to make certain it works.

5. Save your work to your data disk.

From *Hypermedia As a Student Tool.* © 1995. Teacher Ideas Press. (800) 237-6124.

Creating a Button to Link Folders or Pages

When you create buttons to link folders or pages, there are several important things you must remember. LinkWay Live! asks you to use the ID number of a page when you link pages or folders. It does not ask you for the page number. Try this test so you can see the difference. Open any folder to its first page.

1. In the lower left-hand corner you see information about your folder. It shows three things: the name of the folder, the page number, and the ID number (for example, Illinois.1 ID=1 is the Illinois folder, at the first page, and the ID is 1).

2. Go under the Page menu and select New. If you have not created any other pages in this example, it should now say Illinois.2 ID=2. Add another page and you see Illinois.3 ID=3. Now comes the tricky part. Select Go To and click on Previous Page. You are now on Illinois.2 ID=2. Click on the Page menu and select Delete. First you will see a warning that all objects will be removed; then click on YES because you do want to delete this page.

3. Look at what it says. You are now on the second page but the ID number no longer matches. It should say Illinois.2 ID=3.

There will be many times that you may want to delete a page that you had created earlier. It is very important to be certain that you know the correct ID number of the page to which you wish to link.

Linking to Folders works in a similar way. When you create the link, you need to know the name of the folder and the ID number of the page you are moving to. If you put a return button after you move to the linked page, it will return you to where the first button was placed, even if it was in another folder. This is very useful when you create a menu stack and want each of the items in your menu to be in other folders. It is good design to work this way. There may be times when one folder could fit into another project. If everything you create is in one folder, it is harder for you to use the information at another time.

Creating a Graphic in LinkWay Live!

Open your folder. Refer to Starting up the LinkWay Live! direction sheet. The folder name should be in the lower left-hand corner. There should be a border around the page. If it still says ".base," then click on Go To on the menu and select First Page.

Be sure you have selected the c: drive. Now create a graphic to use on this page using LWPaint.

```
Start LWPaint program   YES
                        NO
```

LWPaint selected.

1. LWPaint can be selected by selecting Object menu and then selecting Tools. When the Execute Tool window appears, highlight LWPaint. Notice that LWPaint is placed within parentheses. Click outside the window. A window appears and asks if you want to start the LWPaint program. Click on Yes. A new menu bar appears. The choices are Picture, Draw, Tools, Options, and Color.

2. Select the Picture menu and then New. You will have to name your picture. Pick something easy to remember.

3. Decide what color you want for the bg (background) of your picture just as you did in the Bar Method. From the Option menu, select Bg Color and click on Yes in the dialog box until the color you want is set in place.

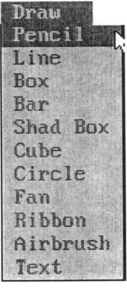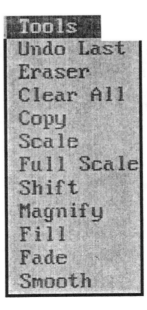

LinkWay Paint menus.

4. Pull down the Color menu and select a color. You can change colors whenever you want.

---

5. Pull down the Draw menu and select Pencil or Paint Brush. Use any of the Paint tools to help you create your graphic.

6. To save the picture on your data disk, go to the Options menu, choose Directory, and type "a:". Go to the Picture menu and select Save. Type in a name and click outside the box. The picture is being saved to your data disk in the a: drive.

7. Go to the Options menu, choose Directory, and type in "c:". Go to the Picture menu and choose Exit Paint. The page you were working on in LinkWay Live! appears.

A sample drawing.

8. Next you will bring the picture you created and put it where you want it on page 1. Go to the Options menu, select Directory, and type "a:".

9. Pull down the Objects menu, select New, and the Object Type menu appears. Click on the Picture, then click outside the box.

10. Click in the place you want to start the window to place your graphic. Drag the mouse toward the lower right. When the window is the right size, click to set. This creates the window for your picture.

11. The Picture menu appears. Select FirstName. Click outside the box. An Adjust window appears. Use the Up, Down, Right, and Left choices to move the picture you created until it fits where you want it. When you adjust your picture, you can take big or little steps. You can choose to move up 1 step or 8 steps. This is true for some of the other moves as well. Once you have adjusted the way you want your picture to look, click outside the box. You can still resize and move your picture through Move + Size in the Objects menu, but you will not be able to use the Adjust window again. If you choose FullPic, you can find out where it is before trying to move it. When it is the way you want it, click anywhere. Look back to page 194 to see the Adjust Menu.

12. Reset the directory to c: to add objects to the page.

Creating a Background in LinkWay Live!

Sometimes you want the same graphic, button, or text to appear on the same spot on each page you create. It is a good idea to do this. It is helpful to those who view the folders you create. It is good design for you to provide the same information in the same place on each page. A good example of this is the use of buttons that help the user navigate through your folder. If the project were about your state, the background you would create might look like the picture below. Remember, you are only creating an example. You would either design your own background or with classmates so that you could use a similar background for all the folders that were going to be linked together.

The background you are going to create will look like this when you have finished:

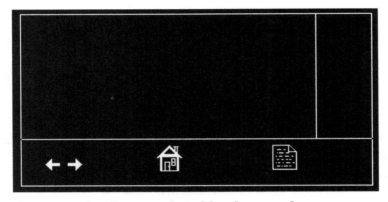

An example of a completed background.

Open LinkWay Live! and create a new folder named for your state. Notice that in the lower left-hand corner it says "*YourState*.1 Id=1." Remember, this tells you that you are on the first page.

1. Click on the Go to menu and select Base Page. Look in the lower left-hand corner. It says "*YourState*.Base." Whatever you put on this page will appear on every page in your folder.

2. Click on the Object menu, select New, and then select Button. The first icon (a small graphic) will take you to the previous page. Draw your button frame in the lower left a little above the name of your state. When Button Type appears, select Go To. Click outside the box. There is no reason to name this button. Click on the —-> until you find a left arrow that you like. When you find it, click on it and then choose Previous in the Go To dialog box. Click outside the box and your first button is in place.

3. Follow these same steps to create your next page button. Remember to select a right arrow and to choose Next in the Go To dialog box.

From *Hypermedia As a Student Tool.* © 1995. Teacher Ideas Press. (800) 237-6124.

4. Create a Link button in the center and select a graphic of a house for your button icon. When you are asked where to Link the button, leave the folder name blank and enter "1" for the page ID. Your first screen will be your title screen and this button will always return your users to this page.

5. A well-designed report provides a bibliography of where the information included in the report was obtained. That is what the icon on the right represents. That will also be a Link button. Create it now. Put it in place and choose the Note Page icon. You will have to edit it when you have completed your folder, and you know the ID of the page it is on.

To edit a button, click on it to select it. You know it is selected because of the dotted-line frame around the edges. Click on the Object menu and select Edit. It will take you through each of the steps again. Be careful that you do not change the icon, and when you come to the Link box, enter the page ID for your references.

When all of these are in place, click on the Go To menu and select First Page. You can add the title of your folder to the main part of the page and some of the topics you will report on in the right-hand frame. The information will only appear on this page. It might look like this:

Adding information to a Base Page.

6. Create a new page from the Page menu. Now you are on ID=2 and ready to test your buttons. There are two ways to test the buttons.

   • In the format Access Level where you are working, double click on the Previous page button. You should be back on ID=1, or the first page.

   • Click on the Folder menu, select Access Level, and click on Read. Don't worry about a password, just click outside the dialog box. This is how your folder will work for your viewers later on. Click "one" on the "next card" right arrow. To get back to the first page, click on the house, or home, icon. Did they all work?

7. You are ready to continue with your folder now. Go back to the Folder menu and select Format from the Access Level dialog box.

13
Multimedia ScrapBook for Windows Support Materials

A First Visit to Multimedia ScrapBook

TO THE TEACHER:

Unlike other programs, Multimedia ScrapBook does not include a tutorial or sample files. If this is the first time you are using Multimedia ScrapBook with students, you may want to go through these lessons and create a small folder with a few examples of the different experiences students will have. You could then create a sheet of pages that ask them to answer questions such as:

1. Can you find a button that makes or shows a picture?

2. Can you find a button that takes you to a page about our school?

3. What is the ID number on the page that has the picture of a mountain?

You will find examples in the First Visit pages for the other programs included in this book.

If you have used this program before, you may already have folders created by students that can be used as an exploration experience for your new students. Link several of them together with a menu and create a set of search questions for students. Either of these strategies should help new students become familiar with Multimedia ScrapBook before they become authors and designers of future folders.

There is a sample ScrapBook file available that will give students an overview of the terminology and application of the terms. The following pages may be given to students to follow to learn about Multimedia ScrapBook. Read them over, try them out, and then make your decision on how you want to introduce your students to this authoring software.

A First Visit to Multimedia ScrapBook

Use the Sample.msb ScrapBook file to learn about many of the terms and their application that are available to you for use in Multimedia ScrapBook.

- Go to the File menu and select Open.
- Select Sample.msb and click on OK.
- Notice that a File=SAMPLE is added to the title bar.

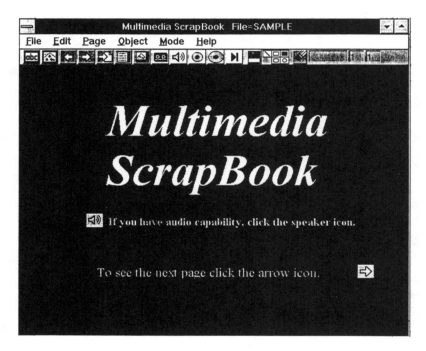

Sample ScrapBook file title page.

- There are two buttons (small squares with simple drawings).
- If you click the audio button (the button closest to the top), and if you do not have a wave device, click Cancel.
- Click on the "forward" button (the box with the point arrow right) to go to the next page.
- Read this page. It explains that you are in a ScrapBook file. That is what Multimedia ScrapBook calls what you or someone else develops.
- A file is made up of pages.
- Pages contain objects.

---

1. What kinds of objects have been added to the title page of the Science Project ScrapBook file?

2. This next page is reached by clicking the right arrow. It explains what the objects are. Were you right?

3. There are many possibilities of working with text. Just remember that too many font styles makes text on the screen hard to read. Why do you suppose this is true?

4. How many picture formats are sources of Picture Objects?

    You may have a chance to try each one when you work on your ScrapBook files.

5. What happens when you click on the picture of the mountain landscape?

6. What kind of button is on page 8 of the file?

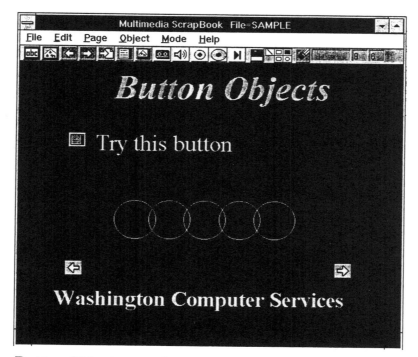

Button Objects sample page.

7. There is a Picture object on the page. Try to create a new circle using Copy and Paste.

8. Multimedia objects work like buttons. What will you be able to add to your projects?

9. Help. Click on Help and select Contents. Then click on "1.1" and "1.4" to find out more about Multimedia ScrapBook.

From *Hypermedia As a Student Tool.* © 1995. Teacher Ideas Press. (800) 237-6124.

Starting Up and Creating a ScrapBook in Multimedia ScrapBook

These directions will help you to start up Multimedia ScrapBook, installed on the c: drive of your computer. You will need a DOS-formatted 3-½" disk, on which you will save the screens that you create. When you create your data disk, be sure you have a directory titled MMSWORK". You will want to store all your Multimedia ScrapBook files in this directory.

1. Turn on your computer. When Windows opens, double click on the Multimedia ScrapBook icon.

2. It is a good idea to name this first scrapbook "Practice" (and use it to try out each new hypermedia skill that you learn). Go to the File Menu and select Save.

   - Click on Drives and select the a: drive.

   - Double click on the MMSWORK folder to open it. If it is not there, use Windows File Manager to create it.

   - Look for the File Name box on the upper left side of the Save dialog box. It will say "*.msb". Highlight the * and enter the name of your file. If you named it "Practice" you should now see "Practice.msb" in the rectangle. Click on OK.

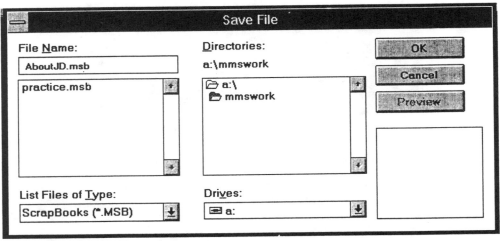

Naming a new ScrapBook file.

   - Look at the title bar at the top of the screen. The file name has changed.

3. Examine the Tool bar, which is located underneath the menu bar, and notice the last three boxes on the right:

The menu (tool) bar in Multimedia ScrapBook.

From *Hypermedia As a Student Tool.* © 1995. Teacher Ideas Press. (800) 237-6124.

The box next to the Eraser icon is the Quick Help box. As the mouse moves over the Tool bar icons, a short description of that icon appears in the Quick Help box window.

The next box is the Page Number box. It displays the number for the current page. This number can be used as part of a Go Page ID button on any other page as a way to return to this page.

The Page ID Number box (the last menu box) displays the ID number of the page in the file. The position of the page may change as you remove or add pages in the file. Page numbers changes as you add or delete pages, but ID numbers do not change.

4. If your file is saved, you can try closing your page and reopening it.

    • Go to the File menu and select Exit. You have now returned to Windows.

    • To reopen a scrapbook file, click on the Multimedia ScrapBook icon. Each time you begin, you start out on an untitled page.

    • Go to the File menu and select Open. The Open file dialog box appears.

    • Click on Drives and go to the a: drive. Remember, this is where your data disk should be.

    • Now you can see your MMSWORK folder. It is a closed folder beneath the open a:\ folder.

    • Double click on the MMSWORK folder. When it opens, you are able to see the scrapbook titles that you have previously saved.

    • Select the scrapbook file you wish to open and click on OK or just double click on the name. When it opens, you are ready to start working again.

You will use many different tools in Multimedia ScrapBook. The figure below will help remind you where everything is located.

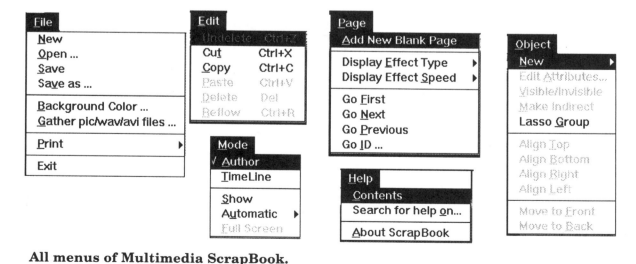

All menus of Multimedia ScrapBook.

From *Hypermedia As a Student Tool.* © 1995. Teacher Ideas Press. (800) 237-6124.

Creating a Border in Multimedia ScrapBook

Now it is time to create the first page of your About Me Multimedia ScrapBook file. You will want to have a border around your page. You will have to "trick" Multimedia ScrapBook into this because it doesn't have a Border tool.

1. Move along the tool bar to the icon for Colors (it is to the left of the Drawing tools); the word "color" appears in the Quick Help box. Click on the Color icon and select the color or pattern you would like for your border. Click on OK.

2. In the Drawing tools there is an empty box and a filled box. The Quick Help box calls the filled box a "bar." When you see the word "bar," you know you are in the right box. Click on the bar. Your cursor has changed to a solid, colored square.

3. With your mouse, move the square to the upper left-hand corner of your screen. When it is in the corner, click on the mouse button and hold the button down. Drag the cursor diagonally to the lower right-hand corner until the screen is filled, leaving a narrow unfilled border along the right edge. See page 209, left lower graphic where band is visible. Release the mouse button and click in the narrow band that is unfilled on the right. You click there so the rectangle will deselect and hold its current color. The band will be closed when the border is complete. If you make a mistake, select the object you want to remake, go to the Edit menu, select Cut, and then redo the steps.

4. Go back to the Color icon to choose another color. Notice that the color you had been using can be seen in the small rectangle below the colors in the Color icon. Select a contrasting color or a pattern. Now click OK and the color changes in that small rectangle. You can always identify the selected color by checking that small rectangle.

5. Now click on the Solid box again ("bar" appears in the Quick Help box). You have another square. With your mouse, move that square so that it is ½" down and ½" to the right of the left corner. Hold the mouse button down and drag the cursor to the lower right-hand corner, leaving the same amount of your first color showing all around the newly created box. Your page should look like step three in the figure below. Don't forget to click in the unfilled band.

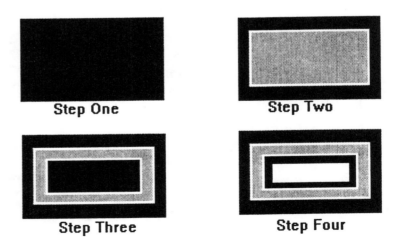

Four steps in creating a border.

6. Repeat the steps for selecting a color, this time make it white, selecting the Solid box (bar) and creating another rectangle. You will have a white rectangle bordered by two colored bands. Your page should look like step four.

7. Click on the Back border color. A blue band appears on the right. Move the arrow over the blue band until horizontal double-arrow appears. Click and drag the rectangle to the right edge of the frame. Now your border is truly complete.

With band still visible   Band closed. Border complete

Border with and without the unfilled band.

8. Save your work by going to the File menu and selecting Save.

Creating Text in Multimedia ScrapBook

When you create text in Multimedia ScrapBook, you can place your text anywhere on the screen, you can use different size fonts, and you can select the color you would like your text to be. All text is placed in a field that you create. You can have more than one text field on the screen.

1. Click on the Objects menu, select New, and then select Text Field. The window closes and a movable rectangle appears. If you got a square picture frame by mistake, press the Escape (ESC) key and you can try again to get the text field.

2. Place the rectangle where you want the field placed. Click once.

3. When the Text Information box appears, click OK.

4. Choose the font and watch the Sample frame to see how it would appear. Experiment until you find the font and size that best fits your project. Choose a font that is easy to read. Click OK.

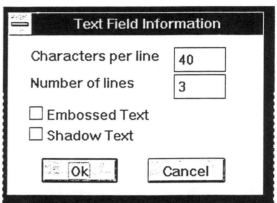

Text Field Information box.

5. Click outside the text field. It appears to disappear, but it is still there. Click once in the center of the field and the frame appears on the screen. This is a good time to size the frame. Make it larger than you think you will need. It is easier to have more room now then to add space for the text later. Place the cursor in the lower right corner until the angled arrows appear. Drag to the right and down to make the box wider and taller.

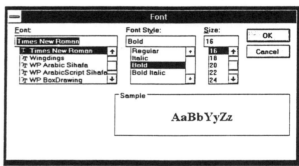

Font style and size choices.

Caution: Words that don't appear in the field now will not appear later. Do not let words go beyond the frame.

6. If the text is to be in color, this is the time to make that choice. Go to the color menu, select the color, and click OK.

7. Now you are ready to begin typing. Double click in the upper left-hand corner of the frame and the typing cursor appears. Click to place the cursor where you want to start typing and enter the text you planned for this field.

8. The arrows can be used to change the size of the text field and to move it where you would like it to be. If the text appears on a colored background, click outside the text box and select Color. Choose the color of the background for the main part of the page. Click OK.

Creating a Graphic in Multimedia ScrapBook

Drawings for Multimedia Scrap-Book can be created in the Paint-brush Program. Paintbrush is a part of the Windows program. Make sure that you are in Multi-media ScrapBook and your Practice file is open.

The first thing you need to do is move into Paintbrush. Press ALT-ESC and find the Paintbrush icon. It may be in your Accessories window.

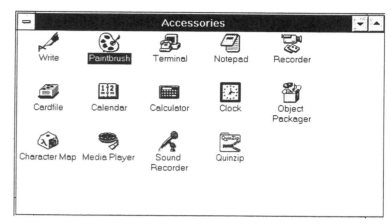

Opening Paintbrush.

1. Double click on the Paintbrush icon to open Paintbrush.

2. Use the tools to create your picture. Make the picture small so that it will not cover your title.

3. When you have completed your drawing, select the Scissors icon with the rectangle in the tool bar. When you move onto the screen, cross-hairs appear. Draw a box around your drawing.

4. Now go to the Edit menu and select Copy To. This will save your picture using less disk space than the regular Save command. You should know that Save also works, but selecting just the picture saves space on your disk.

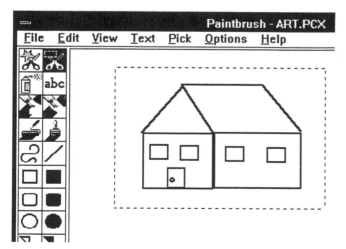

Picture selected.

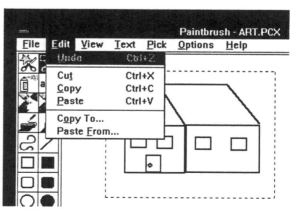

Getting ready to copy the picture.

From *Hypermedia As a Student Tool.* © 1995. Teacher Ideas Press. (800) 237-6124.

Give the picture a name of no more than seven letters. You want to save it in your MMSWORK folder on your a: drive. Be sure to click on Drive and select the a: drive. In your Copy To screen under the word "Directories," you should see "a:\MMSWORK". Save your work with a ".bmp" extension. Your screen should look like the figure below. If this is what you see, click OK.

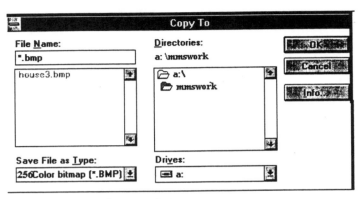

Adding ".bmp" to a picture name.

5. Click File on your Paintbrush menu bar and EXIT, or just press ALT-ESC until you are back in Multimedia ScrapBook.

Placing the Graphic

Now that you have created your picture in Paintbrush, you need to bring it onto your page. You can also use pictures that have been created by others. Sometimes this is called clip art, which you can use later when creating other ScrapBook projects.

There are two ways to use your graphics. In one example, you place the graphic on the screen; in the other, you place the graphic in a pop-up picture window. If you know how to create a pop-up text button, this way will be very easy for you.

1. To bring in a graphic, you can either go to the Objects menu, select New, and click on the picture as a first step, or you can click on the graphic icon located between the text icon (ABC) and the left-arrow button icon.

2. Place the frame where you want the picture to be.

3. You can choose how you want the picture to be treated. This time, click on Clip Picture to Fit and then click OK.

4. The Select Picture File window opens. If you have saved your drawing (*.BMP file) on a data disk, check to see if you are working from the a: drive. If not, click on the Drive icon until the contents of your data disk is displayed. Choose the filename and click OK.

5. Read the next section so that you can use the four object-modifier arrows to frame the graphic and to move it to the place on your page where you think looks best.

From *Hypermedia As a Student Tool.* © 1995. Teacher Ideas Press. (800) 237-6124.

Creating a pop-up picture is a combination of a pop-up button and bringing in a graphic. Try it now. If you have difficulty, reread both sets of directions, ask a classmate, or ask your teacher. You can do it!

Moving Objects

Now that you have brought your graphic onto your page, you might want to move it or change its size. Graphics, buttons, and text fields are all objects and all can be moved and resized in the same way.

1. Click on a graphic once so that it will be selected. You know it is selected when there is a frame around it.

2. Move the cursor around the edge of the frame and watch the cursor change. It started as an arrow but then it became a four-way arrow, a vertical doubled-ended arrow, a horizontal double-ended arrow, and, in the lower right-hand corner, an angled double-ended arrow. Each of these arrows performs a different task.

    a. The four-way arrow—When the four-way arrow is on the top edge of the object, press and hold down the mouse button. Now you can move this object anywhere on the page.

    b. The horizontal arrow—When the horizontal arrow is on the right frame border and the mouse button is held down, you can make the object wider or narrower.

    c. The vertical arrow—When the vertical arrow is on the base of the object and the mouse button is held down you can make the object taller or shorter.

    d. The angled arrow—When the angled arrow is on the lower right frame and the mouse button is held down, the width and height of the object can be changed.

Experiment using these arrows. You will use them frequently.

Creating Buttons in Multimedia ScrapBook

Creating a Button to Display Text

This will let you display text on the screen when a button is clicked.

1. Click on the Objects menu and select New. All the choices will appear. This time you should select Text Pop-up Button.

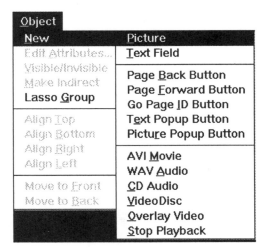

New Objects menu.

If you had wanted to, you could have selected the icon that looks like a paper with a scroll bar, this would have been the first step in creating a pop-up text button. When you finish making this button, place the cursor on that icon and look in the Quick Help box. It will say "text pop-up."

2. You can see the rectangle the size of the final text box. Place it where you want the text to appear.

3. When the Text Pop-up Information window appears, you can choose from the four places listed in the lower part of the frame and decide where the button may be placed in relationship to the text pop-up box. Click on one of the choices. Then, click on Word Wrap ON. You will then be able to write just as you would in the word processor. Click OK. If you want to include more text than would fit in the box, the scroll bar will let you add as much as you need. You have to decide if it would be better for your audience to see all of the text or if the information is important enough for them to scroll through it. These are design questions that you should think about when you create scrapbooks.

---

4. After you clicked on OK in step 3 the Font window appears. Decide how you want the text to appear. You can use the sample frame that appears in the lower right to help you decide what would add the most to your page. Click OK when you are ready to continue.

5. Enter the text. When you are through, click outside the text box. You can see the frame and the button. Double click on the button to test it. If you have looked under the Mode menu, you know that while you have been working you have been in Author mode.

6. There is another way to check your button. Click on the Mode menu and select Show. Now when you click, you can see how your readers will see the button working. Select Author from the Mode menu to continue.

7. If you discovered a spelling error or a word you want to change, it is easy to edit the text in the field. In Author mode, click on the button and open the text box. Just click in the field and you can make any changes that are necessary.

You might prefer to have your button somewhere else on the page. To see how to do this, you must be in Author mode.

1. Click the button once and the text frame appears.

2. From the Objects menu, select Make Indirect.

3. A rectangle appears. Move it anywhere on the screen that you would like to place the button to activate your pop-up text.

4. Now there are two buttons showing. The last step is to hide the first button. Again, from the Objects menu, select the Visible/Invisible choice. That choice is called a "toggle." It can make an object either visible or invisible. Try it. Select the first button by clicking once. Select the toggle choice. Test it by returning to Show from Mode menu. This is how you can tell if the button will be invisible to the reader of your scrapbook.

Creating a Button to Link Pages or ScrapBooks

When you create buttons to link scrapbooks or pages, there are several important things you must remember. Multimedia ScrapBook asks you to enter the ID number of a page when you link pages or scrapbooks. It does not ask you for the page number. Try a test so you can see the difference. Open any ScrapBook file to its first page.

1. In the upper right-hand corner is information about your scrapbook. It shows two things: the page number and the ID number. For example, if this is your first page, you will see a "1" in each of the boxes in the upper right-hand corner.

2. Go to the Page menu and select Add New Blank Page. If you have not created any other pages in this example, there will be "2" in each box. Add another page and there will be a "3" in each box. Now comes the tricky part. Select Page and click on Go Previous. A "2" is now in each box. Click on the Edit menu and select Cut. Because you want to erase this page, click Yes to the question, "OK to erase this page from ScrapBook?" This question makes you think about what you are doing, at times keeping you from making a mistake.

3. Look at what is in the boxes now. You are now on the second page, but the ID number no longer matches. The first box should contain a "2", the other a "3".

There will be many times that you want to delete a page that you had created earlier. It is very important to be certain that you know the correct ID number of the page to which you wish to link.

Linking to ScrapBook files works in a similar way. When you create the link, you need to know the name of the ScrapBook file and the ID number of the page you are moving to. If you put a Return button after you move to the linked page, it will return you to where the first button was placed, even if it was in another ScrapBook file. This is very useful when you create a menu stack and want each of the items in your menu to be another ScrapBook file (this is good design). There may be times when one ScrapBook file could fit into another project. If everything is in one ScrapBook file it is harder to use the information at another time.

Creating a Link to Page Button

On the menu bar there are two arrows. When you place the cursor on them, the Quick Help box shows you that these move you to the next page or the previous page. They make it very easy to create a button that can go from page to page.

1. Be sure you are on the first page of your scrapbook (there will be a "1" in each of the boxes in the upper right). You can move there very quickly by going to the Page menu and selecting Go First.

2. Click on the arrow pointing to the right. Place the rectangle in the lower right-hand corner of the page and click. Now you can see your arrow in place. Test it by clicking twice.

3. Create an arrow pointing to the left and use it to return to the first page. These buttons could also have been created by going to the Objects menu and selecting Page Back Button or Page Forward Button. It is easier to select them from the menu bar.

Creating a Link to Other Pages

You can also move to other pages in your scrapbook, but that is another kind of button. Follow the steps below to see how this works.

1. From the Objects menu, click New and select the Go Page ID Button. After you see the box on the page, you will know which icon to select from the menu bar next time.

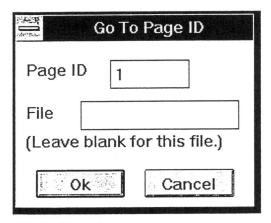

2. Enter the ID number of the page you want to move to in your scrapbook. Click OK and test your button. You may have to find the ID number by using Page options to check each page.

When you want to move from one ScrapBook file to another, use this same button. When you enter the ID number, you must also enter the name of the ScrapBook file into the box after "File". Because you use the ID number as well as the file name, you can

Go to Page box.

go to the title page of another ScrapBook file, but you can also move to any page within the file. An important thing to remember is that when the button takes you to another file, you *must* place a button on that page that returns you to the page you left.

It might seem as though you can only have buttons that look like arrows or pages. Don't forget what you learned when you created your pop-up button—buttons can be made invisible.

Creating a Background in Multimedia ScrapBook

Sometimes you want the same graphic, button, or text to appear at the same spot on each page you create. It is good design to do this. It is helpful to those who view the scrapbooks you create. It is good design for you to provide the same information in the same place on each page. An example of this is the careful placement of buttons that help the user navigate through your scrapbook. You will notice this happening in software that you use in school or at home.

If a project were about your state, the background you would create might look like the picture below.

An example of a completed background.

Remember, this is only an example. You would either design your own background or design one with classmates so that you could use a similar background for all the scrapbooks that were going to be linked together.

Open Multimedia ScrapBook and create a new scrapbook named for your state. The boxes at the upper right end of the menu bar indicate that you are on page 1 and that the ID for this page is 1. There is neither a Background nor a Base Page function in Multimedia ScrapBook, so you will have to "trick" the software into creating a background.

1. Click on the Objects menu, select New and Page Back Button. Move the rectangle to the lower left of the page and click. One button on your background is now completed. Remember that you could select the left arrow from the menu bar as a short cut to do the same thing.

2. Using the selection method you prefer, create a Page Foreward Button. Check the figure above. Are your two buttons on the same level? Do they look like they belong together?

3. The Home button in the figure will always bring you back to this first page. Create a Go Page ID Button using the Objects menu or the shortcut. Place the rectangle in the center and enter "1" into the Page ID box. Look back on page 217

4. Either select Text Field from the Objects menu or click on the shortcut. If you are not sure where it is, use the Quick Help box to find out. After your selection, place the text rectangle above the Go To ID button and click. Enter "10: into the characters-per-line box and click OK.

5. The text for this button does not have to be very large. Select "10" for the size, "Bold" for the Font Style, and "Times New Roman" or another small font. You can see in the Sample box how it will look. Click OK.

6. Type "Home" into the text field. The box can be much smaller.

   - Click outside the field.

   - Click on the word "Home." A blue-framed box appears.

   - Move the arrow cursor to the lower right corner until the angled double-arrow cursor appears.

   - Hold down the mouse button and move the cursor up until the box just surrounds the word.

   - Place the cursor on top of the frame bar until the four-way arrow appears. Hold down the mouse button and place the text field just below the button.

7. There is one last button to create. It is important to provide the reader with the names of the reference sources that were used in a project. That is the purpose of this last button. It is created just as the Home button was. When asked, type "5" into the Text ID box, even though it will have to be edited later. Enter "Reference" or "References" into this text field and place it just below the button.

   Before proceeding to step 8, you may want to copy this page so that every page in your scrapbook file has the four icons. To do this:

   - Go to Edit and Copy

   - Go to Edit and paste. A new page appears; notice that the number has changed.

   - Go back to page 1 using the Home button.

8. Drawing the lines. Find the Line icon on the menu bar. When you click on it, the cursor looks like an angled line. When you draw, the upper left corner of the line is the starting point for drawing.

   - Choose the starting point.

   - Hold down the mouse button and begin to draw a horizontal line above the buttons. Holding down the mouse button while you draw will keep the line straight.

   - Draw the vertical line in the same way.

From *Hypermedia As a Student Tool.* © 1995. Teacher Ideas Press. (800) 237-6124.

9. To test the buttons, create two more pages. Using the Page menu, return to the first page. Click on the right arrow and move to the second page. Is the number 2 in both boxes on the menu bar? Use the Page menu and return to the first page.

Adding Information to the Background

This is an example of how information could be added to a background. The information added to the title page of a history scrapbook, shown in the figure below, is on this page only.

Title page of History Scrapbook file.

You could create an invisible button, just as you did in the pop-up button, to link to other screens. You could place an invisible button over "History" to move to the scrapbook about history. Don't forget to edit the Home button in the History Scrapbook to return to the title page.

Then, if the user were to click on the invisible History button, he or she would now be reading the new ScrapBook file on the History of Illinois.

14
SuperLink

A First Visit to SuperLink

TO THE TEACHER:

Unlike other programs, SuperLink does not include a tutorial or sample folders. If this is the first time you are using multimedia Folders with students, you may want to go through these lessons and create a small folder with a few examples of the different experiences students will have. You could then create a sheet of pages that ask them to answer questions such as:

1. Can you find a button that makes or shows a picture?

2. Can you find a button that takes you to a page about our school?

3. What is the ID number on the page that has the picture of a mountain?

You will find examples in the First Visit pages for the other programs included in this book.

If you have used this program before, you may already have folders created by students that can be used as an exploration experience for your new students. Link several of them together with a menu and create a set of search questions for students. Either of these strategies should help new students become familiar with SuperLink before they become authors and designers of future folders.

Included with SuperLink are application (or directory) samples that include an overview to introduce the basic ideas to students. In addition, there is a sample folder available that will give students an overview of the terminology and application of the terms. The following pages may be given to students to follow to learn about SuperLink. Read them over, try them out, and then decide how you want to introduce your students to this authoring software.

A First Visit to SuperLink

Open SuperLink. Click on Application in the menu bar, choose Open and Samples. You are going to learn about SuperLink and some of the kinds of objects you will be able to create.

1. There are two buttons. Click on Overview.

2. After reading about the SuperLink folder, click on the Forward button (the box with the right arrow) to go to the next page.

3. Read this page. It explains the differences between folders and pages. You will be creating SuperLink folders, or files, for your projects.

    * A folder is made up of pages.

    * Pages contain objects.

4. What kinds of objects are described on the Objects page in this folder? The next page shows examples of the list you made.

5. Click on Pictures. Describe what happens.

6. Click the scroll bar into the Days of the Week field. What happens?

7. What happens when you click in the check box? And when you click again in the check box?

8. As you move through the overview, watch for different page attributes; that is, different visual effects as the pages change. Sometimes these are called transitions. When you create your folder, check these out under the Page menu. When deciding on all the possibilities of working with text, just remember that too many font styles makes text on the screen hard to read. Why do you suppose this is true?

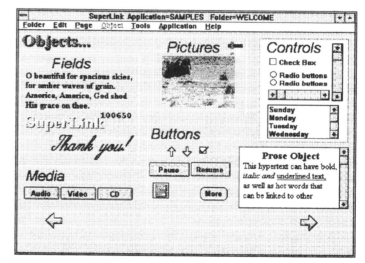

Objects available in SuperLink.

9. How many picture formats are sources? You may have a chance to try each one when you work on your folders.

Starting Up and Creating a Folder in SuperLink

These directions will help you to start up SuperLink, installed on the c: drive of your computer. You will need a DOS-formatted 3-½" disk, on which you will save the screens that you create. When you create your data disk, be sure you have a directory titled "MYWORK." You will want to store all your SuperLink files in this directory.

1. Turn on your computer. When Windows opens, double click on the SuperLink icon.

2. It is a good idea to name this first scrapbook "Practice" (and use it to try out each new Hypermedia skill that you learn). Go to the Folder menu and select Save.

    *   Click on Drives and select the a: drive.

    *   If the MYWORK folder is not open, double click on it to open it. If you do not see the MYWORK folder listed, click on Cancel and follow steps a–c below. If you have the folder go to the next bullet.

    a. Click on the Application menu. An application in SuperLink is the same as a directory. You are going to create a new application, or directory, named "MYWORK". Click on New. When a dialog box asks about saving changes, click on No.

    b. The cursor is in the new application box. Type "MYWORK".

    c. Tab down and type A into the box identifying where the new application should be created. Click on OK.

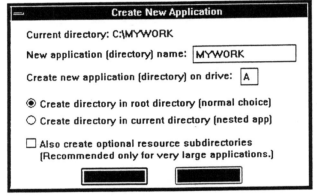

Creating a new application.

    *   Look for the File Name window on the upper left side of the Save dialog box. It will say "Untitled.slf". Select the word "Untitled" and enter the name of your file. If you named it "Practice," you should now see "Practice.SLF" in the rectangle. Click on OK.

    *   Look at the title bar at the top of the screen. The file name has changed.

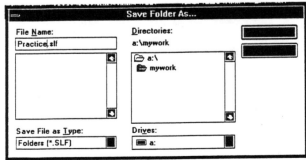

Naming a new folder.

---

3. Examine the tool bar, which is located under the menu bar. You will find graphics tools on the right and a variety of other icons that are short cuts of the many hypermedia skills you will be learning. Along the bottom of the screen you will find other information that is important for you to know. At the lower left is the page number that you are on right now and also the ID number of that page. You will see that, as you add and delete pages, the page number and the ID number will not always match.

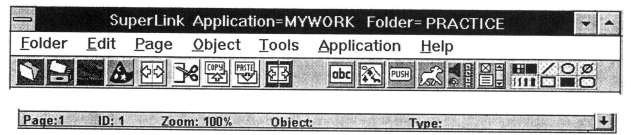

The menu/tool bar and status bar in SuperLink.

If your file is saved, you can try closing your Folder and reopening it. Go to the Folder menu and select Exit. You have now returned to Windows. To reopen a folder, click on the SuperLink icon. Each time you begin, you start out on an untitled page. Go to the Folder menu and select Open. The Open File dialog box appears. Click on Drives and go to the a: drive. Remember, this is where your data disk should be. Now you can see your MYWORK folder. It is a closed folder beneath the open a:\ folder. Double click on the MYWORK folder. When it opens you will see the folder titles that you have previously saved. Click on the folder you wish to open and the name appears in the File Name rectangle. Click on OK (or press the Enter key). When the Folder opens, you ready to start working again.

You will use many different tools in SuperLink. This figure will help to remind you where everything is located.

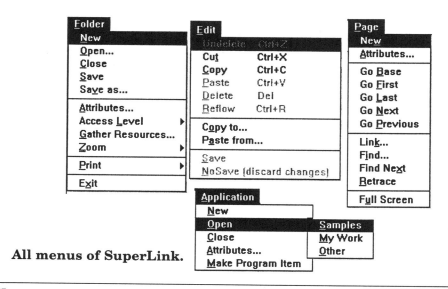

All menus of SuperLink.

From *Hypermedia As a Student Tool.* © 1995. Teacher Ideas Press. (800) 237-6124.

Creating a Border in SuperLink

Now it's time to create the first page of your MYWORK folder. You want to have a border around your page. You will have to "trick" SuperLink into this because it doesn't have a Border tool.

1. Move along the tool bar to the icon for Colors; it is above the line sizes, and the words "drawing color" appear on the lower information (status) line. Before you go further, take a moment to move the arrow across the tool bar icons. Notice the changes in the box where drawing color was. This is the Quick Help feature, which reminds you what each icon does. Back to the border:

   - Click in the "drawing color" box.

   - Click in the color box on the Basic color you want as a background for your border.

   - Click on OK.

2. In the Drawing tools there is an empty box and a filled box. The Quick Help box calls the filled box a draw "bar." When you see the word "bar," you know you are in the right box. Click on the bar. Your cursor has changed to a solid, colored square.

3. With your mouse, move the square to the upper left hand corner of your screen. When it is in the corner click on the mouse button and hold the button down. Drag diagonally to the lower right hand corner until the screen is filled, leaving a narrow unfilled border along the right edge. See page 227, left lower graphic where band is visible. Release the mouse button and click in the narrow band that is unfilled on the right. You click there so the rectangle will deselect and hold its current color. The band will be closed when the border is complete. If you make a mistake, select the object you want to remake, go to the Edit menu, select Cut, and then redo the steps.

4. Go back to the Color icon to choose another color. Notice that the color you had been using can be seen in the small rectangle below the colors in the Color icon. Select a contrasting color or a pattern. Now click OK and the color changes in that small rectangle. You can always identify the selected color by checking that small rectangle.

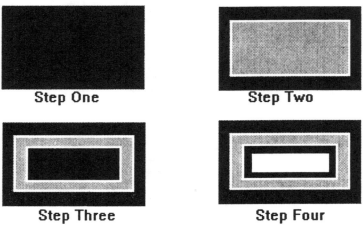

Step One   **Step Two**

Step Three   **Step Four**

Four steps in creating a border.

From *Hypermedia As a Student Tool.* © 1995. Teacher Ideas Press. (800) 237-6124.

5. Now click on the Solid box again ("bar" appears in the Quick Help box). You have another square. With your mouse, move that square so that it is ½" down and ½" to the right of the left corner. Hold the mouse button down and drag the cursor to the lower right-hand corner, leaving the same amount of your first color showing all around the newly created box. Your page should look like step three in the figure below. Don't forget to click in the unfilled band.

6. Repeat the steps for selecting a color, this time make it white, selecting the Solid box (bar) and creating another rectangle. You will have a white rectangle bordered by two colored bands. Your page should look like step four below.

7. Click on the back border color. A blue band appears on the right. Move the arrow over the blue band until a horizontal double-arrow appears. Click and drag the rectangle to the right edge of the frame. Now your border is truly complete.

With band still visible   Band closed. Border complete

Border with and without the unfilled band.

8. Save your work by going to the Folder menu and selecting Save.

Creating Text in SuperLink

When you create text in SuperLink, you can place your text anywhere on the screen, you can use different size fonts, and you can select the color you would like your text to be. All text is placed in a field that you create. You can have more than one text field on the screen.

1. Click on the Objects menu, select, New and then select Field. The window closes and a movable rectangle appears. If you got a square picture frame by mistake, press the Escape key and you can try again to get the text field.

2. Place the rectangle where you want the field placed. Click once.

3. When the Text Information box appears, the characters-per-line and the lines of information provide the default setting. You will see how this changes later. Click OK.

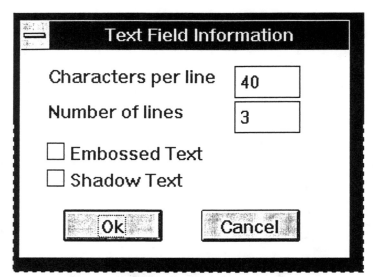

Text Field Information box.

4. Choose the font and watch the Sample frame to see how it would appear. Experiment until you find the font and size that best fits your project. Choose a font that is easy to read. Click OK.

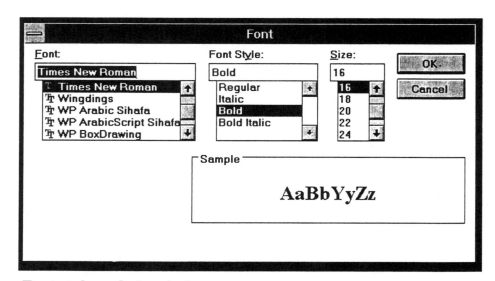

Font style and size choices.

From *Hypermedia As a Student Tool.* © 1995. Teacher Ideas Press. (800) 237-6124.

5. Click outside the text field. It appears to disappear, but it is still there. Click once in the center of the field and the frame appears on the screen. This is a good time to size the frame. Make it larger than you think you will need. It is easier to have more room now then to add space for the text later. Place the cursor in the lower right corner until the angled arrows appear. Drag to the right and down to make the box wider and taller.

Caution: Words that don't appear in the field now will not appear later. Do not let words go beyond the frame.

- Notice that the Edit icon appears on the menu bar to the left of the text (ABC) icon. This icon only appears when an object is selected. A text object is currently selected, so you will see a list of the attributes of that object that can be edited.

- Selecting field attributes: The characters-per-line and number of lines have changed to show the size you created when the field was stretched. Click OK.

- Go through the remaining choices to make any changes you want. Clicking cancel will take you back to the page.

6. If the text is to be in color, this is the time to make that choice. Go to the Edit menu, select Color, make your choice, and click OK.

7. Now you are ready to begin typing. Double click in the upper left-hand corner of the frame and the typing cursor appears. Click to place the cursor where you want to start typing and enter the text you planned for this field.

8. The arrows can be used to change the size of the text field and to move it where you would like it to be.

From *Hypermedia As a Student Tool.* © 1995. Teacher Ideas Press. (800) 237-6124.

Creating a Graphic in SuperLink

Drawings for SuperLink can be created in the Paintbrush program. Paintbrush is a part of the Windows program. Make sure that you are in SuperLink and your Practice folder is open.

The first thing you need to do is move in to Paintbrush.

1. Click on Tools. Select the Execute Window tool. Select Paint.
2. Use the tools to create your picture. Don't make the picture too large. You want other objects on the page.
3. When you have completed your drawing, select the Scissors icon with the rectangle in the tool bar. When you move onto the screen, cross-hairs appear. Draw a box around your drawing.

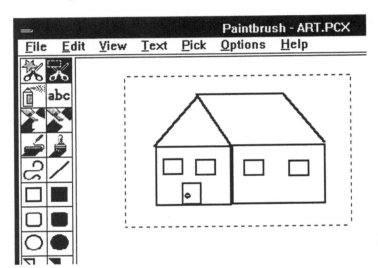

Picture selected.

4. Now go to the Edit menu and select Copy To. This will save your picture using less disk space than the regular Save command. You should know that Save also works, but selecting just the picture saves space on your disk.

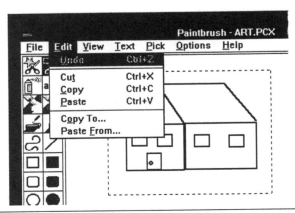

Getting ready to copy the picture.

From *Hypermedia As a Student Tool*. © 1995. Teacher Ideas Press. (800) 237-6124.

Give the picture a name of no more than seven letters. You want to save it in your MYWORK folder on your a: drive. Be sure to click on Drive and select the a: drive. In your Copy To screen under the word "Directories," you should see "a:\MYWORK." Save your work with a ".bmp" extension. Your screen should look like the figure below. If this is what you see, click OK.

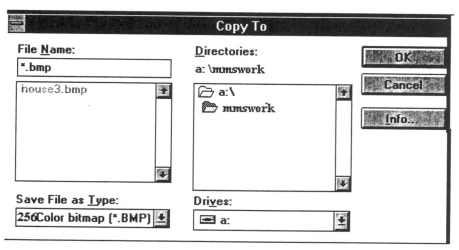

Adding ".bmp" to a picture name.

The File Name window should show "*.bmp." If it does not, click in the Save File As Type window until "256 color Bitmap (*.bmp)" appears, and then select it.

5. Click under File on your Paintbrush program and EXIT. Click on No when asked if you want to save current changes; this returns you to your SuperLink page.

Placing the Graphic

Now that you have created your picture in Paintbrush, you need to bring it onto your page. You can also use pictures that have been created by others. Sometimes this is called clip art, which you can use a later when creating other folder projects.

There are two ways to use your graphics. In one example, you place the graphic on the screen; in the other, you place the graphic in a pop-up picture window. If you know how to create a pop-up text button, this way will be very easy for you.

1. To bring in a graphic, you can either go to the Objects menu, select New, and click on the picture as a first step, or you can click on the graphic icon located between the text icon (ABC) and the Push button icon.

2. Place the frame where you want the picture to be.

3. The Picture Attributes window opens and you can choose how you want the picture to be treated. This time click on Clip to Fit. Click OK.

4. The Select window opens. If you have saved your drawing (*.BMP Folder) on a data disk, check to see if you are working from the a: drive. If not, click on the Drive icon until the contents of your data disk is displayed. Choose the File name and click OK.

5. Read the next Moving Objects section so that you can use the four object-modifier arrows to change the frame size or location of the graphic on your page.

Creating a pop-up picture is a combination of a pop-up button and bringing in a graphic. You will find it easy to do after you have learned about graphics. You already know how to do a text pop-up.

Moving Objects

Now that you have brought your graphic onto your page, you might want to move it or change its size. Graphics, buttons, and text fields are all objects and all can be moved and resized in the same way.

1. Click on a graphic once so that it will be selected. You know it is selected when there is a frame around it.

2. Move the cursor around the edge of the frame and watch the cursor change. It started as an arrow but then it became a four-sided arrow, a vertical doubled-ended arrow, a horizontal double-ended arrow, and, in the lower right-hand corner, an angled double-ended arrow. Each of these arrows perform a different task.

   a. The four-way arrow—When the four-way arrow is on the top edge of the object, press and hold down the mouse button. Now you can move this object anywhere on the page.

   b. The horizontal arrow—When the horizontal arrow is on the right frame border and the mouse button is held down, you can make the object wider or narrower.

   c. The vertical arrow—When the vertical arrow is on the base of the object and the mouse button is held down, you can make the object taller or shorter.

   d. The angled arrow—When the angled arrow is on the lower right frame and the mouse button is held down the width and height of the object can be changed.

Experiment using these arrows. You will use them frequently.

Creating Buttons in SuperLink

Creating a Button to Display Text

This will let you display text on the screen when a button is clicked.

1. Click on the Objects menu and select New, then Button. All of the
   choices will appear. Select Text
   Popup or go to the Push icon and
   select Text Popup.

2. The rectangle that appears is the
   preset size of the popup text box.
   Place it where you want the text to
   appear.

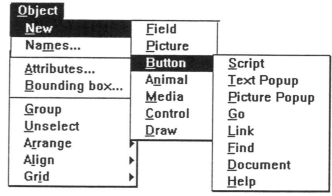

New Objects menu.

3. The Visual Attributes window appears next. Choose the icon that best fits your
   project. One idea would be to name the button "AboutMe" and click on the Sign button.

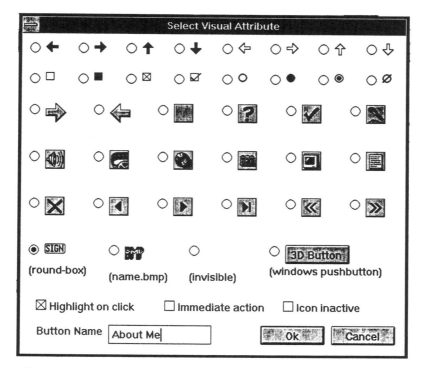

The window for selecting visual attributes.

From *Hypermedia As a Student Tool.* © 1995. Teacher Ideas Press. (800) 237-6124.

4. Click on "Word wrap" in the Text field Attribute window. Click OK.

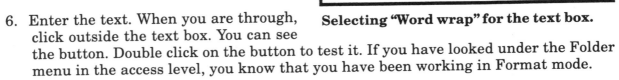

Text Edit Attributes

Word wrap attribute

◉ Word wrap (no horizontal scroll bar)

○ No word wrap (horizontal scroll bar on)

☐ Text Window is Initially Open

[Ok]   [Cancel]

5. The Font window opens and you can decide how you want the text to appear. You can use the sample frame that appears in the lower right to help you decide what would add the most to your page. Click OK when you are ready to continue.

6. Enter the text. When you are through, click outside the text box. You can see

Selecting "Word wrap" for the text box.

the button. Double click on the button to test it. If you have looked under the Folder menu in the access level, you know that you have been working in Format mode.

7. There is another way to check your button. Click on the Access Level in the Folder menu and select Read Only. Now when you click, you can see how your readers will see the button working. Ignore the request for a password and click OK to continue. Select Format from the Access Level menu to continue.

8. If you discovered a spelling error or a word you want to change, it is easy to edit the text in the field. In Format mode, click on the button and open the text box. Just click in the field and you can make any changes that are necessary. There is another, and important, way to edit. This is a good time to learn about it.

Select the Edit icon on the menu bar. Click on the Popup Text button so that a frame appears around it. This tells you that the object is selected. Look on the menu bar. An Edit icon has appeared to the left of the text (ABC) icon. It only appears when an object is selected and has edit features for that particular type of object. Click on it now. Notice that if you do not like the font or the button icon, you can change them here by selecting Font or another appropriate choice.

Creating a Button to Link Pages or Folders

When you create buttons to link folders or pages, there are several important things you must remember. SuperLink asks you to enter the ID number of a page when you link pages or folders. It does not ask you for the page number. Try a test so you can see the difference. Open any folder to its first page.

1. On the status bar at the bottom of the page is information about your folder. The page number and the ID number, for example, will both be "1" if this is your first page.

2. Go to the Page menu and select New. If you have not created any other pages in this example, the status bar will read "2 2." Add another page and it now reads "3 3." Now comes the tricky part. Select Page and click on Go Previous. You are now on "2 2." Click on the Edit menu and select Cut. Because you want to erase this page, click Yes to the question, "Delete this page?" This question makes you think about what you are doing, at times keeping you from making a mistake.

3. Look at what is in the status bar now. You are now on the second page, but the ID number no longer matches. It should read "2 3."

There will be many times that you want to delete a page that you had created earlier. It is very important to be certain that you know the correct ID number of the page to which you are creating a link.

Linking to Folders works in a similar way. When you create the link, you need to know the name of the folder and the ID number of the page you are moving to. Put a Return button after you move to the linked page. It will return you to where the first button was placed, even if it was in another folder. This is very useful when you create a menu stack and want each of the items in your menu to be another folder (this is good design). There may be times when one folder could fit into another project. If everything is in one folder, it is harder to use the information at another time.

Creating a Link to Page button

On the menu bar, select the Push icon. When you place the cursor on it, the Status Bar shows you are on the New Button icon. This makes it very easy to create a button that can go from page to page.

1. Be sure you are on the first page of your folder (there will be a "1" in the page indicator on the status bar). You can move there very quickly by going to the Page menu and selecting Go First.

2. Click on the Push icon and select Go. Place the rectangle in the lower right corner and click. Now select an arrow pointing to the right from the Visual Attributes window. Name your button "Next." Click OK.

3. Click on Next in the Go to Attributes window and click OK.

4. You can test the button by double clicking on it. Another way to test is to go to the Folder menu and change the Access Level to "Read Only."

5. Test your button. On the new page, create a left arrow button to return you to the previous page. Name the button "Previous."

Creating a Next Page button.

---

*You could also have gone to the Object menu and selected Button and Go to create this button. It seems easier to click on the Push icon.

Now that your button is made, click on it. Notice the frame that appears around the button. That indicates that you have selected an object. Now look at the status bar. It still tells the page and ID numbers, and more. It reads "Object: Next" and "Type: Go Button." You named the button or object "Next" and it was a Go button. You can always check the objects on your page by selecting them and checking the status bar.

Page:1   ID: 1   Zoom: 100%   Object: Next   Type: Go Button

The status bar.

6. Create an arrow pointing to the left and use it to return to the first page.

Creating a Link to Other Pages and Folders

You can also move to other pages in your folder, but that is another kind of button. Follow the steps below to see how this works.

1. From the Objects menu, click New and select the Go Page ID Button. After you see the box on the page, you will know which icon to select from the menu bar next time.

2. Enter the ID number of the page you want to move to in your folder. Click OK and test your button. You may have to find the ID number by using Page options to check each page.

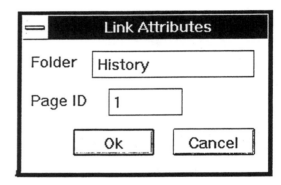

Link Attributes

Folder   History

Page ID   1

Ok   Cancel

The Link Attributes box.

When you want to move from one folder to another, use this same button. When you enter the ID number, you must also enter the name of the folder that you want to link to in the Folder Name rectangle. Because you use the ID number as well as the folder name, you can go to the title page of another folder, but you can also move to any page within the folder. An important thing to remember is that when the button takes you to another folder, you *must* place a button on that page that returns you to the page you left.

Creating a Background in SuperLink

Sometimes you want the same graphic, button, or text to appear on the same spot on each page you create. It is good design to do this. It is helpful to those who view the folders you create. It is good design for you to provide the same information in the same place on each page. An example of this is the careful placement of buttons that help the user navigate through your folder. You will notice this happening in software that you use in school or at home.

If a project were about your state, the background you would create might look like the picture below.

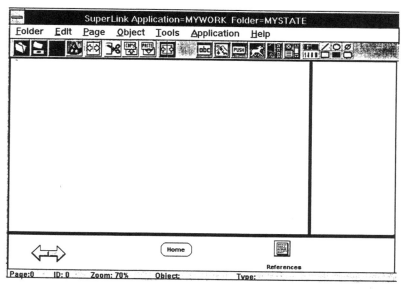

An example of a completed background.

Remember, this is only an example. You would either design your own background or design one with classmates so that you could use a similar background for all the folders that were going to be linked together.

Open SuperLink and create a new folder named for your state. The status bar indicates that you are on page 1 and the ID for this page is 1. Now select Go Base from the Page menu. Check the status bar. Notice that a "0" now appears in both the Page and the ID areas.

1. Click on the Objects menu, select New, select Button, and select Go. Move the rectangle to the lower left of the page and click. Select a left-arrow icon, Previous. Now one button is complete and in place.

2. Create the right-arrow button beside the left arrow just as you see it in the figure. Remember, you can create this button by selecting Go after clicking on the Button or Push icon.

3. The Home button in the figure will always bring you back to this first page. Create a Link button using the Objects menu or the shortcut. Place the rectangle in the lower center of the page. Name the button "Home" and select SIGN as the icon choice before clicking OK. Enter "1" into the Page ID box. Refer to graphic on page 236.

4. Either select Text Field from the Objects menu or click on the shortcut. If you are not sure where it is, use the Quick Help box to find out. After your selection, place the text rectangle above the Go To ID button and click. Enter "10" into the characters-per-line box and check OK.

5. There is one last button to create. It is important to provide the reader with the names of the sources that were used in a project. That is the purpose of this last button. Click the Push (new button) icon and select a Link button. Place it in the lower right corner. Notice that one icon choice in the Select Visual Attributes window looks like a piece of paper. Choose that icon. When asked to provide the ID number, either enter a random number or leave it blank. You will edit that information later when you know the ID number of your References page. Good design suggests that text and graphics together can be useful to the reader. Create a text box to be placed under the piece-of-paper icon. Use a font size no greater than 10 so that the icon will not be overwhelmed by the text. If you are not sure how to create the text box, refer back to you reference sheet "Creating Text in Superlink."

6. Drawing the lines. Find the Line icon on the menu bar. When you click on it, the cursor looks like an angled line. When you draw, the upper left corner of the line is the starting point for drawing.

   - Choose the starting point.

   - Hold down the mouse button and begin to draw a horizontal line above the buttons. Holding down the mouse button while you draw will keep the line straight.

   - Draw the vertical line in the same way.

7. To test the buttons, create two more pages. Using the Page menu, return to the first page. Click on the right arrow and move to the second page. Is the number 2 in the Page and are the ID references in the status bar? Use the Page menu and return to the first page.

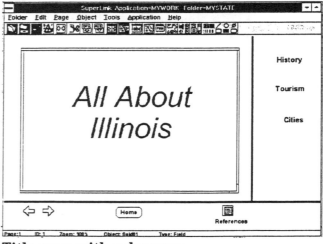

Title page with submenus.

From *Hypermedia As a Student Tool.* © 1995. Teacher Ideas Press. (800) 237-6124.

Adding Information to the Background

This is an example of how information could be added to a background. The information added to the title page, shown in the figure below, is on this page only.

You could create an invisible button to link to other screens. You could place an invisible button over "History" to move to the folder about history. Your Link Attributes window must include the Folder name as well as the Page ID as shown on page 236.

When creating that button, be sure to place it over the text "History," name it "History" in your Select Visual Attributes window, and click on Invisible for a button choice. Create the a copy of the base page in your History folder. Be sure to put the folder name in the Home button Link that returns to the State folder.

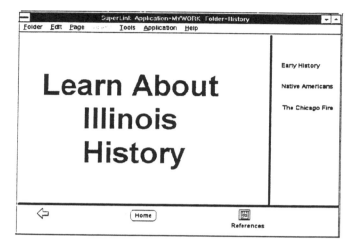

Title page of History Folder file.

Then, if the user clicks on the invisible History button, he or she would be moved to the new folder file on the History of Illinois.

Appendix

A
Assessment Tools

TO THE TEACHER:

Your role as a resource person and guide to your students as they research their content material, communicate their ideas through hypermedia, and as they assess their projects is a critical one. We have found that peer assessment not only helps those whose work is being assessed, but it makes those doing the assessing much more careful about how they create their own projects.

Assessment should be an ongoing endeavor. Set certain times when everyone will assess each other's projects. Criteria could include such things as clear titles on all screens, graphics that complement the text, and certain screens that are to be completed by the date. This gives the authors time to add or change as the project develops.

This book includes three different assessment instruments. They can be used for most projects depending on the criteria you have set forth. They should be adapted to your needs and may give you ideas for an assessment instrument of your own.

Hypermedia Project Evaluation Form

Circle the appropriate numbers or words.

Program Number: 1   2   3   4   5   6   7   8

Title: _____

Evaluation:

	No				**Terrific**
Color	1	2	3	4	5
Text	1	2	3	4	5
Graphics	1	2	3	4	5

Number of Screens: _____

Did buttons work?   Yes   No

Comments: _____

_____

_____

_____

_____

_____

_____

Evaluators Initials: _____

Hypermedia Project Assessment

Name of Project: _____

Author (s): _____

Check the line if the item is included.

1. The title screen includes:
   - _____ a. Name of the project
   - _____ b. Name(s) of the author(s)
   - _____ c. Button that connects to the next screen
2. _____ Table of contents screen
3. _____ Project description screen
4. _____ Buttons operate correctly as indicated
5. _____ Background or border on screens present
6. _____ Original artwork
7. _____ Imported graphics
8. _____ Sound
9. _____ Transitions
10. _____ Number of screens
11. _____ Content is accurate
12. _____ Sources are identified

Give your overall impression. Were the screens well designed? Were the graphics appropriate to the information on the screens? Please express your opinion on the lines below:

_____

_____

_____

_____

_____

Reviewer (s): _____

Peer Evaluation Form

Name of Project: _____

Name of Stack Author:_____

Name of Student Evaluator: _____

Content

1. Give the two most essential pieces of information that the author presented in his/her stack.

2. What did you learn about this topic that you didn't know before viewing this stack?

3. What are the strengths of this stack in terms of content?

4. What are the things that need improvement?

Design

1. What design elements enhanced the viewing of the stack? Why?

2. Did any design elements have a negative effect on your viewing of the stack? If so, what are they and why did they cause this negative reaction?

3. What are the strengths in the design of this stack?

4. Was viewing this stack any different from using a book? If so, how does the technology (hypermedia, CD-ROM, etc.) make it different? If not, why didn't the technology change the experience?

Appendix
B
Generic Planning Sheets

Project Development Guide for Teachers

Title:

Curriculum Connection:

Purpose:

Content Goals:

Planning Forms (List Titles):

Student Experiences:

Hypermedia Skills Needed for This Project:

Social Skills Emphasized in This Project:

Suggested Time-Frame:

Description of Sessions:

Assessment Strategies:

Additional Notes:

Extensions:

Screen Planning Form

Card Name: _____

Border: _____ Color: _____

Opening Transition: _____

What transition is between pages (cards)? _____

What buttons are on your page? Where do they go?

Pop-up: _____ to _____

Sound: _____ to _____

Link to next screen? _____ to _____

Other: _____ to _____

Notes: _____

_____

_____

_____

Mapping Your Stack

FOR THE TEACHER:

One of the most difficult concepts for student designers to understand is the nonlinear nature of hypermedia. Students, at the beginning, create the stacks and move from card to card in a linear fashion, much like reading a book. It is not an easy task to help children learn how to think and learn in a completely new way. There are several different approaches that we can suggest as you begin introducing this idea to your students.

As students work on a stack, they tend to view it in isolation—as the work of the individual or pair working on that one stack—and not as a part of a whole, a bigger picture. The stack mapping guides that follow can help students see the bigger picture as well as help them in their planning. Notice that the first page is a template that each student or student pair can use to monitor their stack as it grows. It also suggests one of the many ways all stacks should be designed—with their navigational buttons in the same place.

One way we have found to successfully introduce these concepts is to ask the students how they think others might want to use the information when all the stacks have been linked together. This can begin as early as the About Me stack in chapter 1.

In this lesson, students might think that users would wish to look at each of the stacks or cards in a linear fashion, from beginning to end. But after some discussion, they can come to realize that a user may also want to be able to find stack of a particular student without going through all the others. This is a good way to introduce the menu as a nonlinear path through the stack.

The two sample pages that follow demonstrate one way in which students can begin to visualize how the pieces fit together. A project on the United States lends itself to this example. The first sample Maps shows how the title page links to a table of contents stack. It also shows that each of the states would have its own stack, and as demonstrated by the double-headed arrow, would all link back to the table of contents. The second sample page moves from the single part of the larger stack, Illinois, on the original sheet to a screen planning form for the stack devoted solely to Illinois. Illinois has now moved from being on the peripheral to being the center focus around which the other cards develop. Arrows indicate both the linear path a user might take as well as the nonlinear routes available. All the user needs to do is click on the topic of interest. It is important to point out to students that when a user goes from card to card in a stack linearly, the *designer* has decided the route through the information. But when there is a menu with choices, then the *reader* is in control of choosing his or her own path.

Mapping Your Stack (Samples—United States, Illinois)

Mapping Your Stack

Illinois

Screen Name: Illinois
Button Names: One for each topic, TOC
Button Types: Invisible over text
Links: Links to cards

This is a new stack

Table of Contents

Screen Name: TOC
Button Names: 1. States 2.Students
Button Types: Invisible over text
Links: Links to cards

This is a new stack

Our United States

Screen Name:Title
Button Names: 1. Contents
Button Types: 1 -Invisible (over icon)
Links: 1 - TOC Stack

This information should appear on each
card as you r map as the stack grows:
Screen Name   Button Name
Type of Button   Links to/from

Mapping Your Stack

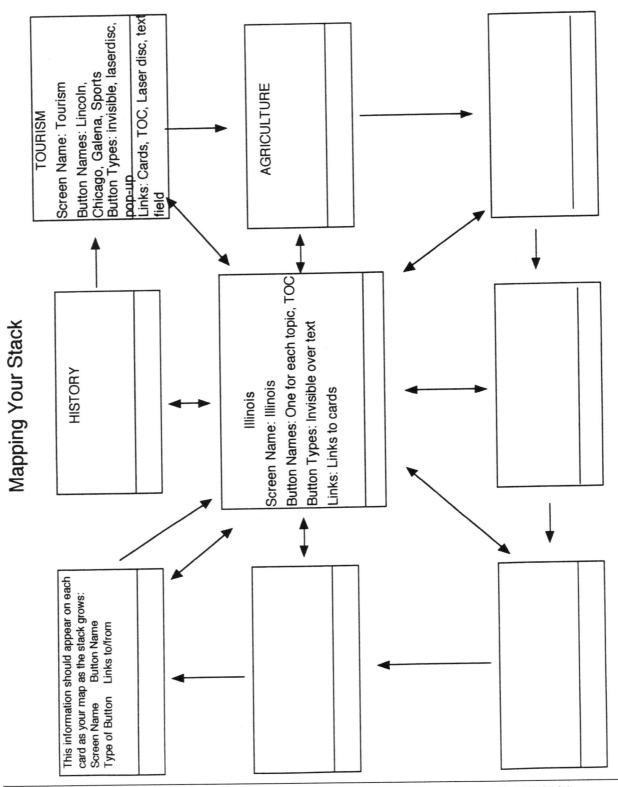

TOURISM
Screen Name: Tourism
Button Names: Lincoln, Chicago, Galena, Sports
Button Types: invisible, laserdisc, pop-up
Links: Cards, TOC, Laser disc, text field

AGRICULTURE

HISTORY

Illinois
Screen Name: Illinois
Button Names: One for each topic, TOC
Button Types: Invisible over text
Links: Links to cards

This information should appear on each card as your map as the stack grows:
Screen Name   Button Name
Type of Button   Links to/from

From *Hypermedia As a Student Tool.* © 1995. Teacher Ideas Press. (800) 237-6124.

Topic Web Form

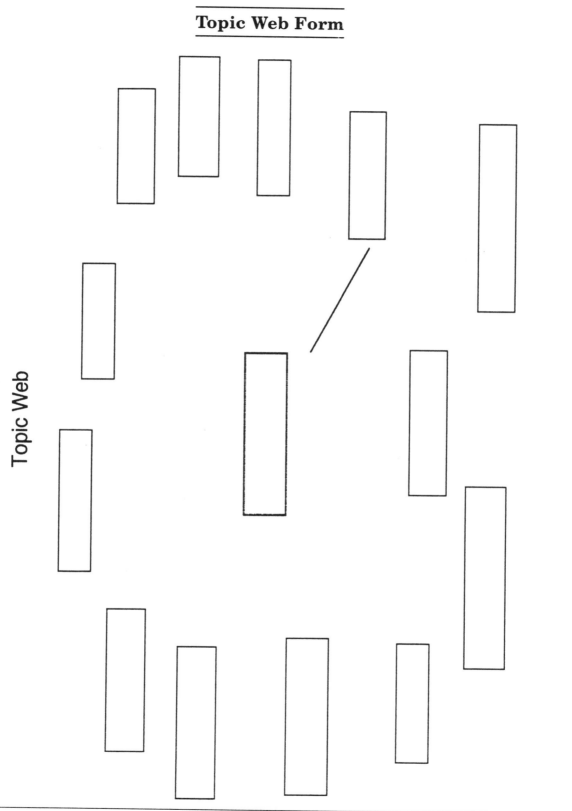

Navigation Planning Form

Navigation Planning Sheet

Appendix

C

Teacher Support Materials

Creating a Menu Stack

The menu stack is a stack that connects many other stacks around a common theme. In planning a menu stack, the teacher and the students must determine the appropriate metaphor for the particular stack. For example, the menu for a group of stacks created by students on each of the planets and other elements of the solar system may use a graphic of the entire solar system as a one card menu stack. Invisible buttons placed on each of the planets or elements would act as the user's navigational tool through the stack.

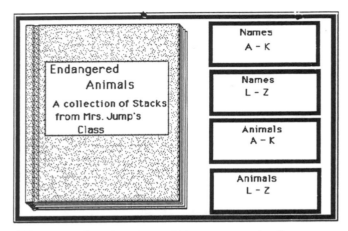

The opening screen of the menu stack.

Other metaphors might take several cards to achieve, such as using a graphic of a closed book as the opening title card and the pages of the book with specific menu lists to provide the navigational tools that users will need. The graphics used in these menu stacks may be created by the students or may be clip art or graphic backgrounds.

Invisible buttons are on each of the four navigation buttons on the right side of the card. Each of these buttons moves the user to another card in this stack.

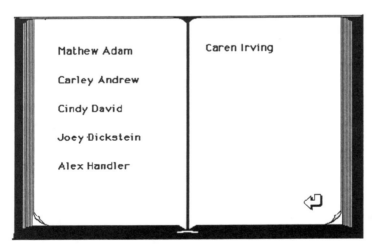

The second screen of the menu stack.

Invisible buttons on each of the names link the user to the stack created by the student that has been selected. The curved return arrow in the lower right-hand corner of the selected stack should contain the button to send the user back to the first card of this stack.

Classroom Display and Recording of Computer Presentation a.k.a. The VCR As a Printer

Written by Roger Wagner

This booklet is designed to help you explore the exciting new idea of using your classroom TV/monitor for computer-based presentations, and using the VCR as a "printer" for the computer. Once set up, you'll be able to record student presentations and send them home to parents; you can record class projects and share them with other teachers and administrators; you can create training tapes for other staff members in your school or district; you can even create "portfolios" of projects to take to conferences and other meetings to share what you've been doing with computers— without having to take any more equipment than a single videotape!

If unable to find locally, please contact:

Roger Wagner Publishing, Inc.
1050 Pioneer Way
Suite P
El Cajon, CA 92020
(619) 442-0522

Plans for Making a Fabric Quilt from Hypermedia Designs

The graphic tools that are part of every hypermedia program can be used to create quilt tops. Simply have the students use the graphic tools to create a screen. Either color or black and white images can be used.

Insert a four-color (or black) heat transfer ribbon into your ImageWriter printer. They are available from many sources. We have purchased them from Educational Resources in Elgin, Illinois. Their number is 1-800-624-2926.

Print the screen. The paper is then used as an iron-on. Be sure to follow the ribbon directions as to content of fabric. Be aware that text will print backwards, so text should either be avoided or carefully arranged.

The squares of fabric on which the graphics have been printed can then be sewn together to make a hypermedia quilt.

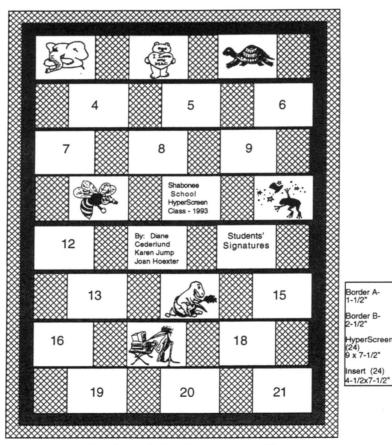

HyperScreen Quilt - Scale: 4 inches = 1/2"

Muslim for HyperScreen : 2-1/2 yards   Insert: 1-1/2 yards
Muslim for backing: 3 yards   Small Border: 1 yard
Border: 1 yard   Batting: 3 yards

Plans for Making a Hypermedia Quilt Design: Teacher-Created Templates

Steps to creating a template:

1. Open your hypermedia software.

2. Create a new stack.

3. Move the Tools menu onto your screen if possible.

4. Use the Rectangle tool to create a square.

5. Use Copy from Edit (or press Command-C on the Macintosh) to make a duplicate (it's on the clipboard).

6. Paste the copy (Command-V) and align it.

7. Repeat the Paste command until you have six squares.

8. Use other tools to create your design or use patterns to fill in alternating squares.

9. Save the stack.

You can print out the single card or past it into the scrapbook (on a Macintosh) and paste it into a word processing document if you want to give students written directions.

Students may complete a single square that represents their story. It would then be repeated or perhaps have patterned or colored squares in between.

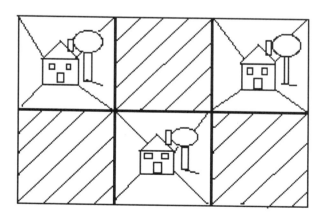

Comparison of Multimedia Programs

Program Titles	List Price	Run Time Version	Import Graphics	Import Text	Spell Check Available	Sound	Create Animation	Color Capability	Access Video Discs	Access VCR Clips	Sample Files Included	Hardware Required
HyperScreen Scholastic, Inc. 2931 E. McCarty St. Jefferson City, MO 65101 1-800-541-5513	$89.95	No	Yes. Additional graphics available from Scholastic. Public Domain DOS 3.3 Print Shop Graphics	No	No	Yes. W/ program & additional sound available through the publisher	No	Yes	Yes	No	Yes. Sample files & a short tutorial are included.	Apple IIe Apple IIGS MS-DOS w/256 graphics card
HyperStudio (Apple IIGS) Roger Wagner Publishing 1050 Pioneer Way, Suite P El Cajon, CA 92020 1-800-497-3778	$125.00	No	Yes	Yes. Text files from word processors.	Check before import.	Yes. Within program or using a microphone.	Yes	Yes	Yes	No	Yes. Sample files & a tutorial are included.	Apple IIGS. At least 1MB RAM. At least 1 3.5-in. drive. Is GS/OS compatible & can be networked.
HyperStudio (Macintosh) Roger Wagner Publishing 1050 Pioneer Way, Suite P El Cajon, CA 92020 1-800-497-3778	$125.00	Yes	Yes. Any PICT, TIFF, EPSN, or MacPaint, clip art from other sources.	Yes. Text files from word processors.	Check before import.	Yes. Within program or using a microphone.	Yes	Yes	Yes	Yes. Can access Quick-time clips.	Yes. Sample files & tutorial included.	Macintosh w/ at least 2MB RAM using System 6.0. At least 4MB RAM using System 7.
HyperCard (Macintosh) Apple Computer Co. 20525 Mariani Ave. Cupertino, CA 95014 1-800-776-2333	$99.00	No	Yes	Yes. Text files from word processors.	Check before import. In HyperCard can check using Hyper-Spell by Heiser.	Yes. Imported or create using a microphone.	Yes	In ver 2.2. In 2.1 thru Hyper-Color from Heiser.	Use Videodisc Toolkit from Apple or Video-Stack from Voyager.	W/ Voyager Video-Stack.	Intellimation has many stacks available to use as samples or purchase Education Home Card from Intellimation.	Macintosh using System 6.01 or higher.

Program Titles	List Price	Run Time Version	Import Graphics	Import Text	Spell Check Available	Sound	Create Animation	Color Capability	Access Video Discs	Access VCR Clips	Sample Files Included	Hardware Required
Digital Chisel (Macintosh) Pierian Spring Software 5200 SW Macadam Ave. Suite 250 Portland, OR 97201 1-503-222-2044 FAX 1-502-222-0771	Educator Price—$119.00 Site license—$995.00	No	Yes. Libraries on an included CD-ROM & others available from Pierian. Photo-CD access.	Yes.	Check before import.	Yes. Import or add your own. Many included.	Yes	Yes	Yes	Yes	A tutorial is included as well as a demo.	Macintosh System 6.01 or higher. 6-8 mgs RAM to use QuickTime.
Multimedia ScrapBook (Windows on IBM PC or a compatible PC w/ Windows) Alchemedia, Inc. P.O. Box 1061 La Conner, WA 98257 1-206-466-5946	$200.00 Site license—$1,600	One time license is $400.00 to make unlimited copies.	Yes. Additional graphics from any source, PCX, or use a scanner.	Yes. Copy & paste	Check before import.	Yes. W/ program, additional sound through the publisher AV Form on Windows machine. CMI machines need sound.	No	Yes	Yes & CD-ROM discs. Photo CD.	Yes	No. Great help files.	Minimum requirements compatible w/ Windows 3.1.
Linkway Live (MS-DOS) IBM, EduQuest 1000 NW 51st St. Boca Ratan, FL 33429-1234 1-408-372-8100	$130.00	Yes	Yes. Any PCX, PCM, PCV, PCJ, PCZ graphic can be brought in.	Yes.	Check before import.	Yes	Yes	Yes	Yes	Yes.	A tutorial included, no sample files.	Mouse must be properly installed. EGA IBM-486 Windows version available.
SuperLink (Windows) Alchemedia, Inc. P.O. Box 1061 La Conner, WA 98257 1-206-466-5946	$400.00 Site license—$2,000	Yes	Yes. Any PCX, BMP, DIB, GIF, JPEG, FIF, PCM, PCV, PCJ, or PCZ graphic can be brought in as well as photo-CDs	Yes. Use any font installed on the computer. Cut & paste.	Check before import.	Yes.	Yes. Any media w/ Windows CMI driver can be directly controlled.	Yes. Displays up to 24-bit true color mode.	Yes & CD-ROM discs, photo CDs.	Yes	No sample files. LinkWay Live folders can be brought in.	Minimum requirements compatible w/ Windows 3.1 minimum 386 & 4MB memory.

Reference and Resource Lists

References

Abernathy, B., D. Andre, A. Bass, and J. Sonnenberg. 1993. *Hands-on multimedia for teachers: Bringing learning to life with HyperCard and HyperStudio.* Carpentersville, IL: MediaTech.

Abramson, G. W. 1993. Linkway features and design. *The Computing Teacher* 21 (2): 16–18.

Adams, D. R. 1990. *HyperCard and Macintosh: A primer.* New York: Mitchell McGraw-Hill.

Allen, G. D. 1993. What's in a name: The power of naming in HyperCard. *HyperNexus* 3 (3): 19–20.

Apple Computer. 1989. *HyperCard stack design guidelines.* Reading, MA: Addison-Wesley.

Baugh, Ivan. 1994. Hypermedia as a performance-based assessment tool. *The Computing Teacher* 21 (6): 14–17.

Beekman, G. 1990. *HyperCard in a hurry.* Belmont, CA: Wadsworth.

———. 1992. *HyperCard 2 in a hurry.* Belmont, CA: Wadsworth.

Belk, Rebekah, and Margaret Mara. 1994. Problem solving in HyperStudio: Strategies and tips. *The Computing Teacher* 22 (3): 65.

Boyer, B. A., and P. Semrau. 1993. Selecting and evaluating interactive videodisc programs in art. *The Computing Teacher* 21 (3): 28–30.

Brooks, J. G., and M. G. Brooks. 1993. *In search of understanding: The case for constructivist classrooms.* Alexandria, VA: Association Supervision.

Brown, A. 1993. Hypertext, cooperative learning, and peer resourcing. *The Computing Teacher* 21 (2), 36–37.

Bull, G., and J. Harris. 1991. *Hypercard for educators: An introduction.* Eugene, OR: International Society for Technology in Education.

Byron, Elzabeth. 1990. Hypermedia (multimedia). *Teaching Exceptional Children* 22 (4): 47–48.

Carter, Bruce, and Karin Wiburg. 1994. Thinking with computers. *The Computing Teacher* 22 (1): 7–10.

———. 1994. Thinking with computers II. *The Computing Teacher* 22(2): 6–9.

Chaney, J. 1993. Alphabet books: Resources for learning. *The Reading Teacher* 47 (2): 96–104.

Culp, G. H., and G. M. Watkins. 1993. *The educator's guide to HyperCard and HyperTalk*. Needham-Heights, MA: Allyn and Bacon.

D'Ignazio, F. 1993. Student multimedia book talks: Illuminating on a shoestring. *The Computing Teacher* 21 (3): 31–32.

Dunn, S., and R. Larson. 1990. *Design technology: Children's engineering*. New York: Falmer Press.

Forman, G., and P. B. Pufall, eds. 1988. *Constructivism in the computer age*. Hillsdale, NJ: Lawrence Erlbaum Associates.

Grabinger, R. S., J. C. Dunlap, and S. Heath. 1993. Learning environment design guidelines. Paper presented at the Annual Meeting of the Professors of Instructional Design & Technology, May 14–17, 1993, in Bloomington, IN.

Goodman, D. 1990. *The complete HyperCard 2.0 handbook*. New York: Bantam Books.

Harel, I., and S. Papert, eds. 1991. *Constructionism*. Norwood, NJ: Ablex.

Higgins, K., M. O'Keefe, and D. Klimas. 1989. *HyperStudio: Hypermedia system for the Apple IIGS*. El Cajon, CA: Roger Wagner.

Hofmeister, J., and J. Rudowski. 1989. *Learning with HyperCard*. Cincinnati, OH: South-Western Pub.

Improving, not standardizing, teaching. 1991. *Arithmetic Teacher* (September): 18–22.

Jones, M. 1983. AB(by)C means alphabet books by children. *The Reading Teacher* (March): 646–48.

Lamb, A. 1993. *IBM LinkWay Plus LinkWay Live Authoring Tool*. Orange, CA: Career.

Lamb, A., and D. Myers. 1991. *HyperCard creativity tool for writing, organizing and multimedia*. Orange, CA: Career.

Land, M. 1990. To scan or not to scan: Get the picture?: Common questions concerning the legal use of scanned images. *HyperNEXUS, Journal of HyperMedia and Multimedia Studies* 1 (1): 21.

McCain, T. D. E. 1993. Teaching graphic design in all subjects. *The Computing Teacher* 21 (3): 21–23.

———. 1993. *Teaching graphic design in all subjects*. Eugene, OR: ISTE.

McMullen, D., and R. A. Jensen. 1993. HyperCard and gifted students: An opportunity for divergent thinking and creative production. *HyperNexus* 3(3): 15-16.

Myers, D. and A. Lamb. 1990. *HyperCard: Authoring tool for presentations, tutorials & information exploration.* Orange, CA: Career.

Natal, D. 1993. Peer collaboration in an elementary school lab: Problems and how they are solved. Paper presented at the Annual Meeting of the American Educational Research Association, 1993, in Atlanta, GA.

National Committee on Science Education Standards and Assessment. February 1993. *National science education standards: An enhanced sampler.* Washington, DC: National Research Council.

Romberg, T. A. 1993. NCTM's standards: A rallying flag for mathematics teachers. *Educational Leadership* 50 (5): 36–41.

Sponder, Barry, and Robert Hilgenfeld. 1994. Cognitive guidelines for teachers: Developing computer-assisted instruction. *The Computing Teacher* 22 (3): 9–15.

Turner, S. V., and V. M. Dipinto. 1992. Students as hypermedia authors: Themes emerging from a hypermedia study. *Journal of Research on Computing in Education* 25 (2): 187–199.

Turner, S. V., and M. Land. 1994. *Hypercard: A tool for learning.* Belmont, CA: Wadsworth.

Ventura, F. n.d.. *HyperCard projects for teachers.* Newbury Park, CA: Ventura Educational Systems.

Wileman, R. E. 1993. *Visual Communicating.* Englewood Cliffs, NJ: Educational Technology Publications.

Winograd, K. 1992. What fifth graders learn when they write their own math problems. *Educational Leadership* 49 (7): 64–67.

Yoder, S., G. L. Bull, and J. Harris. 1991. *LinkWay for Educators: An Introduction.* Eugene, OR: ISTE.

Software Resources

Apple Computer 1990. *Educators Home Card.* Santa Barbara, CA: Intellimation Software.

Dover Clip-Art Series. 1982–1990. New York: Dover Publications, Inc. A wide range of titles with line graphics that are very good for scanning.

Heyer, T. 1993. *Add impact with graphics: Clipart Collection II.* Grand Rapids, MI: Abacus. PC clipart graphics in PCX format.

Hyperstudio Forum. HyperMedia Associates, Inc., T/A HyperStudio Network, Box 103, Blawenburg, NJ 08504.

Inside HyperCard. The Cobb Group, 9420 Bunsen Parkway, Suite 300, Louisville, KY 40220. Subscribtion information available at 1-800-223-8720.

League, V. 1989. *Graphics at your fingertips.* Palatine, IL: Graphics at Your Fingertips. These graphics are available for the Apple and Macintosh computers.

The Voyager Company, 1351 Pacific Coast Highway, Santa Monica, CA 90401. This is the source for *Dominos, An Uncensored Journey Through the Sixties* (and other useful videodiscs).

Index